# THE SKY'S THE LIMIT

# THE SKY'S THE LIMIT

PASSION

AND

PROPERTY

IN

MANHATTAN

## STEVEN GAINES

LITTLE, BROWN AND COMPANY

*New York   London*

Little, Brown and Company
Time Warner Book Group
1271 Avenue of the Americas, New York, NY 10020
Visit our Web site at www.twbookmark.com

First Edition: June 2005

Library of Congress Cataloging-in-Publication Data

Gaines, Steven S.
     The sky's the limit : passion and property in Manhattan / Steven Gaines — 1st ed.
          p. cm.
     Includes bibliographical references (p.     ) and index.
     ISBN 0-316-60851-3
     1. Residential real estate — New York (State) — New York.  2. Apartment houses — New York
(State) — New York.  3. Apartments — New York (State) — New York.  I. Title.

HD268.N5G34   2005
333.33'8 — dc22                                                                      2004026614

                              10 9 8 7 6 5 4 3 2 1

                                    Q-MART

                         Book design by JoAnne Metsch

                    Printed in the United States of America

FOR BERNARD BERKOWITZ

# CONTENTS

CARRIAGE TRADE     1

PRIVATE CLUBS     33

TURNED AWAY     61

SUTTON PLACE     85

BROKER TO THE STARS     112

THE CONCIERGE AND THE LANDLORD     150

THE ANSONIA HOTEL     173

BILLION-DOLLAR BROKER     206

NUMBER 1     227

A NOTE ON SOURCES     255

ACKNOWLEDGMENTS     257

INDEX     259

Though one could dine in New York,

one could not dwell there.

—*Oscar Wilde, 1887*

# THE SKY'S THE LIMIT

# ONE

# CARRIAGE
# TRADE

On that day in June 1999 when Tommy Hilfiger got into 820 Fifth Avenue, on the Upper East Side of Manhattan, where these kinds of things duly matter, the news was examined and deciphered like some sort of a social Rosetta stone. The ladies with the tanned, slender arms in their sleeveless Carolina Herrera dresses picked over the details — the square footage, the price, his wife, his money — along with the cheese soufflé every day at lunch that week at Swifty's. Why would eightyish society nabob Jayne Wrightsman, who reportedly controlled everything at 820 Fifth Avenue, down to what color the lampshades were in the lobby, let Tommy Hilfiger in? What did that *mean?* Was Fifth Avenue turning into Central Park West?

Fifth Avenue is the address against which all others are measured. It cleaves Manhattan down the middle, East from West, the geographic arbiter of status. It divides the Croesusean rich from the merely wealthy, the influential from the truly powerful. From its southernmost tip, at Washington Square in Greenwich Village, to Ninety-sixth

Street, where it stops mattering, it is six and a half miles long, most of it high-end retail space and skyscraper office buildings. But on the mile and a half facing Central Park, from Fifty-ninth Street to Ninety-sixth Street, in sixty-three co-operative and five condominium apartment buildings, there lives the greatest consolidation of private wealth ever assembled in one place. Of that stretch of the avenue, 820 Fifth Avenue was one of the top two "great houses," as the old-time management referred to the buildings they lovingly tended.

"I would have thought Eight-twenty Fifth was *the* best address in the city," Edward Lee Cave, the don of the carriage-trade brokers sniffed, meaning pre-Hilfiger. At the carriage-trade brokerage houses, selling an apartment at 820 Fifth Avenue is the equivalent of receiving the real estate Légion d'Honneur. The building is so exclusive, the co-op board so difficult, that even the loftiest plutocrats have been repelled from its doors, including three billionaires — Revlon chief Ronald Perelman, financier Asher Edelman, and oilman Frederick Koch. Yet there it was, that Wednesday in June 1999, in a big, black bold headline in the salmon-colored *New York Observer*: TOMMY BOY'S BIG ADDRESS: O.K.'D AT 820 FIFTH. The article confirmed that "baggy-clothing" designer Tommy Hilfiger had been approved to buy, for $12.5 million, an eighteen-room, six-bedroom apartment at 820 Fifth Avenue from the estate of the poet Louise Crane and that "high end brokers were in shock."

Truth be told, nothing seemed shocking anymore on Fifth Avenue. It was safe to say that there wasn't a coupon-clipping WASP dreadnought in sight. The real high-WASP families had long ago moved to quiet little buildings on fashionable side streets where the building profiles were lower — and so were the maintenance fees. As for "real society" on Fifth Avenue, well, the old saw is that "real society" died in 1908 with

Mrs. William Backhouse Astor Jr.* In any event, Tommy Hilfiger was hardly the first new face to stake his claim to a "rung in the social ladder," as one character in Edith Wharton's *House of Mirth* describes a Fifth Avenue address. The history of Fifth Avenue has always been that of new money being trumped by newer money. The only difference now is that the cycles come much more quickly, the people are much richer, and new money smells better than it used to. Gertrude Vanderbilt once cautioned her grandchildren about men who made their money from oil and livestock: "It takes three generations to wash off oil and two to exterminate the smell of hogs." She also longed for a more genteel time when "Society was still Society" and not "a hodgepodge of tradesmen and stockbrokers." Men who made their money in oil or steel were known as "shoddyites" and nouveau riche families were nicknamed the McFlimsies. The moneymen who got rich on Wall Street were disparaged as "bouncers." In the 1890s Ward McAllister was still trying to separate the "nobs" of breeding and position and the "swells, who had to entertain to be smart." Entertaining to be smart meant a great deal on Fifth Avenue. All of the generations of Fifth Avenue residents — "Fifth Avenoodles," as the newspapers mocked them in the 1800s — were always furiously social people who showed off their wealth and class by being voracious collectors of art, food, furniture, and clothing and givers of grand parties and balls.

When the name FIFTH AVENUE, in capital letters, appeared for the first time on the historic Commissioners Plan of 1811, it was only a

---

*The last of New York's original "Old Guard" aristocracy to actually live in a Fifth Avenue mansion lingered until 1949, when Augustus Van Horne Stuyvesant, the last living male bearing the name of the first governor of New York, ended his days in a town house at East Seventy-second Street, deaf and alone, sitting all day in front of a portrait of Franklin Delano Roosevelt and cursing.

designated number on a map, without any special distinction other than it started at what once was a potter's field called Washington Square Park and ran straight up the island, all the way north to the Harlem River. The street's association with the rich began in 1834 when millionaire farmer and landholder Henry Brevoort, age eighty-seven and known as the Old Gentleman by his family, built himself a two-story, flat-roofed Georgian mansion on the corner of Ninth Street and Fifth Avenue, then three miles north of the center of the city, and chained a bear to a stake on his front lawn as entertainment.* Six years later, one evening in February 1840, Brevoort inaugurated the street as the home of lavish entertaining by giving the second masked ball ever to be held in Manhattan, according to the next day's newspapers, for 500 people. Legend has it that two young guests eloped — the British consul's daughter, who wore a costume "of floating gauzes, bracelets, a small coronet of jewels and a risoe[sic]-colored bridal veil," and a lad from a wealthy southern family, who wore "cap and bells and cockle shells aglistening all in a row," according to one account — and caused such a scandal that society banned masked balls for years to come.

Upper Fifth Avenue of today is a big residential boulevard, 100 feet wide, with mostly tall apartment buildings and hardly a mansion (or a ballroom) for blocks. There are roomy twenty-foot-wide sidewalks on either side of the street — the park side is cut pavement stone — and

*Brevoort evidently was the only property owner able to thwart the grid of 1811. An old grove of Brevoort's favorite trees stood on his farm where the city engineers were going to grade West Eleventh Street between Fourth Avenue and Broadway, and Brevoort was said to have stood in the doorway of his farmhouse with a loaded blunderbuss, threatening to blow away any man who touched one of his trees. More likely, Brevoort was rich and powerful enough to persuade the corrupt politicians to leave his farm alone. In any event, that the street stops for one block is the only anomaly of the system, and where East Eleventh Street should be, Grace Church now stands instead, which, not coincidentally, was designed by Brevoort's grandson James Renwick.

a center asphalt motorway sixty feet across, which is during the day a tangle of taxis, limousines, and buses headed south. At night the street is less crowded, sleeker, and a little surreal in its Stonehenge-like majesty. The silver-gray apartment buildings, especially the stately limestone fortresses, seem unapproachable and unoccupied. It is rare to see any movement, or even a person, in the windows of an apartment on Fifth Avenue, and oddly at times there are only a few people walking on the street. People who live on Fifth Avenue invariably never stroll on it but walk one block east to Madison Avenue, where there are interesting shop windows and fashionable restaurants. On many a clear spring night you can see for a mile down Fifth Avenue with not a soul in sight, except maybe a jogger or dog walker headed for Central Park. Most people go from taxi or limousine to the protective shield of a building canopy and disappear into the lobby, the portals guarded by uniformed doormen who monitor the street from behind the wrought-iron filigree covering the thick glass front doors.

There are also a few formidable heavy wooden street-level doors along Fifth Avenue, some banded with metal. These are the entrances to one of the city's most luxurious residential treats, a maisonette, literally, a "small house" that is carved out of the larger building surrounding it. Maisonettes are usually triplexes, most with their own private gardens, and they can also be entered from the main building lobby, which is the way most owners prefer (for security purposes). Other doors lead to the many professional offices of a variety of doctors and dentists that populate street-level Fifth Avenue. If Fifth Avenue doctors are not necessarily the best in their specialties, they are at least the most financially successful in being able to pay the rent for their offices, sometimes as much as $35,000 a month for a suite of rooms facing Central Park. The avenue is particularly known for its corps of vanity physicians — dermatologists, cosmetic dentists, diet gurus, and plastic surgeons offering youth-restorative services. For over thirty years the superfine needles used by Dr. Norman Orentreich and his staff at 909 Fifth Avenue have been legendary fonts of wrinkle-filling collagen and Botox injections that smooth out the worry lines of troubled clients such as Elizabeth Taylor. At 1009 Fifth Avenue plastic surgeon Dr. Gerald Imber prefers to start nipping and tucking clients while they're still in their late thirties, so instead of their getting dramatic middle-age overhauls and looking pulled tight, he simply arranges it so that over the decades his patients maintain their youthful visage. One of Fifth Avenue's largest maisonettes, a fifteen-room triplex at 817 Fifth with forty feet of frontage facing the park, was for many years the home and office of Dr. Howard Diamond, the grand master of rhinoplasty in New York in the 1960s and 1970s. Thousands of princesses from all five boroughs and New Jersey made the pilgrimage to Dr. Diamond's subterranean operating rooms to sleep under anesthesia for a few hours and awaken with the doctor's famously all-purpose ski-slope nose with his distinctive planed bridge. The maisonette was bought by the late pediatrician and philanthropist Dr. Anne Dyson, who gutted it; installed new wiring, central air conditioning, and six phone lines; and put it on the market for $15 million.

Like every fashionable center of life, Fifth Avenue has had its share of white-collar scandal, but once the frisson of schadenfreude passes, manners and civility prevail and a brisk "howdyado?" (as Dominick Dunne captured the perfunctory greeting) is always offered in the elevator or lobby. The two impermissible breaches of conduct for a resident of a Fifth Avenue building are suicide and murder — either to be the victim or the perpetrator causes neighbors distress, although Ann Woodward's taking her own life at 1133 Fifth Avenue years after she accidentally shot her husband at their country estate gave the building more cachet than it ever had before. But there was no small feeling of satisfaction when Serge Rubinstein, the infamous crooked financier, was strangled to death in his art-filled town house at 814 Fifth Avenue, where, noted the newspapers, there were "nineteen pieces of furniture and fifteen paintings in the murder bedroom alone." Claus von Bülow had the good taste to sell his eighth-floor apartment at 960 Fifth Avenue after he was acquitted of attempting to murder his wife, Sunny, at his second trial, thereby depriving his neighbors of the pleasure of snubbing him in the lobby. At the time of his murder, Wall Street financier Ted Ammon was suing his neighbors at 1125 Fifth Avenue, including actor Kevin Kline, claiming he had lost an $8.5 million buyer for his tenth-floor apartment because of the co-op board's failure to give his buyer a board meeting in a timely manner. When Ammon was found bludgeoned to death at his Middle Lane mansion in East Hampton in October 2001, the attorneys for his estate dropped the lawsuit and the apartment was quickly and quietly sold for $10 million to a partner at Goldman Sachs.

Despite the persistent notion that Fifth Avenue is somehow not welcoming to Jews, there is at least one Jewish family in every building, although the majority dwell in the newer, post–World War II buildings that are easier to get into. Rich Jews first claimed the street in the late nineteenth century. Clothing manufacturer Isaac V. Brokaw assembled a family compound: a French Renaissance mansion with turrets for himself at Seventy-ninth Street and Fifth Avenue, twin houses next door for his two sons, and one for his daughter around the corner. Felix and Frieda Schiff Warburg's Gothic mansion at Ninety-second Street was so grand that it was turned into a museum housing the greatest collection of Judaica in the world. The banker and patron of the arts Otto Kahn, one of the most admired Jewish men of his time, built the last private house on Fifth Avenue in 1918; and to be different, he sheathed his 13,000-square-foot mansion in limestone imported from France. The present Temple Emanu-El, built in 1929 on East Sixty-fifth Street, is considered one of the richest Jewish temples in America, with more seats than Saint Patrick's Cathedral, and it stands on the exact spot where the apex of society once stood, the home of John Jacob Astor IV.

The avenue was also once the home of the Union of American Hebrew Congregations at 838 Fifth, a building whose interior has been gutted and transformed into luxury condominiums that start at $9 million (maids' rooms in the first-floor rear can be purchased separately for $500,000 each) by one of the street's most prominent Jewish residents, Alfred Taubman, the seventy-nine-year-old shopping-mall developer and former chairman of Sotheby's, who lives right next door at 834 Fifth Avenue. Taubman has left intact the commandment chiseled across the facade of the old Hebrew Congregations' building, "Love thy neighbor as thyself," which is pretty much what his neighbors at 834 did after he was incarcerated in a federal penitentiary for seven months for price-fixing between his company and the auction house Christie's. He returned home to his building without the least bit of diminution in his social standing.

Of course, the people at 834 Fifth, a building that rivals 820 for supremacy on the street, are getting used to high-profile hijinks. In 1991 one of the building's best-known highfliers, John Gutfreund, the so-called King of Wall Street, was forced to resign as the chief executive of Salomon Brothers because of his complicity in a Treasury bond scandal. Ten years before that, the building was in the spotlight because John DeLorean, the inventor of the gull-wing automobile that he named after himself, was arrested for laundering drug money so he could raise development funds for his car. DeLorean went bankrupt and was forced to sell his apartment — which was bought by one of the few people of color to own an apartment in a "Good Building" on Fifth Avenue, Reginald Lewis, an African American who was chairman of Beatrice Foods, and his Filipino-born wife, Loida.*

The most famous person of color who lived on Fifth Avenue, now moved away, was a longtime resident at 1158 Fifth — the actor Sidney Poitier. It was the broker Dolly Lenz of Douglas Elliman who brought Poitier to see the apartment in the WASPy building, booking the appointment using the maiden name of the actor's wife. Lenz's colleagues scoffed about Poitier's chances of getting into such a posh building, but the admired actor had letters of recommendation from Disney chairman Michael Eisner, television icon Bill Cosby, and actor Gregory Hines, and he was not only accepted by the board of the building without hesitation but was given as a gift a silver key chain on which to hang his new apartment key. Poitier became the best-known African American co-op owner on Fifth Avenue, but because his building was above Ninety-sixth Street, the real estate status line, Fifth Avenue aficionados don't think it counts.

The most highly discriminated-against group on Fifth Avenue is neither the Jews nor people of color, but those who toil in the fashion industry — "cloak and suitters," as they used be more politely called, or "garmentos," as they are now known. Although Fifth Avenue residents are in love with fashion and being fashionable, they don't want people who actually work in that business to live next door to them. There was only one really big name in fashion who lived on Fifth Avenue, and that was Ralph Lauren, who resided on one of the floors of the original fifty-four-room triplex built for Marjorie Merriweather Post at 1107 Fifth.

But Tommy Hilfiger was no Ralph Lauren.

*The open-minded constituency of 834 has been attributed to the liberal influence of Laurence Rockefeller, who lived in a triplex apartment (with its own running track on the roof) that recently was sold for over $44 million to publisher Rupert Murdoch.

Mr. Hilfiger had not revived fashion nostalgia for a more elegant era, nor did he use a polo player for a logo or sell cashmere deck chair throws for $2,700 at a boutique on Madison Avenue in the old Rhinelander mansion. Mr. Hilfiger was the designer and marketer behind a company that manufactured or licensed $2 billion a year in clothing and accessories for urban ghetto kids. Hilfiger's baggy-trouser trademark shape — one could hardly call it a silhouette — the kind that teens wore hung down low, so the crack of the buttocks showed, with the crotch around the knees, was like an urban teenage uniform. In school yards across America, a garment with Hilfiger's name and tricolored flag logo stitched on it was considered as haute a fashion accessory as a Hermès crocodile clutch on Fifth Avenue, yet it is safe to assume that there was not a soul who lived at 820 Fifth Avenue who had a single article of Tommy Hilfiger clothing hanging in his or her cedar-lined closets.

A few days after news of the sale, more details began to leak and it became clear that the formidable Alice Mason, the doyenne of all the carriage-trade brokers in the city, had had her hand in it. But even for Alice Mason, getting Hilfiger into 820 was quite a trick.

## I I

"THIS IS HOW I do it," Alice F. Mason said with the satisfied smile of a magician about to divulge the clever secret of her favorite illusion.

"I sit eight people here, and I have eight here, eight there, and eight here," she said, wending her way through the modest-size rooms of her apartment, pointing out assorted occasional tables. "Then I put this under here and take this out," she explained obscurely, gesturing to a sideboard. "That's sixteen, twenty-four" — she counted guests aloud — "and then twenty in here in the library" — she turned into a room almost bare except for the built-in banquettes under the windows — "well, it would be the library, but I don't have any books." She laughed.

Mason, a jowly seventy-two, was demonstrating how she would manage to seat sixty people at one of her black-tie dinner parties in her compact, eight-room flat on East Seventy-second Street. She was dressed to receive a visitor in a smart, tailored black Armani pantsuit and a big burst of expensive white costume jewelry around her neck, and Fluffy, her twelve-year-old white Pekingese, was tucked under her left arm, just like in the portrait of them on the wall of her living room. She loves showing people around her apartment because it has long been one of the little ironies of New York real estate arcanum that Mason, the esteemed broker who practically invented the modern carriage-trade end of the business, lives in a rent-stabilized apartment and pays only $1,500 a month for rent. What is more striking is that this "back-elevator" apartment, with its bleak view of Lexington Avenue, is legendary as one of the great salons of the city. Over the past thirty years the literary, political, and diplomatic elite of the time have converged on Mason's unpretentious digs to participate in dinners that are so mannered, they qualify as social kabuki — "Evenings that are like plays," she said. "Their aim was to give you a mental high that lasted for days."

She got the idea to give regular parties in the 1970s when the writer Norman Mailer, a friend, told her, "If I knew I was coming to your house for dinner the second Tuesday of each month, I could save myself four or five lousy dinners." Mason's parties always followed the same cast-iron mold. They were called for 8 P.M. and guests were expected to be prompt. Dress was formal. There was no such thing as being fashionably late, although sometimes there would be a crush in the small elevator. She would greet her guests, usually dressed in a gown by James Galanos, standing just inside a small, laquered red entrance foyer whose walls are tiled with mirrors. Her daughter, Dominique, forty-four, who began assisting her mother with her parties when she was fifteen years old, would stand nearby, handing out place cards and table seatings, although there would be a small chart on the wall for backup. Mason would urge her guests into her simply decorated living room of Louis XIV–style furniture and a fake ficus tree for an hour of hors d'oeuvres, cocktails, and chatter until, precisely at 9:00 P.M., in a busy scurry of waiters and waitresses, a transformation occured. The rooms would be disassembled, the fold-out tables opened, linen and place settings would appear, the library be reconfigured, and voilà, dinner for sixty, catered by Daniel Boulud, the latest *chef de la maison.*

There were always sixty; thirty men and thirty women, and Mason did not feel obligated to invite husbands with wives (or vice versa) if one of them was boring. ("I try for fifty-six people who are interesting," she once confided to *New York* magazine about her standards, "and four who are boring.") When Richard Ivor, the British ambassador to the United Nations, asked if he could bring his wife, Mason told him, "Tell her it's a working dinner." Mike Nichols and Diane Sawyer were one of the few married couples invited together — others were Norman Mailer and Norris Church, Betsy and Walter Cronkite, and Barry Diller and Diane Von Furstenberg, but they were separated at dinner at different tables in different rooms. Twice in the course of Mason's dinner parties, guests fell in love. Louise Melhado and editor in chief of Time Inc. Henry Grunwald, who married in 1987, met at a Mason dinner party, as did Francesca Stanfill and Peter

Tufo, former managing director of investment banking at Merrill Lynch & Co. and the U.S. ambassador to Hungary.

Dinner guests were seated in tight groups of six or eight around tables so small that each guest could have only one glass and one plate in front of him or her at a time, and wineglasses needed to be removed with each course as a new wine was introduced. In this deliberately intimate setting guests were expected to share one topic of conversation among the table and not engage in private discourse with the person to their right or left, contrary to custom. "It's not like a bon-mot thing," Mason once explained, "where one wit is trying to outwit the other." It was also understood that one person held the floor at a time, and at each table an unofficial monitor, or "host," usually a regular such as Gloria Steinem or Helen Gurley Brown, enforced the rules. The tables might be small but the conversation never was, especially when the knee-to-knee guests included Dominick Dunne, Steve Kroft, Carl Bernstein, Peter Jennings, Arianna Huffington, Alan Greenspan, and Barbara Walters. There were never any movie stars — save for Woody Allen, who in later years was allowed to bring his young bride, Soon-Yi. Mason wanted stimulating conversation, not pretty faces. Sometimes, but rarely, the events were fund-raisers for her favorite Democratic Party candidates, including Bill Clinton and Jimmy Carter, whose framed photographs with her are displayed on tables throughout the apartment.

She always tried to arrange unusual and hopefully productive pairings at the same table. She has seated representatives of Yasser Arafat with such prominent New York Jews as Loews Corporation magnate Laurence Tisch and *New York Daily News* publisher Mortimer Zuckerman, whereby they were able to have an unusually free exchange of ideas in a collegial atmosphere. There was an unspoken rule that political conversation must not get too heated, which is why one night columnist Sidney Zion had to pop up several times from his table at a Mason party (this one held off-premises at Regine's) to cool down. When author Dotson Rader broke protocol and wandered from room to room, Mason was so piqued that she announced he would never be invited back. (Mason herself is not the easiest dinner guest. *W* magazine reported that she sat "stone silent" during a Park Avenue dinner party because she was miffed about being seated at a B table. She let herself out the back door without saying good night to the hosts. "I know the way out," she was quoted as saying, "I sold them the apartment.")

Dinner would be over at 10:45 P.M. and the guests were expected to leave the way they arrived — promptly, except for one night in 2003, when the Iraqi invasion was about to begin, Bill Clinton discoursed until nearly 1 A.M. and held the crowd "mesmerized," Mason said.

The net effect of the parties was that Mason became one of the city's most unusual power brokers, a combination Elsa Maxwell–Pearl Mesta cum political operative who raised millions of dollars for Carter and Clinton. The press lapped her up and she reigned in the 1980s. ALICE IN POWERLAND, *W* called her in a big spread; ALICE MASON'S BIG DEAL DINNERS, her feature in *New York* magazine was titled; and she was the MASON DU JOUR, in *Manhattan, Inc.* The publicity generated a powerful halo effect; her well-heeled guests and their friends thought of her first when they wanted to buy or sell, such as Woody Allen, whose town house Mason sold for $27 million. While some brokerage houses half Mason's size spent as much as $50,000 a month to advertise, she rarely had to place a paid ad in a newspaper. The publicity about her parties made them legitimate tax-deductible write-offs — at around $15,000 each back then, a real bargain.

But the parties were hardly just a marketing tool; they were also an affair of the heart. Mason had been giving dinner parties long before Norman Mailer suggested she hold them on a regular basis. Mason started entertaining at home in the late 1950s, when she first got into the real estate business. She grew up in a suburb of Philadelphia; her mother was a Cuban American from New York, her father a Chestnut Hill dentist, and she attended Colby College in Maine. Although the details of her background have been disputed in gossip columns and magazines, the small mysteries of her past only enhance her mystique. She is thrice divorced — the first a six-month marriage to a distant cousin in 1952 with whom she shared her maiden name of Mason — and she is not inclined to talk about any of her husbands. She finds the whole subject of marriage "a very boring thing." *Boring* is a key word in Mason's vocabulary and her psychology. "You only have so much energy," she once told a reporter, "and I don't want to put mine into marriage. Also, I loathe companionship. I get bored so easily with that. . . ."

"In a way, the dinner parties are like romances for her," said her daughter, Dominique, who runs the company, Alice F. Mason Ltd., from their small, crowded offices on Madison Avenue, big enough for only a dozen or so desks. Dominique is the daughter of Mason's second husband of four years, Francis Richard, a director of the Berlitz School whom she married in 1957. "You plan the dinner parties and you write them down," Dominique said, "and you rework the seating and you call everybody and see if they're going to come, so it was like replacing a romantic factor in her life, and they had all the aspects of a romance." Even in Mason's freshman days in the real estate business with a small firm called Gladys Mills, handling mostly rentals or town house sales, Mason invited her clients to dinner at her apartment — then a one-bedroom on the Upper East Side. The guests, who included Marilyn Monroe, for whom she arranged a sublet at 2 Beekman Place, and Alfred Gwynne Vanderbilt Jr., were forced to eat their dinner from trays while sitting on Mason's bed.

Mason was thrilled that she had Alfred Vanderbilt as a client; he had recently divorced his wife, whom he left behind at 820 Fifth Avenue, which was then a rental, and he needed his own place. "I thought, 'Finally I have a great client,'" Mason said, settling into a French-style upholstered sofa in her living room, "and I'll be able to get him into one of the good co-op buildings. Then I discovered that he wasn't in the *Social Register*, for some reason or other, and a lot of better buildings wouldn't consider him."

The "some reason or other" that Vanderbilt wasn't in the *Social Register* was that he had demanded his name be removed from the infamous black book with red lettering as a matter of principle, as had several other men of good conscience. The *Social Register*, sometimes referred to as a stud book, is simply an alphabetical list of the names and addresses of people deemed to be in society. It had its precedent in the 1883 *Society-List and Club Register*, which was a directory to the homes of the old English and Dutch families of New York and who was "at home" to receive guests on what days. It no doubt influenced Mrs. Astor's self-appointed arbiter elegantiarum, Ward McAllister,* who first uttered the number four hundred as the amount of people who "mattered" and who could comfortably fit into her ballroom, to compile his own list of the famous Four Hundred six years later. (He suggested that perhaps "our good Jews" could put together their own social list. They didn't.) The modern-day *Social Register* that confronted

---

*When McAllister eventually published the Four Hundred, it had only 319 people on it, and when he died, not even that many showed up at his funeral, while his benefactor, Mrs. Astor, gave a ball on the eve of his burial.

Alice Mason was first published by Louis Keller, of Short Hills, New Jersey, the son of a patent attorney and a former dairy farmer with a fetish for the rich. After Mr. Keller died in 1922, various functionaries, including one ancient woman, Mrs. Edward C. Burry, who collected clips of marriages and deaths from an office on Park Avenue South until she died in 1960, kept up the tradition of compiling the *Register* for fifty years. Every entry includes the surname of the patriarch, matriarch, and offspring of each clan, along with their alma maters and years of graduation in parentheses. Town and country addresses and phone numbers are also supplied. New additions had to be nominated by an existing member, seconded, and recommended by letter. For many years the *Register* was completely white and Protestant, with a few Golden Clan Irish Catholics. For a time Bernard Baruch's name was in the *Register*, but not because he wanted to be, and John Hay Whitney also demanded his name be deleted from the book as a matter of conscience, as did the publisher Alfred A. Knopf, who called the existence of the *Social Register* a "travesty of democracy." Sometimes people were removed for unseemly behavior. When the 1966 edition was published, the headline of Suzy Knickerbocker's column in the *New York Journal American* was a relieved '66 SOCIAL REGISTER OUT AND NO ONE'S DROPPED. It hardly seemed a portent of late-dawning equality when in 1999 African American entertainer Bobby Short was listed for the first time. A more egalitarian version of the *Social Register* continues to be published today, albeit with some embarrassment, by the publishing empire of Forbes Inc.

It was a stunning discovery for Mason to learn that inclusion in the *Social Register* could hold absolute sway over who was able to live where in New York. "All of these buildings had managing agents," she said, "and all the managing agents were in the *Social Register* themselves, and they only hired brokers who were also in the *Social Register*, and they weren't allowed to sell to anyone who *wasn't* in the *Social Register*." Mason eventually got Alfred Vanderbilt into 31 East Seventy-ninth Street, "and he had to give *all* his relatives as references," she said.

The *Social Register* turned out to be only one of Mason's many frustrations. She discovered that New York co-operative housing was a morass of prejudices and shibboleths. A 1959 survey conducted by the Anti-Defamation League of B'nai B'rith reported that of 175 luxury co-ops in New York, one-third had no Jewish residents, achieved by a "gentleman's agreement" that owners sell only to their own kind. "It wasn't just Jews that certain buildings didn't want," Mason said, the frustration of those days creeping back into her voice. "They wouldn't take *anybody*. They didn't want big-time WASPs from California, or the Midwest, or Texas. They didn't want people with vowels in their names, like Italians or Greeks — no matter how rich they were — or people who came from countries whose names had too many vowels, like Scandinavians. The 'Our Crowd' Jews had their own building anyway. The Straus family — one *s*," she pointed out, "who owned Macy's department stores built Seven-twenty Park Avenue for themselves, and they lived there until they died and kept everybody out. Eight ninety-five Park and Seven-thirty Park were also for 'Our Crowd' Jews. Six-fifty Park was built for the rich Irish."

Mason shrugged. "I thought, 'What is this all about, this *separation* of everybody? It's so *amazing*. I'd really like to learn something about this.'"

Mason bought herself a copy of the reverse directory, a phone book available from the telephone company that lists names and phone numbers by address. Mason began to compile a catalog of the top 150 buildings on the Upper East Side of New York on a stack of yellow legal pads. For each address, she made a subjective evaluation of the complexion of the building, analyzing it financially, socially, and psychologically. She counted how many names sounded Jewish or Italian or foreign. She noted the difference between a building where there was one German Jewish name like Schiff and buildings where there were several Greensteins and Rosensweigs, who were clearly Eastern European Jews. She learned that some boards didn't mind taking "achievers," as she called them, first-generation rich who had made their money in admirable ways, and that certain boards had a reputation as "do-gooders," who were open to accepting someone "new." For instance, 834 Fifth was a very liberal building in terms of religion and new money despite being one of the most desirable on the street.

"I made it my business to meet a key person on all the important boards," Mason said. "Not the whole board, just a key person, and I developed many relationships so I could call a key person on the board. I started by getting 'Our Crowd' Jews into Fifth Avenue buildings because they were bankers and they had everything in common with all the people who were in there already. They just weren't in the *Social Register*, so I didn't break barriers with some furrier." Although, truth be told, she did slip in a few furriers. Dominique Mason told of a wealthy furrier who wanted to buy an apartment at 655 Park Avenue and had the money but not the breeding. Mason advised him to transfer all his bank accounts to a branch office on Fifth Avenue and Fifty-first Street where she did business. Then she met with him and his wife and gave them a copy of the *Social Register* and said, "I don't care how long it takes, go through every single name. Anybody you ever met in your life that knows anybody in this book, you find me four people!" Mason also took the man's wife, who had a terrible hairdo and wardrobe, to Bergdorf Goodman and made her buy a suit for the board interview. And as for her Bronx accent, Mason said, "When you go to the board meeting, say you've got a cold — COUGH — and you can't talk."

It was also a revelation to Mason that one of the most difficult kinds of people to get into co-operative buildings were diplomats, with some good reason. Diplomats hold frequent cocktail parties and receptions, can indulge in controversial politics, and in general make bad neighbors. And they have diplomatic immunity as well, so even if they tie up the elevator every night and make too much noise or stop paying their maintenance fees, there is no way to evict them. Mason's third husband was a Dutch diplomat ("I married him in December and divorced him in May," she told *New York* magazine), and that brief marriage ignited her fascination with the United Nations. In 1971, when the People's Republic of China was admitted to the United Nations, she remembers thinking what an exciting time it was in New York and she wondered where all those new Chinese diplomats would live — or where any diplomats lived, for that matter. In 1977 billionaire Prince Saud al-Faisal, an heir to the Saudi throne and Saudi Arabia's foreign minister, was turned down at 640 Fifth Avenue on a thirteen-room apartment that belonged to Bruce A. Norris, the president of the Detroit Red Wings, because other residents feared demonstrations. When the U.N. ambassador from Zaire applied for an apartment at 32 East Sixty-fourth Street, a board member said he heard "the ambassador liked to drink, he liked to entertain, and he would go into the closet and throw spears" and the board had to say no.

Mason got out her trusty yellow pads and researched where all the diplomatic residences were located. Then she had a map of Manhattan with the location of 145 diplomatic missions drawn up, each identified with its national flag. She named the map the "Alice Mason Map of Permanent Missions and Observers to the United Nations, New York" and sent one to "all the missions at the U.N. plus foreign leaders," she said, with a note saying that she would be happy to represent them in finding housing, despite the problems. No real estate broker had ever solicited foreign nationals before, and for the past twenty-five years Mason has been the United Nation's de facto real estate broker, a valuable niche market upon which no other broker has been able to encroach.

When all else fails, Mason turns to a higher power for board capitulation. She believes in "astral projection" and in chanting as a way of influencing opinion. "That's how I got Jack Kaplan into Seven-sixty Park Avenue," she said. Kaplan was a controversial man, the former owner of Welch Grape Juice Company who sold his company to a cooperative of workers. In 1964 a congressional panel accused him of helping funnel $1.25 million through one of his personal charities, the J. M. Kaplan Fund, for use in building a CIA training camp in Costa Rica. "Jack Kaplan was not the profile of that building," Mason said with a meaningful nod. "I knew that board wouldn't want him, but I had this method in the sixties that nobody else had. Every day I went to my yoga class and I chanted, 'You want the Kaplans, you want the Kaplans . . . ,' figuring that somebody in that yoga class would be in astral contact with someone on the board of Seven-sixty Park Avenue." Jack Kaplan was unexpectedly accepted, and a few weeks later one of the board members ran into Mason on the street and said to her, "We can't believe we let Jack Kaplan in. I must have been in a trance. At the meeting I suddenly said, 'We want the Kaplans!' Why did I want the *Kaplans?*"

Mason's favorite story of astral projection took place in 1969 when she was trying to get Eddie Gilbert into the penthouse at 1133 Fifth Avenue. Gilbert was *Time* magazine's former "Boy Wonder of Wall Street" who had fled to Brazil with over $20 million he borrowed to cover bad margin calls, which he repaid after he returned to the United States to do some time in Sing Sing. He was still very rich and needed a place to live. "Gilbert had been in jail for six months for fraud," Mason said, "and he married an airline hostess, but he was dying for that apartment at Eleven-thirty-three. He told me, 'Oh, Alice, if you could only get me that apartment.' I said, 'The head of the board is a judge named Kaufman, and I want you to say over and over again to Judge Kaufman, 'Eddie's paid his dues, he's paid his dues, you should let him in, he's paid his dues. . . .' And when Eddie went for his board meeting with Judge Kaufman, the judge said, 'Well, Eddie, you've paid your dues . . .' and they let him in!"

Mason chuckled. "But that was 1969. I haven't done that in a while," she said, smiling, hoping it did not sound foolish. "And I did not chant Tommy Hilfiger into Eight-twenty Fifth Avenue," she added.

## I I I

EIGHT-TWENTY FIFTH AVENUE is a vortex of desire in Manhattan residential real estate. Situated on the corner of East Sixty-third Street and Fifth Avenue, it looks like money — a stately fortress of glistening gray limestone crowned with a modest copper cornice. It is one of the great works of architects Starett and Van Vleck. A prim white canopy, its number 820 flapping in the wind, stretches from the curb to the entrance. The double front doors are glass set behind a thick bronze filigree and attended by two doormen liveried in dark gray uniforms with black stripes down the side of their trousers.

The building has only twelve apartments, one per floor, and in each one the paneled wood and mirrored elevator opens directly onto a forty-three-foot-long entrance gallery with parquet de Versailles floors — the architect's breathtaking introduction to the lavish sensibility and size of the apartment. Lining this enormous entrance gallery are sets of double doors leading to an enfilade of reception rooms overlooking Central Park: living room, den, library, sitting room, and dining room, each with its own fireplace. The volume of the rooms is such that if it were not for the spectacular view of Central Park across the street, the sensation is of being not in a building in New York City but in a French country château suspended in the ether. It is unique even among the great buildings of New York because the apartments have never been subdivided and for the most part are in their original, unadulterated 1916 layouts, each with seven servants' rooms and a back servants' hallway so the staff can go about their lives and tasks unseen.

Not only is 820 Fifth Avenue physically handsome, it is regarded as the kind of a building where the residents lead "a privileged and a congenial way of life," Nancy Richardson, the former wife of financier Frank Richardson who lived on the fifth floor and whose apartment was for sale for about $18 million, told a reporter. Since it was built in 1916, the building has sheltered some of the most powerful men in the United States, including Alfred E. Smith, the former governor of New York; Arthur and Kathryn Murray, the owners of the dance studios; and one of the richest men in the city, Robert Goelet, whose sprawling family owned much of the land under what is now Rockefeller Center and who once gave a party in his apartment for 350 guests, including the Jay Goulds, three princesses, and Prince Matchabelli. Alfred Sloan Jr., chairman of General Motors, died in his apartment at the age of ninety. Pierre Lorillard, the son of the tobacco billionaire, and Eberhard Faber, the man whose name is on the millions of pencils his company manufactures, both lived in the building until their death at age eighty-seven.

The building is also associated with CBS president William Paley, who lived on the eighth floor with his best-dressed wife, Babe, a leader of society and in whose entrance gallery once hung Picasso's 1906 *Boy Leading a Horse*, then worth only about $125 million. The horse was an appropriate image, because one of the first occupants of the eighth floor was the utilities baron and horseman C. K. G. Billings, who had become famous in New York in 1903 for giving a dinner party in the Grand Ballroom of Sherry's restaurant for thirty-six guests seated on horseback with small tables affixed to their saddles. The horses were brought oats for dessert. In later years the eighth-floor apartment was owned by the much-married Stavros Niarchos, the billionaire Greek shipping magnate whose estate sold the apartment for $15 million to Goldman Sachs mergers and acquisitions co-chairman Jack Levy. Eight-twenty Fifth Avenue is so special that it has even had an imaginary tenant: the con man in the play and movie *Six Degrees of Separation* who passed himself off as the son of Sidney Poitier gave it to the police as his home address.*

Some say the building's exclusive reputation began to change in June 1996 when Terry Semel, the co-CEO of Warner Brothers, bought the eighteen-room, 7,000-square-foot seventh-floor apartment of Ann and Gordon Getty for $12.5 million. It was reported in the press that the venerated Jayne Wrightsman didn't want Mr. Semel in the building, embarrassing everyone involved. Semel was show business, although he was also smart and a gentleman, as well as enormously rich — so rich, in fact, that some years earlier he had given up his seat on the Time Warner board rather than comply with the Securities and Exchange Commission's requirement that he reveal his compensation package. He would have had no trouble meeting the co-op board's reputed demands that buyers have $100 million or at least twenty times the

*The locale of the apartment of the duped art collector in *Six Degrees of Separation* is given as 1049 Fifth, the building where radio commentator Rush Limbaugh now lives, and as previously noted, Sidney Poitier's real address was once 1158 Fifth.

price of the apartment in assets. It also happened that Semel and his beautiful wife, Jane, were avid art collectors, and it was intimated in the press that Semel was able to bypass Mrs. Wrightsman's objections to him and get approved by the building's tough co-operative board by currying favor with the board president, William Acquavella, a prominent art dealer, by buying art at Mr. Acquavella's Madison Avenue gallery. This caused what *Avenue* magazine called an "internecine squabble" between Mrs. Wrightsman and Mr. Acquavella. In fact, Mr. Semel had never bought art from Mr. Acquavella's gallery. Yet this issue of being able to curry favor with Mr. Acquavella, who bought his own eleventh-floor apartment in 1993 for $9.8 million, was one that vexed the building and justifiably infuriated Mr. Acquavella, who demanded and received a correction from the publication that printed it. But as Mark Twain said, "Scandal sticks to rebuttal like tar."

In any event, word on the street is that the highly honorable Mr. Acquavella doesn't make the final decisions about 820 Fifth anyway. Although Mr. Acquavella is the putative president of the building's co-op board, conventional wisdom is that the octogenarian Mrs. Wrightsman, who lives on the third floor, runs the place. The elegant, small-boned rara avis of society is the widow of Oklahoma-born oilman Charles Wrightsman, who died in 1986 at the age of ninety. It was Mrs. Wrightsman who has been credited with bringing the newly widowed Jackie Kennedy to Fifth Avenue only six months after the assassination of President Kennedy when she tipped off the former First Lady that Mrs. Lowell Weicker had put her fifteen-room apartment on the market at 1040 Fifth and that it would be an appropriate home base for her. It was not far from the apartment of Jackie's sister, Lee Radziwill, who had recently moved to 969 Fifth Avenue, and her in-laws Patricia and Peter Lawford, who lived at 990 Fifth, and Jean and Stephen Smith, who lived at 950.

Mrs. Wrightsman and Jacqueline Kennedy met when they were both young housewives in Palm Beach, with Wrightsman a lot greener at the game of Palm Beach housewife than Jackie but a lot richer. Wrightsman was born Jayne Larkin, in Flint, Michigan, and in the 1940s she was a saleswoman at a perfume counter in a Los Angeles department store when she met Charles Wrightsman, a divorced man thirty years her senior, with grown children. Wrightsman didn't have many social credentials, but he did have social ambition and barrels of Oklahoma crude, along with a twenty-eight-room Palm Beach villa that he gave to his young wife as an anniversary present in 1947.

It was in Palm Beach that the young Mrs. Wrightsman began a remarkable transformation. She hired tutors for herself in the arts, literature, and French, in which she became fluent. She began to work tirelessly for charities, garnered a reputation as a warm host and a good friend, and started to study eighteenth-century French furniture — also an interest of her new friend Jackie Kennedy — becoming a connoisseur of the period. She would later be declared the "queen of the French decorative arts" when her collection was put on permanent display at the Metropolitan Museum of Art in 1969, including the Rubenses, Vermeers, and Louis XV's red lacquer desk that passed through the Palm Beach estate. When Jackie Kennedy was First Lady she appointed Mrs. Wrightsman to a committee to help find period pieces to decorate the White House, and over the years the women became so close that Mrs. Wrightsman stood vigil with the family in the apartment when Mrs. Onassis died. The Wrightsmans eventually abandoned Palm Beach as a home base for a suite at the Pierre Hotel, and frequently visited with the Baroness Renée de Backer, a Rothschild who lived at 820 Fifth Avenue, whose apartment they eventually bought.

At 820 Fifth Avenue, these many decades later, Mrs. Wrightsman is said to have total say, not just over who moves in but over what kind of wood paneling is in the elevator or what color the flowers are in the vase in the lobby. She is so powerful, it is said in jest, that she has influence over who gets into the building next door, 825 Fifth.*

She certainly controlled the fate of the fourth-floor apartment, right above her, which had been put on the market in February of 1998 for $13.5 million. For over seventy years it had been the home of the family of Mrs. W. Murray Crane, the widow of U.S. Senator Winthrop Crane of Massachusetts. Mrs. Crane cofounded the Museum of Modern Art in 1929 with Mrs. John D. Rockefeller Jr., as well as the Dalton School, and lived in the apartment with her daughter, Louise, until she died at the age of ninety-eight. Louise Crane, who died in 1998, was a noted poet and arts patron as well, and more philanthropy for music and art in the city of New York was generated out of that apartment than almost any other place in the city. The apartment deserved an occupant worthy of its provenance, and even just to show it to potential buyers, real estate brokers had to make appointments through Mrs. Wrightsman's lawyer, to be preapproved — the logic being, why even bother showing the place if the client was someone Mrs. Wrightsman wasn't going to let buy it?** Among those who didn't pass muster was peripatetic Johnson & Johnson heiress Elizabeth "Libbet" Johnson, who for a moment was fixated on buying both the Crane apartment and Nancy Richardson's fifth-floor apartment

*A trustee of the Metropolitan Museum of Art, she has so much clout at the museum that she was able to get it to ditch the considerable presence of Madonna. When Versace died, the next clothing gala turned into a virtual paean to him, at which Madonna was supposed to perform. Mrs. Wrightsman thought Madonna unseemly and got her knocked off of the show.

**In a few rare instances buyers are asked to "prequalify" before seeing an apartment where there might be curiosity value, as was the case when Jacqueline Kennedy Onassis's apartment was for sale at 1040 Fifth. Buyers were asked to present financial and social accreditation to her estate's representative — in this case, her son-in-law, Edwin Schlossberg, before the family would consider allowing a stranger to see her private quarters and lavatory.

above it for a total of $27 million and combining them into the largest trophy apartment on the street — 14,000 square feet. But because renovation work is allowed only during summer months, it would have required five summers to complete the scope of Ms. Johnson's extensive makeover. Mrs. Wrightsman said something like "over my dead body," and Ms. Johnson was told to move on.

And so, the fourth floor of 820 Fifth Avenue languished empty and dark for over a year, a magnificent palazzo unable to find the perfect suitor, when one June day Tommy Hilfiger stepped across its doorway.

# I V

"IT WAS A moment that happened," Alice Mason said, by way of explanation. "And it was an exception."

"It was very intricate," explained Dominique, who had joined her mother in the living room and lit a cigarette, much to her mother's disapproval. "It was about a million pieces to a complicated puzzle that my mother figured out."

Tommy Hilfiger had been represented in the deal by Alice Mason's top producer, Deborah Grubman, the wife of high-profile entertainment attorney Allen Grubman, who has represented almost every major figure in the music industry, from P. Diddy to Tommy Mottola to Madonna. Deborah Grubman had a reputation as being a smart, honest broker, and her husband's tentacle-like business connections were a never-ending source of real estate clients for his wife. When Deborah Grubman first suggested to Alice Mason the pairing of Hilfiger and 820, "I said, 'I don't think so,'" Dominique recalled. "Then she had gone and showed it to him anyway, and when he wanted to buy it, Mom figured out whether or not he was feasible and then she figured out how it became feasible."

Mason did not pick up the phone and call Jayne Wrightsman. "I was barely acquainted with her," Mason said, and calling ahead for an on-the-spot decision is never a good idea. "Do I want a fast no?" Mason asked. "Or do I want to try for a slow yes, and see what I can do?"

What Mason did was to build a portrait of Tommy Hilfiger in his board package that she knew would appeal to Wrightsman's sensibilities. Her most important tools were the letters of recommendation she assembled, which read like a mini-biography of Hilfiger's life after she got through editing and tinkering with them. Mason asked Hilfiger to get a long, descriptive letter from a childhood friend, a clever touch that presented the homespun Tommy Hilfiger — a self-made man from a modest background in Elmira, New York, where he was one of nine brothers and sisters of a hardworking Catholic family, his father a watchmaker, his mother a nurse. He married his high-school sweetheart, Susie, and they had three polite, well-behaved children. The letters made it clear that he made his money not on some clever business deal, but the hardscrabble way, opening first one retail shop in upstate New York and soon ten of them, before selling them and venturing to Manhattan, where he started a company that tapped into the style zeitgeist of 20 million teenagers. Perhaps the most important letter in the package was a recommendation from Leonard Lauder, whose cosmetics company, Estée Lauder, manufactured and distributed Hilfiger's highly successful perfume. In the echelon of Manhattan status, "you can't get much better than a letter from Leonard Lauder," Dominque said.

But you *can* get better — if it turns out, just providentially, that a few years earlier you had made a substantial seven-figure contribution to the Costume Institute at the Metropolitan Museum of Art, a museum that is one of Wrightsman's great passions. Hilfiger also made a well-publicized $2.5 million donation to the Fresh Air Fund, another of Wrightsman's favorite charities, which sends city kids to summer camp. It bode especially well that the donations had been made years before he even thought about 820 Fifth Avenue. "Mrs. Wrightsman liked that," said Dominique. "She liked that it wasn't tit for tat."

As for his personal finances, Mason decided to present Hilfiger's assets through his holdings in his namesake company, rather than his personal assets, as the crucial part of his financial qualification, although he showed both to the board. Published reports were that Hilfiger's salary per annum was about $25 million — not very much for a building like 820 Fifth Avenue. However, Hilfiger's $2-billion-a-year company was very cash-rich, with a reported $500 million in a war chest that Hilfiger had accumulated to buy out other companies. When the final figures came in, Dominique Mason said, "Hilfiger showed us his money, and it was *a lot*."

Tommy Hilfiger being accepted by the board of 820 Fifth Avenue would have been one of Alice Mason's greatest triumphs — if only he had ever moved in there, even for only one night. Instead, Hilfiger came to loggerheads with the board about his renovation plans, and while they were dickering about what he could tear down and rebuild and when, the baggy-pants craze passed and his business fortunes waned. Although Hilfiger switched to a more classic look, his sales kept plummeting and the company lost more than half of its market value; eventually the bonds used to back his company were reduced to junk status. His business was not the only thing that faltered — so did his longtime marriage. Within a few months of closing on the apartment, Hilfiger and his wife of twenty years started divorce proceedings and Hilfiger wound up in a bachelor pad with the other veterans of the co-op wars in TriBeCa, where he bought a 4,500-square-foot condominium penthouse for a mere $3.5 million. Less than a year after buying the apartment at 820, he put it back on the market, with Alice Mason as the broker, this time priced at $20 million — close to a 100 percent increase in less than a year. "That was the right price for it at the time," Mason huffed. "Hilfiger had underpaid."

Even at that exalted price she found a buyer right in the building — Lily Safra, the billionaire banking widow, who bought Hilfiger's apartment for $18 million for her daughter to live in. It was a handsome profit for Hilfiger and yet another commission for Mason. Safra spent another few million dollars renovating the place and had new wiring, plumbing, lighting, and flooring added. However, like Hilfiger, her daughter never moved in and Mrs. Safra put it back on the market in 2002, "decorator ready," asking $30 million. It was sold for a reported $24.5 million in the fall of 2003.

Deborah Grubman has since left Mason's employ and is now a managing partner at the Corcoran Agency, where she is one of its most successful brokers.

Jayne Wrightsman appears to have learned her lesson. When in March of 2000 Steve Wynn, who sold his Mirage Resorts in Las Vegas to MGM Grand for $4.4 billion, tried to buy socialite Nancy Richardson's fifth-floor apartment for $17.5 million, Wrightsman put her foot down and said, "Forget it."

Mason said she's satisfied with the Lioness in Winter portrayal of her in a recent issue of a society magazine, and she agreed that she has cut back drastically on her business responsibilities and simplified her personal life. She lunches occasionally at her corner table at Le Cirque (and chants for a cab to pick her up and drop her off) and she sells real estate when it's necessary for the boss to make a cameo appearance, but most days she stays in her apartment and some days she doesn't go out at all. She has cut the dinner parties back to only one a year, making them more exclusive than ever.

"There are three reasons why she stopped giving the parties," Dominique said. "She entertained everybody she ever wanted to have dinner with. People complained to her everywhere she went that they weren't invited. And people didn't invite her back."

"Invited back?" Mason cried when she heard this analysis. "If I had to sit through somebody's boring dinner party, I'd want to kill myself." She mimed putting a gun to her head.

Boring. That word again. In truth, her own parties began to bore her, like her romances. "People aren't as interesting now, don't you think?" she asked. "Today everybody is famous or very rich, and beyond a certain amount of money, what difference does it make?"

# T W O

## PRIVATE
## CLUBS

Everybody jumps and says to me, '*Oh, I can't wait to read your book when you write it,*'" Edward Lee Cave said in a falsetto voice, trying to mimic a cloying sycophant. "Well, it ain't gonna be written!" he thundered, the twang of his Virginia accent rising along with his indignation. He clasped his hands in front of him on his desk to stop them from shaking. "I consider this business a sacred trust. We are like the private banking division of the real estate industry," he intoned, like a priest chanting Sancta Maria. "Our clients do not like to read about themselves in books or newspapers. And neither do co-op boards! If it's gossip you want, you can get that from any Park Avenue housewife, not from me."

Cave, sixty-one, fixed his piercing blue eyes on a visitor sitting across his polished desk like a marksman taking aim, and there was a meaningful silence except for the tapping of rain on the windows of his office and the muffled sounds of traffic on the street below. Cave is a handsome man, with a strong jaw, short-cropped silver hair, and broad shoulders. He was elegantly dressed in a bespoke pinstriped gray suit, a hand-tailored, pink spread-collar shirt, and red braces that matched the color of the initials ELC embroidered on his shirt's breast pocket.

Suddenly, he took several deliberate, deep breaths and then held the last one, his cheeks flushing. He had been fighting a chronic case of the hiccups and he was determined to beat them. "I am going to the opera tonight," he explained, exhaling, "and I can't have the hiccups."

Another thing Cave can't have are uninvited strangers to his offices. While most brokerage houses intentionally have street-level offices with lit displays of glamorous apartments in their windows to catch the interest of people walking by, Cave's offices are inconspicuously tucked away behind a numbered door on the third floor of a nondescript white-brick office building on Madison Avenue in the Sixties. The offices are handsome but functional. There is a large conference room with a circular mahogany dining-room table and twelve upholstered dining-room chairs around it; a communal room for his brokers with desks, telephones, and low partitions; and a cozy inner sanctum, his small office, the walls covered in William Morris fern wallpaper, a pattern that has adorned every office he's had in the past thirty-five years. On the walls are photographs of some of the most beloved objects he sold as an auctioneer during his tenure as a vice president of Sotheby's, including a southern plantation that he sold for $1 million, and an ormolu candelabra with Meissen statuettes of parrots that fetched $65,000 and are now worth perhaps $1 million. "I spent my life appraising what other people have made," he said, "and I know where everything is that I ever sold." On the windowsill, visible from the street, are two life-size marble busts from the estate of legendary art collector Ben Sonnenberg, one of them a cleric in a wig and one of them William Pitt, the British prime minister, looking down his snooty nose.

"I don't *want* people we don't know asking us to help them," Cave said pleasantly, "because we don't know where we can *put* them. I have sold only two apartments in twenty years through advertising. The only reason why we even occasionally advertise is to remind our friends that we're still here. There are only twenty-five people at this firm and they say that our gang here was either married to, is related to, or went to school with, *all* of our clients. Why, Armin Allen, one of our brokers, is president of the Newport Preservation Society, and I've known him for *thirty-five years.* Polly Peabody had been a broker here *forever.* Our clients are our *friends.*"

Cave's clients are also rich. Sitting on his desk are three oversize Rolodexes, each bulging with the names, addresses, and phone numbers of "the richest, most powerful people in the world," as he told the *Wall Street Journal* in 1987 in a feature article about his phenomenal success. He cultivated these names from his seventeen years at Sotheby's, and another seventeen years as the owner of his own real estate company, Edward Lee Cave Inc., which secured him the reputation as the "crown prince" of New York real estate, as *Vanity Fair* magazine dubbed him. "My first year in business, nineteen eighty-two, I represented the most expensive apartment sold that year in New York, for two million dollars," Cave said. "It was the top floor of Four East Sixty-sixth Street" — one of the most prestigious addresses in the city on the corner of Fifth Avenue — "and I have sold the same apartment three times since, the last time, five years ago, for thirteen million." Cave discreetly did not say that the buyer was the cofounder of Microsoft, Paul Gardner Allen, the third-richest man in the United States, whom the board voted to allow in despite his wearing blue jeans to his interview. Cave's firm has also sold one of the most expensive co-ops in the world so far, the thirty-four-room triplex of financier Saul Steinberg at 740 Park Avenue, to a relatively obscure fifty-three-year-old invest-ment banker named Stephen Schwarzman for over $30 million. In typical inside New York real estate style, the broker who handled the deal at Cave's office was Saul Steinberg's former sister-in-law, Kathryn Steinberg.

Cave likes to say that the kind of apartments he specializes in is the "spectacular," but what he means is that they are spectacularly expen-sive. He personally will not deal in apartments below a certain price, which he will not name, but $5 million seems to be the minimum to rouse his interest. What's more, Cave won't just represent any apart-ment in any old building; his métier is in Good Buildings, or GBs, as the ladies who lunched at the restaurant in Bergdorf Goodman used to call them. Nobody had really defined exactly which the GBs were until they were given flesh (and brick and mortar) by writer Tom Wolfe, who in a 1985 *Esquire* magazine article named forty-two GBs. "What drives people wild at bottom," Wolfe wrote, "is the simple fact that le monde is sheerly divided into Good Buildings and those that, for whatever reason, are not Good. It may have nothing to do with space, construction or grandeur." All of these GBs, save for five strays along the East River, can be found in an area Wolfe called the Triangle, defined by three unbreachable lines of status beginning with Fifty-seventh Street from Sutton Place to Fifth Avenue on the south, up Fifth Avenue to Ninety-sixth Street on the west, and a sharp diagonal back to Sutton Place on the east, effectively cutting out a huge swath of the Upper East Side, including much of Carnegie Hill and upper Park Avenue. There are no GBs at all on the West Side of Manhattan, not even on Central Park West, with the venerable Dakota and the ele-gant towers of the San Remo and the Beresford, and none of the GBs have names, which would be considered gauche, except for River

House (which insiders refer to by its street number anyway). The addresses of GBs speak for themselves.*

While in every city and village around the world social status is determined in part by what side of the tracks people live on, in Manhattan where one lives, by choice or by fate, becomes a prism through which people are defined. Psychologists believe that before people choose a specific house or apartment, they are drawn first to a type of neighborhood where the tone and character reflect the way they want the world to perceive them. This can be a tricky choice in Manhattan, where there is simply not a "posh" side of town, or a "best" neighborhood, but many neighborhoods and distinct enclaves with scores of nuances and gradations. The location of an apartment half a block in either direction, the age or construction of a particular building, what floor you live on, even your zip code, can peg your social and financial status, your religious or ethnic background, or your sexual preference. If your zip code is 10011, which encompasses sections of the West Village and Chelsea, and you're a single male, chances are you're gay.** If your zip is 10021, a slice of the Upper East Side that used to be known as the Silk Stocking District, odds are you are white, earn seven figures per annum, and worship in a church and your mailing address is eagerly sought by credit card companies and retailers of prestige luxury goods.

---

*Wolfe's GBs are: 1 Beekman Place; 10 Gracie Square; 1 and 120 East End Avenue; 550, 555, 635, 640, 720, 730, 740, 765–75, 770, 778, and 812 Park Avenue; 810, 820, 825, 834, 953, 960, 998, 1020, 1030, and 1040 Fifth Avenue; 435 East Fifty-second Street (River House); 4 and 131–35 East Sixty-sixth Street; 2 East Seventieth Street; 4, 19, 36, 117, and 160 East Seventy-second Street; 50 East Seventy-seventh Street; 21, 39, 66, and 79 East Seventy-ninth Street; 25 Sutton Place North; and One Sutton Place South.
**In the 2000 census, demographers found that 10011 had the highest concentration of male same-sex households in the city, seven times the norm.

Middle-aged, upper-middle-class families who can't afford prime-time property on Fifth or Park console themselves with the "neighborhoody" feel of Carnegie Hill, north of Eighty-sixth Street and therefore beyond the cusp of the fashionable. Far east above Seventy-second Street is known as the "Yupper East Side" because it is stuffed with high-rise, cookie-cutter apartment buildings occupied by upwardly mobile Yuppies looking to marry and mate and move on. Intellectual wives pushing baby strollers and husbands hoping to make partner are drawn to the roomy "classic six" co-ops in the two miles of unmemorable buildings on West End Avenue on the Upper West Side, which all face other unmemorable buildings. It is a truism that the East Village is filled with young pale hipsters, poor gays, computer geeks, druggies, and neurasthenics who smoke cigarettes and otherwise. The rich, aging gays live in gentrified town houses on the charming streets of the West Village along with a younger generation of upscale married couples with young children. The sybaritic, muscled Chelsea Boys of the newest generation of gay men have made Chelsea, the West Side between Fourteenth Street and Thirty-fourth Street, their stomping ground. TriBeCa is so trendy that it's barely a real place; it's a "destination neighborhood" invented by real estate developers out of the old egg-and-butter-district warehouses and its name is an acronym for the "Triangle Below Canal Street." It is one of the city's most expensive diasporas, a neighborhood with huge lofts for those too unusual or private to qualify for an apartment uptown, rap moguls such as Jay-Z, and those hard-to-categorize inveterate New Yorkers like the late John F. Kennedy Jr.

Some delineations of class and status are obvious to the eye — for instance, the abrupt change north of Ninety-sixth Street on Park Avenue, where railroad tracks rise out of the ground and the pristinely kept co-operative doorman buildings of Carnegie Hill suddenly give

way to tenements and bodegas. But there are also more muted differences. There is a "better" side of Park Avenue (the western side, where
most of the superior buildings were built and many of the so-called
back apartments have unparalleled views of Central Park), and less-
prestigious buildings are made of brick, although a few Good Buildings (720 Park Avenue, for example) start with two stories of limestone
before turning into brick. Important buildings are all above Sixty-first
Street on Park or Fifth Avenue, away from the commercial district.
At one time, above Seventy-ninth Street on Park Avenue used to be
snidely known as the Irish Gold Coast, but no more, although it is
decidedly less classy than south of that cross street. On Central Park
West apartments above Eighty-second Street are worth $100,000 less
per room, for no discernible reason other than being north of an
invisible social demarcation that defines "too far uptown." And while
Fifth Avenue might be "the best address," if your apartment is on a
floor below the "tree line," usually the fourth floor, and your view of
the park is blocked by leaves in the summer or bare branches in the
winter, yours is a shabby lot compared with the neighbors above you,
whose apartments are worth hundreds of thousands of dollars more
per floor the higher you go. However, the opposite can be true on Park
Avenue, where the view from the windows of the higher apartments is
only of the windows of another building, but below the fifth floor
the viewer is greeted with the cityscape of the handsome avenue, divided by its meridian and seasonal plantings, the flow and stasis of
Manhattan traffic, and the life of the city passing close by — but not
too close.

Cave himself lives in a smartly decorated flat in a small town house
on East Ninety-first Street that he bought twenty-five years ago. Contrary to the impression that Cave was to the manner born, he grew up
in Arlington, Virginia, the son of a successful Volkswagen dealership

owner. When asked if his family was middle-class, Cave scowls and intones, "If you asked my grandmother, Anna Blanche Compton Cave, if we were middle-class, she'd *destroy* you." After attending boarding school in New England and studying in Geneva, he received a degree in decorative arts from Columbia University in New York, which didn't cheer his family. "My father said, 'Edward, why don't you take law?'" Cave recalled. "And I said, 'One thing I promise you, Daddy, I'm never going to have an antiques store in Greenwich Village." He did, however, take a job decorating the apartments of the very rich for Parish-Hadley, the WASP decorating company, which was his introduction to the *intime* peculiarities and peccadilloes of the way very rich people lived. But choosing wallpaper and buying antiques for customers who didn't properly appreciate them was anathema to Cave, and in just a year's time he left decorating for Sotheby's, where he became the firm's most trusted connoisseur of English period furniture and Chinese porcelains, as well as one of its star auctioneers. In 1976, drawn to beautiful houses and apartments the way he was drawn to smaller treasures, he created Sotheby's new International Real Estate division. "We've sold them Monets," he cheerily told the *Wall Street Journal*, "now we'll sell them the walls to hang them on."

As it would turn out, when Cave left Sotheby's in 1982, the walls would soon be just as expensive as those Monets and just as good an investment. Only a few years before, you couldn't give away apartments in New York City. After twenty years of statewide fiscal mismanagement and two liberal mayoralties, the city was in financial and social turmoil. One million citizens were on the welfare roles, crime rates were at historic highs, and the prostitutes in hot pants and the muggings in Central Park had became comedy fodder for late-night TV talk-show hosts. One million middle-class people fled the city during the 1970s, mostly into the surrounding suburbs. They called the exodus the "squeegee effect," after the men who appeared out of the shadows on New York City street corners to wash car windows for change. In October 1975, with the tax rolls depleted and the short-term, high-interest debt over $6 billion, Moody's Investors Service downgraded all New York state and city securities and bonds, and it was thought that 100 banks might fail. That month an indifferent President Gerald Ford turned down New York's plea for a federal bailout and declared in an address to the National Press Club that perhaps the best thing that could happen was for New York City to go bankrupt and be restructured. The following day the *New York Daily News* ran the classic headline FORD TO CITY, DROP DEAD.

"You could have bought any apartment in the city for two hundred and fifty thousand dollars," Cave marveled.

Not for long. By the 1980s the hungriest, most powerful generation in history — the baby boomers, who were moving through time and space like the proverbial elephant in the snake — burst upon the U.S. economy. There were 76 million baby boomers, and they had turned all the idealism and pacifism of the 1960s inside out into naked ambition and greed. The most ambitious of the boomers were inevitably drawn to New York in the 1980s, where the bull market on Wall Street was a cornucopia of cash. Tens of thousands of boomers became part of the engine that made the bull market run, and the workers who tended that good-time engine — the bankers, lawyers, brokers, traders, money managers, accountants, and all those employed by the myriad tributary industries fed by greenbacks — were compensated gloriously and beyond imagination. Men and women who were only thirty or forty years old got rich quickly. Very rich.

In 1982, according to the U.S. Census Bureau, there were only 12 billionaires in America. By 2003 there were 262 billionaires — with 48 of them making their home in New York City. The rest of the nation was rich, too. At the turn of the twenty-first century there were 6.5 million millionaires in America, one-third of them under thirty-nine years of age. By 2001, according to one analysis, there was a total of 9.8 million millionaire households.* People were so loaded that to register on the Forbes 40 richest list, you had to be worth more than $430 million. The word *millionaire* itself lost all meaning, and the publisher of *Millionaires* magazine added a new title called *Opulence*.** All that money was so confusing that the *New York Times* tried to differentiate between the merely affluent, whom it defined as earning $1 million to $10 million a year, from the superrich, who had assets of $10 million to $100 million.

The mantra "greed is good" was first uttered by the fictional, corrupt überstockbroker Gordon Gekko, portrayed by Michael Douglas in the movie *Wall Street*. As it turned out, greed was certainly good for some, but prosperity also proved that money couldn't satiate some people, or perhaps that avarice was infectious. Prosperity itself, explained an economics professor at New York University, "has created this mania to be rich." All this cash generated what the *Wall Street Journal* dubbed the "wealth effect" — a change in the psychology of consumers marked by a need to spend on big-ticket items — "affluenza," as one wag described it. The wealth effect was proof again of one of the tenets of Thorstein Veblen's *Theory of the Leisure Class*: the whole point of conspicuous consumption is that it's conspicuous. Despite the constraints of good taste, there is allowable pleasure in showing off wealth and possessions, sometimes even joy. Thus, the

---

*NFO WorldGroup, a market-research firm, put the number of "cash" millionaire households in America — excluding the value of houses and retirement funds — at an astounding 3.8 million in 2003.

**The word *millionaire* was coined by a newspaper in 1843 upon the death of tobacco farmer Pierre Lorillard to describe the amount of money he made by selling snuff.

very new, very rich scrambled for shiny things to own and show off —
every sort of status bauble on the planet: private jets, muscle cars,
Aspen vacation chalets, Hamptons beach houses, and trendy expensive
wristwatches galore, a different color face for every day of the year.
NOTHING LEFT TO BUY? snidely asked a *New York Times* headline in a
business section article in March of 2000, which quoted a recent Ivy
League graduate as saying that he aspired to owning not one but a fleet
of planes by the time he was thirty.

Of all the vainglorious purchases, the single greatest public represen-
tation of financial success, the one that comes before money is put
away for the children's education or before buying a trophy mansion in
the country, is a status address in Manhattan. All the pent-up desire
in New York at the end of the twentieth century was focused on real
estate, on displaying a special piece of turf in the richest, toughest
town in the world; and with all that desire and all that money, it made
prices for top apartments nonsensical. By the 1990s the cost of an
apartment in New York no longer held any relationship to the true value
of the space it represented. It was like the mass hysteria of the tulip
mania of Holland in the seventeenth century, when buyers were mort-
gaging their homes just to own a single root of a rare tulip that only
they and a few of their friends would ever see bloom. New York real
estate brokers marveled in 1980 when the first apartment over $1 mil-
lion dollars was sold at 834 Fifth Avenue, a four-bedroom, fourteen-
room duplex for $1.6 million. Even as prices escalated over the next
decade, $5 million for an apartment had remained the high end until
the late 1990s, when things really got crazy and apartments started to
sell for more than $20 million in the top buildings. Although the mar-
ket held its breath after the terrorist attacks of 2001, only two years
later co-op prices were expanding by 20 percent. Nowadays there is an
average of better than fifty apartments for sale in Manhattan above

$5 million, with at least two dozen for sale over $10 million on Fifth Avenue and Central Park West, and a dozen in the $25 million range. There is no shortage of takers in these price ranges, either, only a shortage of apartments. When the apartment of the late Fiat chairman Giovanni Agnelli at 770 Park Avenue went up for sale for $20 million, the first week it came on the market it was shown twenty-two times to prospective buyers and was eventually bought by Vornado Realty Trust chairman Steven Roth for about $25 million. Publisher Rupert Murdoch paid $45 million for his penthouse apartment at 834 Fifth.

Prices have escalated at an even greater rate in the condominium market. At One Central Park, the new Time Warner Center on Columbus Circle, one apartment sold for $30 million to a California doctor, and a duplex on the seventy-fifth and seventy-sixth floors went for $42.5 million to a forty-six-year-old British financier. Just across Columbus Circle, at Trump International Hotel & Tower, where Janet Jackson lives, Johnson & Johnson heiress Libbet Johnson has put her 20,000-square-foot condominium apartment on the market for $62 million.

Edward Lee Cave does not like to deal in condominiums, where anyone can buy in and there is no board approval. He embraces the cooperative plan of apartment ownership that is the bane of most other brokers. He regards the gauntlet of the co-op board as an indispensable protection, and because he does, the boards trust that he won't try to sneak the "wrong person" past them just so he can get a fat commission. "And may I tell you," Cave said, "as much as co-op boards may drive us crazy, because they are cautious, in days like today when the stock market is down and the market is tight, it's a godsend, because there is nothing on Park Avenue for sale because of distress — *nothing* — and so the prices never go down.

"Co-ops are no different than private clubs," Cave said. "Only private clubs aren't as personal as where you live. The co-op board is trying to figure out two things when somebody comes to buy an apartment. First, they want to know that you are nice people who will behave yourself and that your kids are not going to go screaming up and down the halls. Second, they are trying to make sure you're financially okay, because you're going into a very tight real estate deal — sometimes you've got as few as twelve other tenants in the building with you, who want to know that you can always meet your obligations and pay your dues and also afford to help put a new roof on the building if necessary." Which sometimes happens. Journalist Mike Wallace of *60 Minutes* and Viking Press publisher Tom Guinzburg, both apartment owners at 32 East Sixty-fourth Street, were chatting in front of their building one day when Wallace said, "Is there something wiggling at the top of the roof?" It was the cornice, which was loose and in danger of falling. For the next two years the building was enmeshed in scaffolding while the cornice was restored at a cost of $1.5 million. The burden was shared among the owners at close to $100,000 each, tacked onto their monthly maintenance costs.

"You must remember," Cave said, "these aren't just apartment buildings. They're not just brick and mortar. They are not investments, like stocks and bonds. They are vertical *neighborhoods*. I'm not selling brick," he said, wagging his finger again. "I'm selling lifestyle."

# I I

IT IS THE intimacy of Manhattan that makes the thorny housing arrangement known as the co-operative plan the most prevalent form of apartment ownership.

If the adage is true that a man's home is his castle, then the moats of Manhattan's dwellings are no bigger than a carpeted hallway. In Manhattan, people live on top of one another, quite literally; it's a tight, vertical world, with only twenty-two square miles of land crammed with a population of more than 1.5 million. Although it's not exactly Bombay, the next person's turf is never much more than a membrane away. One man's ceiling is another's man's floor. And as anonymous a place as the city pretends to be, it is actually a very intimate place in which to live. Even in the best apartments on Park and Fifth Avenues you can hear through the walls in the still of the night: the muffled sound of a toilet flushing, a cough, or the harsh voices of a quarrel. From the window of every apartment you can see into the windows of neighbors, in the next building, across the way, on another street, people whose names and identities you do not know, yet the rituals of their daily lives become the background tapestry of your own.

In every other city in the world, the condominium model, in which you buy the four walls and floors of the space you live in and pay common carrying charges based upon its size, is the usual form of ownership. With the co-operative method, people do not really own the walls and floors of their apartments — they own stock in a private corporation that owns the entire building. The number of shares of stock they own represents the square footage of the physical apartments they occupy, and owners are assessed monthly maintenance fees based on their number of shares. Every shareholder is obligated to behave according to a set of commandments outlined in the "proprietary lease," a codex of policies and ordinances enforced by the board of directors that cover almost every situation imaginable in a Manhattan apartment building, from the obvious, such as not leaving garbage on the floor of the incinerator room or allowing children to play in the hallways, to the more obscure, like the interdiction of offensive odors emanating from one's apartment (be it frying fish or marijuana smoke) or not eating in the elevators or not sitting on the chairs in the lobby while waiting for guests, or the prohibition of holiday decorations on doors in common hallways. United Nations Plaza once had a rule prohibiting residents from cooking in a wok, and another that all drapes had to be lined in white so the building would look orderly from the outside. In one landmark case, plastic surgeon Ronald Levandusky sued the co-op board of One Fifth Avenue, which tried to stop him from moving a steam pipe in the kitchen four feet during a renovation of his co-op, claiming that the board's intransigence about where the pipe should be was part of a personal vendetta against him by a board member. The court found that whatever its reason, the board was within its rights to tell Dr. Levandusky where to put the pipe and that the board "may significantly restrict the bundle of rights a property owner normally enjoys." Broadway producer Arthur Cantor once told the *New York Times* about his co-op at the Dakota: "It's a form of living under a dictatorship. . . . In a sense you're half-slave and half-free." Socialite Charlotte Ford, who lives in a leaky penthouse on Sutton Place, told a reporter, "I'm always saying to myself, I'm going to move to a condo. . . . The way the boards function — ridiculous."

The proprietary lease also spells out causes for eviction from the building for inappropriate behavior, but that seldom happens, except on the rare occasion a resident is repeatedly drunk or unruly in the lobby or urinates in the elevator. Even more rarely a shareholder can be evicted over a morals issue, as when the board of 1 Beekman Place voted in 1982 to evict the seventy-year-old A&P heir, Huntington Hartford, from his twenty-room apartment for "dissolute, loose or immoral character" after he and his former wife attacked his secretary. (When Hartford was forced to put the apartment up for sale, brokers discovered that a locked door separated every room, and the eccentric supermarket heir demanded that in order for brokers to show prospective buyers the apartment, each door had to be locked behind them as they went from room to room. A. Laurance Kaiser IV was showing the apartment to a client when he opened the unlocked door to Hartford's bedroom; there Mr. Hartford sat, naked, his silver hair disheveled, looking out at the East River. Kaiser's customer said, "Mr. Kaiser, Mr. Hartford has a small problem, let us leave." (The apartment was eventually sold in 1984 for $1.5 million, and the new owner flipped it the following year for $4 million.)

The court of appeals recently upheld a decision of a West Side co-op board to evict a prominent Wall Street bond seller who had antagonized his neighbors by being a relentless troublemaker in a building where the neighbors had lived peacefully until he moved in. In a much-admired building just off Fifth Avenue in the Seventies a man managed to buy a very expensive apartment with a completely false board package, including forged letters. A charming and well-behaved neighbor, he lived in the building for several years before it was discovered that he had made his money in video pornography and had practically invented the idea for 900-number phone sex. The board forced him out, and now one of the city's most active social couples resides in the apartment instead.

Another reason for the co-operative plan's popularity in New York is the great tax advantage to the building — only stock changes hands, so the holding corporation pays no capital gains taxes, no matter how much the property accrues in value. Because buying stock in a private company is a private transaction, there is no public listing of sales or prices, so all figures quoted in the industry — and in this book — are the word-of-mouth figures that filter through the porous real estate community and wind up in brokers' computers, sometimes unsubstantiated. (The prices of town houses and condominiums are recorded deeds and are available in city records.)

But most of all, the co-operative plan is popular because the co-op board of directors has the right to reject whomever it pleases, without explanation, as long as there is no civil rights violation. It is the ultimate exclusionary tool in American housing, institutionalized and legal. This legal right to blackball people from buying an apartment without explanation was affirmed by a landmark 1958 New York Court of Appeals ruling when Sidney Weisner, an attorney, and his wife were rejected by the co-op board at 791 Park Avenue and Weisner sued the board to find out why they had been turned down. "There is no reason," the court wrote, "why the owners of the co-operative apartment house could not decide for themselves with whom they wish to share their elevators, their common halls and facilities, their stockholders' meetings, their management problems and responsibilities and their homes."

Of course, there are civil rights violations taking place all the time in co-ops — people are frequently turned away because of their religion or color or their age. In 1964, before profession became a protected class, the co-op board of 117 East Seventy-second Street turned down actor Peter Lawford and his wife, Patricia, who was the sister of President Kennedy, it was said, because he was "an actor and a Democrat." The city's Commission on Human Rights refused to investigate, saying that no law protected Democrats or actors. "The power of co-op boards is sweeping," said broker Dolly Lenz. "They can turn you down because you have green eyes if they want."

Because co-op boards are not bound to state the basis of a rejection, unless some big mouth on the board lets it leak, it's next to impossible to prove a civil rights violation. In one of the few successful cases against a co-op board an African American attorney who worked at the silver-spoon firm of Skadden, Arps, Slate, Meagher & Flom and his wife, who was white, were awarded $640,000 in damages in May 1977 by a Manhattan jury who believed their rejection from a building at 425 East Fifty-first Street was racial, in part because one of the board members scribbled "black man" on a pad. The following year another interracial couple, a white physician and his African American wife, demanded $1 million for being turned away from 180 East End Avenue when the board questioned the doctor's "financial ability" to pay his mortgage and maintenance. The case was settled out of court for only $12,000. In a 1982 incident, a Jewish couple sued a Park Avenue co-op, saying they were turned down because of their religious beliefs, and lost. There is currently a bill in the New York state legislature that would compel boards to say exactly what the basis of their rejection is, but the powerful real estate lobby that represents various players in the $2.5 billion residential market — mostly big real estate agencies and management firms who like the "old boy" business run just the way it is — will probably keep it tabled. In any event, almost all the grievances presented to the Commission on Human Rights are about rentals, and just a small percentage are about co-ops — only two or three complaints a year — and rarely are any of those against the top buildings, certainly never a Good Building, where people who are snubbed would just as soon as walk away with some dignity rather than fight to live where they are not wanted.

It used to be that only rich people who could afford to pay cash for co-ops lived in them. That's because until 1971 New York State didn't allow banks to give mortgages for co-operative apartments: it was believed imprudent to lend money based on shares of a privately held corporation. Buyers were forced to secure personal loans, often with a five-year payoff limit and a $150,000 cap. In 1979 the *New York Times* estimated that there were only 100 co-ops along Fifth, Madison, Park, and Lexington Avenues, or along the East River. That was about to change with the introduction of new laws allowing rental buildings to "convert" to co-ops, which ignited a multibillion-dollar business. Hundreds of speculators descended on the residential real estate inventory of the five boroughs and began buying up tens of thousands of small rental buildings on the cheap and converting them into co-ops. Tenants who lived in the building were given a choice by the so-called sponsor of staying on as renters or buying their apartments for an "insider's price," a huge discount off the purchase price — often as much as 40 percent — as an inducement to stay. The converters made billions of dollars in the 1980s and changed the way middle-class New Yorkers live, giving them the peace of mind of owning their own living space. Co-operative buildings are everywhere now — about 9,000 of them in all five boroughs, with nearly half in Manhattan.

But only forty-two of them are Good Buildings.


# I I I


THE PRIMARY METHOD by which a co-op board scrutinizes a prospective buyer is called the board package. Nominally, it's an assets-and-liabilities statement, but in reality this financial curriculum vitae turns into an intrusive examination of the life of the applicant, who is forced to endure inspection by a group of complete strangers with the hope that he or she will be found sufficient to live under the same roof with them. The apotheosis of this process may be the time the board of 755 Park Avenue asked prospective owners as part of their board package to write a short essay on why they aspired to live at that particular address.

For a wealthy man applying for a co-op at a top building, the cost of assembling a detailed financial statement can easily reach $10,000 in accounting and legal fees, plus another $2,500 for the copying and binding of the ten copies that most boards demand. A completed board package can weigh as much as five pounds, and it's not unusual for brokers to have them delivered by bonded couriers in secure file transfer boxes to the building's lawyer or to the apartment of the chairman of the co-op board.

Some few Croesusean souls are so rich that it's impossible to compute and document their exact wealth for a board. "An asset/liability statement on Henry Kravis would take a year and a half to prepare," Cave scoffed. "Men of that kind of wealth don't even know themselves how much they are worth. When I have clients with a great deal of money, I ask them to get a letter from their accounting firm attesting they have net liquid assets in excess of one hundred million dollars, of which thirty-five million is in General Electric stock. That's usually enough. Although I once had a client who was a very rich man who wanted to get into Thirty-two East Sixty-fourth Street, and I suggested that if he showed too much money, it was going to get the board's noses out of joint. Yet when his papers came in, it showed his full worth, eighty-five million dollars. I said, 'Why did you do that?' and he said, 'Well, I made it! Why shouldn't I show it?' And, you know, I kind of liked the guy for that."

Thirty years ago it might have been enough for a buyer to send the co-op board a bank letter saying that the prospective owner was a "valued customer." Today's toughest boards want the previous three years of an applicant's tax returns; statements from all savings and retirement accounts; an accounting of all financial liabilities, including personal debts, loans, mortgages, credit card balances, and alimony payments; and the last three months' canceled checks. Canceled checks in particular are scrutinized for incriminating evidence, such as regular large amounts written out to the Sherry-Lehmann liquor store on

Lexington Avenue, which can indicate that an applicant entertains or drinks too much. Or canceled checks can be simply socially embarrassing — for instance, the monthly checks made out to one of the city's best-known Botox doctors or a popular psychopharmacologist whose practice is just up the block. If a board is not satisfied with the amount of paperwork received, it can demand statements from further back. Buyers never know what kind of revelation might trip them up. One man was rejected because he had once applied for a JC Penney charge card, a store that one of the board members felt was too downscale. He was asked at the board interview exactly what it was he bought at JC Penney and the man said, "Underwear," which was not as acceptable as answering, "A snowblower for my Aspen ski house," thus sealing his fate. Sometimes even a noble disclosure backfires. One married couple's income tax records revealed a large contribution to the Coalition for the Homeless, which alerted the board of a Park Avenue building that the wife also counseled homeless people as a volunteer. The board decided that perhaps the wife might invite homeless people to the building, and the couple was declined admittance.

It goes without saying that in Good Buildings buyers are expected to pay cash for their apartment. "I've never gotten a mortgage for anyone, *ever*," Cave huffed, his nose in the air almost as high as the one on the bust of William Pitt. In addition, each building has a "number." This number is an amount that the buyer must show in liquid assets in addition to the cost of the apartment. Depending on the building, the "number" is either a multiple of the price of the apartment or sometimes just a minimum amount. "The rule of thumb," said Cave, "is the 'number' is three times the purchase price but, believe me, it changes with every building."

At 834 Fifth (Sotheby's chairman Alfred Taubman, socialite Carroll Petrie, Bing Crosby's son Harry) and 740 Park (Courtney Sale Ross, widow of the late Time Warner chief Steve Ross; perfume magnate Ronald Lauder), the "number" is ten times the price of the apartment. The threshold number at 4 East Sixty-sixth Street (Veronica Hearst), 2 East Sixty-seventh Street (publisher Arthur Carter, cosmetics magnate Leonard Lauder), 820 Fifth (banker Michael David-Weill), and 960 Fifth (art dealer Richard Feigen, divorcée socialite Anne Bass) is $100 million. Applicants need only $50 million to get into 720 Park (financier Henry Grunwald, Revlon chief Michel Bergerac), 950 Fifth (publisher Mort Zuckerman, Loew's Hotel scion Jonathan Tisch), 998 Fifth (Wall Street honchos Steven Rattner and Joseph Perella), 1030 Fifth (director Mike Nichols and television commentator Diane Sawyer), and 1040 Fifth (actress Candice Bergen and her husband, Marshall Ross, and billionaire David Koch).

To raise the gold standard even higher, boards demand that these enormous sums be truly liquid, in money market accounts, Treasury bills, or blue-chip portfolios. Boards won't accept "single-asset" portfolios in which holdings are all of one New Age–type stock and they generally disregard the value of 401(k) retirement plans, paintings, jewelry, antiques, boats, and country homes — anything that might take time to convert to cash in a rocky business environment. An applicant's showing $30 million in collectible motorcycles as part of his assets when he applied for an apartment at 2 East Sixty-seventh Street, notoriously one of the most thorough boards in the city, was a "red flag," said Arthur Carter, the *New York Observer* publisher who is one of the board's three members. So was the portfolio of another would-be buyer who showed $400 million in one stock. "I told him, 'You should short this stock,'" Carter said, "'because I would have shorted all of it.'"

Carter, who made a personal fortune of $200 million as an investment banker, owns the fourth floor at 2 East Sixty-seventh and runs the board with cosmetics magnate Leonard Lauder, who has owned the penthouse for thirty years, for which he originally paid $300,000 and is easily worth $25 million on the open market. Real estate brokers consider Carter the greatest tyrant of any director of a co-op board, and he takes great pleasure in his building's tough reputation. He will not refute that he orders a dossier on prospective apartment owners, compiled by a team of detectives, with revelations from as long ago as smoking pot in high school or getting a DWI (driving while intoxicated) citation coming home from the country club. Carter feels he's maintaining a tradition. "When Charles Allen was president of the board he turned down fifteen people who wanted to buy apartments, including Neil Sedaka."

What are the "red flags" to a top board? Carter enumerated: "No litigious types. No one who is so public a figure they require security or are followed by paparazzi. No one who is in a lunatic marriage, or a second marriage, and no one who is single, because you never know whom their spouses are going to turn out to be," Carter said, despite the fact that he is thrice married. Also, the women on co-op boards do not want divorcées in their building, especially wealthy and pretty ones; the wives of rich men do not want their husbands riding on the same elevator with them. Finally, Carter explained, buildings also worry about having "too many Jews" and being known as a "Jewish building." Brokers openly agree with him that although none of the top buildings have prohibitions against Jews altogether, there is a perceived quota before a building gets pegged as "Jewish" and loses prestige and value. ("This is the way it works," explained Alice Mason. "There is one Jewish person on the board, and that Jewish person is the one who vetoes all the other Jewish people.")

Many brokers feel that since everybody is so rich these days, sometimes being wealthy isn't enough to impress, and in those instances the requisite "letters of recommendation" that the board demands can be

crucial tools for acceptance. Most buildings demand at least five letters of recommendation, usually three from personal friends and two
from business associates. In putting together a board package, most
brokers ask their customers to solicit as many as fifteen letters and let
the broker cull the best. Brokers make specific suggestions on what to
ask for in the letter. It's no longer good enough to write a letter that
says the applicants "are a lovely couple" and sign off. Personal letters
must be paeans to the steadfastness and honor of the buyers, their
quiet and accommodating presence; brokers think nothing of editing
these letters and sending them back for revisions. Business testimo-
nials are from the applicants' bankers (and not the kind that manage
the local branch), stockbrokers, business managers, and lawyers, attesting to a long-term fiduciary trust. This is also a moment when some
vicious malicious mischief takes place, and it's real estate urban legend
that co-op boards frequently receive anonymous uncomplimentary
letters about applicants.

Finally, even if your credentials pass muster, so must you in person.
No matter how rich or exalted, every buyer is obligated to appear for
face-to-face scrutiny by the board, euphemistically called the "board
meeting." This final hurdle is traditionally held at 5:30 P.M. on a weekday in the apartment of the board president, who is invariably top dog
in the building and who tends to represent the building's cultural profile. Sometimes the board comprises as few as six in a building such as
the Beresford, an unusually small number for a building that takes up
an entire city blockfront. Only a few influential members of the board
join the president, and the entire meeting lasts no more than one
nerve-racking hour. Boards usually try to be humane, although legend
has it that one building unexpectedly conducted board meetings in
French to see if the prospective owner became flustered. Years ago the
board of 1125 Park Avenue came up with the clever idea of holding the

board meeting at the apartment of the buyer, so they could really get an intimate impression of how their prospective neighbor lived.

Brokers coach and rehearse clients for the crucial board meeting, including advice on wardrobe — some even shop with clients for appropriate, low-key clothing in muted shades. Conventional wisdom has it that women should not wear furs or diamonds; a single strand of pearls is sufficient. One broker arrived at the apartment of his client to give her the once-over shortly before she left for her board interview, and when he saw that she was wearing a pastel-colored outfit he cried, "It's all wrong! It's all wrong!" He made her change her clothes. "Can you imagine?" marveled the woman, who was moving to New York from Paris, where she had lived and dressed fashionably most of her life. When "broker to the stars" Linda Stein was working with the pop star Sting on a $4.8 million apartment at 88 Central Park West, she gave him orders to shop for a conservative suit at Brooks Brothers for his board meeting and made him promise to "think Central Casting businessman and father," which he dutifully did. Dominique Mason Richard tells with delight the story of a woman who carried with her to a Park Avenue board meeting what she believed was a smart knockoff of a designer pocketbook that she bought from a street vendor. Weeks after being rejected she discovered that the scrawl across the pocketbook wasn't the designer's name or initials but actually read, "screwyouscrewyouscrew."

Hall F. Willkie, the president of Brown Harris Stevens Residential Sales, tells his clients to "dress like you're going to a funeral" and warns them not to be too charming or outgoing, that "too much personality" can turn off a board. "Never elaborate" is Willkie's credo. He recalled a client who was asked at his board meeting if he liked dogs. Thinking that dogs would present a problem in the building, he said, "Oh no, I hate dogs, absolutely can't stand them." It turned out he was talking to one of the great benefactors of the New York Association for the Society of Prevention of Cruelty to Animals and was summarily rejected.

Conventional wisdom also holds that clients must never accept an alcoholic drink at the interview, even if the board members themselves are drinking. If someone at a board meeting asks if the buyer intends to do major renovation work on the apartment, the answer should always be "Hardly anything at all, that's why we like it." (Although in the better buildings buyers always fess up to ambitious renovation plans if they are smart, and in any event, plans ultimately need board approval.) If a board member inquires about the applicants' entertaining habits, the response should invariably be "We live very quietly and rarely entertain." When one couple was asked at a board meeting what their hobbies were, the wife answered cheerfully, "We love to go to Atlantic City and gamble," and they were rejected. If a member of the board asks if there are any questions, the answer is "No." Deadly inquiries include whether the lobby is going to be redecorated or how often the windows are washed, or to mention that one of the lightbulbs is burned out in the elevator. Some applicants, however, can do no wrong. When Christie Brinkley was a single model, before she married Billy Joel, she signed a contract to buy an apartment at the very uppity 50 East Seventy-seventh Street, where most observers didn't think she'd get through the front door. However, the mostly male board of the building couldn't wait to meet her, and she was approved with ease.

While it's true that buyers don't have to parade their children for approval at a board meeting, it is sometimes the moment when the family dog must make a personal appearance to be tested for friendliness and comportment to make certain that what's described as a cocker spaniel in the application doesn't turn out to be a pit bull with long ears. At one building on East Seventy-fourth Street it was the job of a board member who was a psychologist to take each dog in the elevator to the lobby to see if it obeyed the doorman's command to sit. Terrified owners sometimes feed their pets tranquilizers before the interview. Thousands of mid-level co-operatives ban dogs altogether, or limit their size and weight — twenty-four inches tall or twenty-two pounds is a common standard, slightly larger than a Louis Vuitton purse. A notarized letter from a veterinarian attesting to the dog's actual weight is sometimes required, but some proprietary leases specify only that the dog must be "carry-able." Some buildings have a bylaw rule that if the board receives more than two written complaints by other residents about a dog, it's evicted. Many of the better buildings along Park and Fifth Avenues have more lenient rules about canines. Dogs have always been an accoutrement of the gentry, and like Parisians, wealthy New Yorkers dote on their pets. Mrs. Marcellus Hartley Dodge, the daughter of William Rockefeller, who lived in a private home at 800 Fifth Avenue, built one of the first dog runs in the city on the roof of her house, and in the 1950s Mrs. J. Denniston Lyon ordered her butler to make weekly trips to her estate on Long Island and dig up patches of her lawn, on which her Pekingese, Peaches, preferred to relieve himself, to bring to the city. In fact, rich people rarely have only one dog of a breed, and two or three dogs, most with pedigrees older than their owners, is the Fifth Avenue norm. Even in the best of the Good Buildings there is no canine occupancy limit, either; at 820 Fifth one owner recently had seven miniature dachshund puppies in her entourage.

Finally, to add insult to injury, if you do make it past the sentinels, most buildings demand a "flip tax," which is not a tax at all but an assessment the buyer must pay the building upon becoming an owner. The flip tax is usually 1 percent of the sales price of the apartment, but it can be as high as 3½ percent, the tariff for entry at Central Park West's San Remo. Putatively, the flip tax covers the internal costs and disruption the building suffers from the burden of people packing and leaving and newcomers moving in, but most apartment buyers think of it as an initiation fee and consider themselves lucky.

# THREE

# TURNED
# AWAY

T ry as one may, there is still about a 5 percent turndown rate in Manhattan luxury real estate. The rejection rate paces the economy; the hotter the market, the more emboldened the boards are to say no. Rejections of the rich and famous are now so commonplace that they are rarely accompanied by displays of schadenfreude, nor are they as humiliating as when in 1982 actor Werner Klemperer, who played Colonel Klink on the TV show *Hogan's Heroes,* was rebuffed on an apartment at 5 Riverside Drive. "I don't involve myself in the rock scene, the dope scene," the mortified actor told the *New York Times.* "It makes me almost think back on the fifties when people could insinuate something about other people without saying anything."

Others could care less what people were saying about them as long as they were saying it. Given all the gossip about Madonna and her marriage to actor Sean Penn, she seemed completely unfazed when she was turned down in July 1985 on a $1.2 million twelve-room apartment by the board of the celebrity-packed San Remo, the same month *Penthouse* and *Playboy* ran pictures of her standing buck naked in the middle of a Miami street. It somehow didn't impress the board that she showed up for her interview in a little black dress with pearls and two large gold crucifixes dangling from a chain around her neck. Despite the building's reputation for lenient admissions standards, "if we let her in," one board member told the *New York Daily News*, "we'd have to let *everybody* in." Actress Diane Keaton was reportedly the only San Remo board member to vote to let Madonna in. Not that the San Remo board had any regrets, but down the street at Harperly Hall, 41 Central Park West, where Madonna moved instead, her presence in the building immediately raised the value of all the apartments in the building by 25 percent, brokers estimated.

Neither Klemperer nor Madonna need have been dismayed: there is little logic in terms of true moral, ethical, or financial judgment in many turndowns. Try to figure out why the board of humdrum but dignified 770 Park Avenue felt that *60 Minutes* journalist Mike Wallace wasn't its kind of neighbor and wished him on his way, which led him to a much more distinguished palazzo-like apartment at the venerated Verona at 32 East Sixty-fourth Street. The showbizzy Dakota board welcomed Rex Reed, John Lennon, Leonard Bernstein, and Roberta Flack* but closed its gates to Billy Joel and Cher. (More understandably, over the years it has also turned down long-tongued Gene Simmons of the seventies rock group Kiss and actress Joey Heatherton, who kept canceling board meetings.) Many years ago the board of 927 Fifth Avenue rejected entertainer Barbra Streisand despite her presenting personal letters of recommendation from Governor Nelson Rockefeller, Attorney General Louis Lefkowitz, and Mayor

---

*Flack incurred the ire of the board as well as the city's Landmarks Preservation Commission when she removed original building blocks from the Dakota's thick walls to install new air-conditioning units; she was allowed to keep the new air conditioners but was ordered to put the original blocks in storage to be replaced at some future date.

John V. Lindsay. The singer and actress was rejected, confided one board member to the press, "because she'd probably give a lot of parties."

They were wrong. Streisand moved instead to a seventeen-room triplex penthouse at the Ardsley, at 320 Central Park West, where she never gave parties and hardly ever entertained. In fact, she would have been a model tenant at the Ardsley had she not earned a reputation as the building's chief kvetch and critic, for whom nothing was quite good enough, including the way the lobby was decorated. It was also from the Ardsley that for twenty years she restlessly conducted a search for her dream apartment on the Upper East Side. Unfortunately, her reputation as a diva preceded her and whenever she showed any interest in a Good Building, she was invariably advised that she would have a hard time getting past the board. Streisand was furious when it was reported in the press that the board at 2 Beekman Place had turned her down when she hadn't even made a bid on an apartment.

In the meantime, her Ardsley penthouse had turned into one of the great white elephants in the annals of New York real estate, mocked in the press for being on the market for more than a dozen years without finding a buyer. Once people got past the cachet of its being Barbra Streisand's apartment, they discovered that it had a bad layout and a leaky roof, it mostly faced the rear of the building, the price tag of $10 million was inflated, and there was an omnipresent smell of stuffed cabbage being cooked, evidently a favorite of Streisand's son, Jason, who also lived in the building.

In July 1998, when Streisand married fifty-seven-year-old actor James Brolin at her Malibu, California, home, where they were going to live year-round, she became what is known in real estate parlance as a "motivated seller," meaning she wanted to dump the apartment (along with her past life) more than ever. So when the twenty-nine-year-old pop singer Mariah Carey, part of the next generation of divas, showed up and offered $8 million in cold cash, Streisand said yes, if she could get informal assurance from the board that Mariah Carey wouldn't be rejected out of hand. Carey was the cynosure of media attention at the moment, newly divorced from Sony Records CEO Tommy Mottola and pursued by photographers. Her every mood fluctuation was documented in supermarket tabloids. In short, she was a co-op board's nightmare. The board at 91 Central Park West had already turned her down even though that normally celebrity-friendly building's residents included actor Liam Neeson and his wife, actress Natasha Richardson.

Streisand was assured by a member of the board that it was not predisposed to blackballing the young singer on principle and would give her a chance, but six months dragged by after Carey signed a contract and put down an $800,000 deposit before a face-to-face meeting was scheduled. When the appointed day finally arrived, Carey showed up not "dressed for a funeral," as her broker Dolly Lenz had instructed her, but in an outfit with a bare midriff, chaperoned by three hulking African American bodyguards, all of whom she insisted sit with her during her board interview, which the board must have found odd indeed. One of the board members, trying to be hip but making a fool of herself, asked Carey if "Mr. Biggie" might be visiting the building, meaning the Notorious B.I.G. (aka Biggie Smalls,) a rap impresario who had been murdered.* Carey responded blithely, "Mr. Biggie, he be dead."

She be dead, too, with the board. Carey didn't look back. She headed downtown, banished to the multimillion-dollar confines of the lofts of TriBeCa, where she dropped $9 million for a penthouse

---

*The woman who asked the question later admitted that it was Puff Daddy she meant to ask about but couldn't remember his name.

triplex on the seventeenth floor of 90 Franklin Street and hired the uptown "Prince of Chintz," Mario Buatta, to decorate the three floors so they looked like a junior version of Streisand's grown-up triplex uptown.

Back up at the Ardsley, Streisand was fuming. "If an artist can't live on the Upper West Side," she said in a statement to the press, "where can they live?" She considered suing the board, or donating her apartment to a charity and taking the tax deduction and letting the charity contend with the board. Eventually, fourteen years after she first put it on the market, Streisand sold her apartment to a single woman for $4 million — half the price Mariah Carey had offered for it — and went to live happily ever after in Los Angeles.

Perhaps the all-time chump of malicious New York co-op board turndowns was Richard Milhous Nixon, who was one of the most hated men in America in 1979 when he tried to buy a place to live in New York. He had spent the previous five, post-Watergate years in ignominious exile at Casa Pacifica, his San Clemente, California, ranch — enough time, he thought, for him to reemerge in public life as an "elder statesman," and he believed New York City was the place to do it. It was first announced that he was looking for a house in Connecticut, so it took the city by surprise when in July the *New York Times* reported that Nixon and his wife, Patricia, had received the approval of the twelve-member board of 19 East Seventy-second Street to purchase a nine-room penthouse for $1 million. There was an immediate insurrection among the thirty-four other residents in the building. "He is very controversial," Mrs. Jane Maynard complained to a newspaper about the disgraced ex-president. "Just imagine if the shah of Iran visited him." More than a little embarrassed, Nixon withdrew his offer and next tried to buy a condominium with no board to turn him down — Abe and Zipora Hirschfeld's $1 million, eleven-room apartment at 817 Fifth Avenue. Hirschfeld was a millionaire developer of Manhattan parking lots who would later court controversy by reneging on his $1 million offer to Paula Jones to drop her sexual-harassment lawsuit against President Bill Clinton, as well as serving a prison sentence for plotting to kill his business partner. At first Hirschfeld reveled in the publicity that the sale of his apartment generated, but soon anonymous threatening letters started to arrive. "You creeps," one letter read. "God will punish you." Another said, "When I see you, I hope you are dead."

It turned out that Richard Nixon got lots of letters like that, and so would his neighbors. Nixon was in constant danger from a multitude of would-be assassins who wanted the honor of taking him down, and wherever he chose to live, the Secret Service was obliged to make the premises safe for him. At 817 Fifth Avenue the Secret Service wanted to control the roof, the basement, and the front lobby, where they intended to establish a twenty-four-hour command post to intercept anyone suspicious. This would also entail occasionally checking the identity of guests of other residents. The $300,000 security tab it would take for all this was going to be paid by the American taxpayers, but the other residents of 817 Fifth would pay with their peace of mind. A group of owners at 817 filed a lawsuit in New York State Supreme Court to bar the sale of the Hirschfeld apartment to Richard Nixon, claiming loss of value to their apartments, as well as their diminished quality of life. Humiliated again, Nixon withdrew his offer, but this time he lost most of his $92,500 deposit, which Hirschfeld refused to return.

Nixon eventually turned to Edward Lee Cave for help. Cave advised him to give up trying to find a co-op and instead to purchase a private home. Cave found Nixon a town house at 142 East Sixty-fifth Street, which turned out to have once been owned by the great federal judge

Learned Hand, a progressive who no doubt was spinning in his grave. Nixon spent a few unhappy years in the house before moving to Saddle River, New Jersey, where Pat died, and eventually he moved to Yorba Linda, California, where he died in April 1994. The East Sixty-fourth Street house now belongs to the Syrian government, which uses it as a residence for its chief delegate to the United Nations.


I I


NIXON MADE THE right move by backing down when he was rebuffed. The worst thing anyone can do is to sue the board of a co-operative after being rejected. It's the inverse of Groucho Marx's paradox about not wanting to belong to any club that would have him as a member; why would you sue for admission into a building where the people don't want you? How badly can you want a particular apartment?

One assumes very badly, in the case of Gloria Vanderbilt, when in a moment of rejection rage she sued the board of directors of River House for nixing her purchase of a $1.1 million apartment in 1980. Vanderbilt had evidently swooned over the building's famed tower apartment, 24–25 C, the lower two floors of the seventeen-room tower triplex once owned by Mrs. Marshall Field III, the ex-wife of the department-store heir. The multilevel lair had 360-degree views of the city, four bedrooms, six bathrooms, four maids' rooms, an entrance foyer with a spiral staircase, and one of the most startling drawing rooms in the city — forty-six feet long and twenty-two feet wide — with a breathtaking wall of double-height windows overlooking the East River.

River House, built in 1930, is one of the few Good Buildings that lie outside of Wolfe's "triangle," and although it is a glamorous and romantic place to live, it's not for everyone, because it is so far off the beaten path. Even inveterate New Yorkers can't tell you exactly where River House is located, despite its palatial size, because it stands, improbably, at the edge of the East River on a cul-de-sac between two dead-end streets, East Fifty-second and Fifty-third Streets. Its out-of-the-way location hides its two fifteen-story wings and twenty-six-story tower, which are only fully visible from the river. This location also affords River House one of the most elegant and unusual entrances of any building in the city. Beyond tall wrought-iron gates and twin concrete sentry boxes topped with brass art deco eagles, there is a landscaped cobblestoned courtyard with fountains and statuary used as a turnaround for limousines and taxis dropping off and picking up passengers. Every time a car enters this courtyard a chime rings inside the lobby to warn one of the three uniformed lobby men that a visitor is approaching, and he steps outside to open the car door. Visitors pass under a small green canopy into the plush reception hall. Ahead is a wall of glass doors; beyond, a prettily landscaped courtyard perched above the East River. Although the Biedermeier and Directoire furniture that Ernesta Beaux first used to decorate the lobby and landings has disappeared, the inky-green marble floors and the mirrored murals by Mexican artist Jan Junta remain, as does the regal ambience of old-world charm.

The large brass plaques with the word PRIVATE that are embedded into the concrete sentry boxes mean just that; River House is one of the most famously discreet buildings in the city. It is a tradition among the staff and apartment owners to be protective of the building's privacy. Co-op owners who are trying to sell their apartments are not even allowed to use the address or give the name of the building in newspaper advertisements, and brokers who break this rule are blacklisted from selling apartments in the building. (There are currently only four brokerage houses allowed to represent apartments in River House.) The board also reprimands owners who give interviews to the press, and it virtually terrorized *Chicago* producer Marty Richards into not mentioning in interviews that his $25 million maisonette was for sale — and not selling.

The kind of people who live at River House do not appear in bold-face type in gossip columns, either. The mix of owners has included a meritocracy of American industry and finance whom most people never heard of: Owen Cheatham, founder of the Georgia-Pacific Corporation; Clyde Weed, chairman of the board of Anaconda Copper; George Champion, chairman of the Chase Manhattan Bank; Carl Mueller, a vice president of Bankers Trust, who was the board president when Gloria Vanderbilt applied. The building's most recognizable resident is the former secretary of state under Nixon, Henry Kissinger, who owns a sixth- and seventh-floor duplex in the north wing.* The board is notoriously anti-celebrity, and rejects over the years include the Aga Khan and the actress Diane Keaton (because she was an unmarried actress who was then dating Woody Allen). Legend has it that Joan Crawford, then on the board of the Pepsi-Cola Corporation, was rejected because Robert Woodruff, the president of Coca-Cola, lived in the building. To spite Woodruff, so the story goes, Crawford built the famous Pepsi-Cola neon sign in Long Island City that is so prominent on the horizon from the building.

For a building that abhorred attention, Gloria Vanderbilt was getting lots of it. She was more famous at that moment than at any time since she was a child, when as the subject of a famous custody fight between her mother and her aunt, the newspaper headlines had called

*When Dr. Kissinger walks his dog in the neighborhood, a security man walks behind him and cleans up after the dog because it would be undignified for the former statesman to be seen scooping up dog poop.

her the "Poor Little Rich Girl." At the time she put in her offer at River House, every night millions of Americans saw Gloria Vanderbilt literally shake her fanny on their TV sets, hawking $36 five-pocket Murjani blue jeans for middle-aged women. "Vanderbilt jeans hit all the right places," Gloria said in the commercial in her bright finishing-school accent, "your waist, your hips, your rear." The jeans also hit Gloria's pocketbook. Vanderbilt reportedly had a piece of the action worth $19 million.

If her newfound fame was going to be a problem with the board of River House, nobody told her. Vanderbilt signed a contract and was waiting for her board meeting to be set up when her attorney received a phone call from the building's management firm inquiring if Gloria Vanderbilt intended to marry her pal Bobby Short, an urbane saloon singer who was a fixture at the Carlyle Café, where he sang recherché Cole Porter tunes. He was also a fixture on Vanderbilt's arm, accompanying her to parties at Studio 54 and to charity costume balls. He was also black, and upon examination, there were no black residents of River House. "We're not planning to get married," an embarrassed Bobby Short told a reporter when the story was leaked to the newspapers. "But frankly, I don't think it's any of their business at all what we do."

Perhaps not. Many residents of River House insist that Bobby Short being black or Vanderbilt's celebrity was not a factor in what happened next and that the real issue was that the apartment hadn't been offered first to other River House co-op owners, as specified in the building's bylaws. In any event, a short time later Gloria Vanderbilt was told there would be no board meeting, and her application to buy an apartment in River House was denied.

Thus was unleashed one of the greatest public washings of Frette sheets the city had seen in a long time. For the shrinking violets at

River House, it was purgatory. "People have never gone through anything like this before," a rattled board member told the *New York Times*. "It's a new and painful experience." Another resident tried to explain: "This is not one of your chichi buildings. We don't like the limelight."

Vanderbilt, devastated to lose her dream apartment and bent on public vindication, hired the notoriously aggressive law firm of Saxe, Bacon & Bolan, the legal muscle behind her Studio 54 buddy attorney Roy Cohn, which immediately unleashed five different kinds of hell on the building. First her attorneys got the New York State Supreme Court to issue an injunction stopping the building from selling the apartment to anyone else — the only time anyone in the real estate business can remember that happening. Next they lodged two racial-discrimination complaints with the Commission on Human Rights, charging racial prejudice because Short was black and sexism because Vanderbilt was a woman; demanded that the commission subpoena the chairman of the co-op board; and asked that the board packages of other tenants be subpoenaed. They reported the building to the New York City Department of Buildings for renovations that had been made by a previous tenant without a permit, and it was also leaked to the press that an ex-con lived in the building, a man who was a disbarred lawyer and had used a fake name to buy his apartment. "It's absolutely astonishing," Vanderbilt's lawyer piously told a reporter. "They allow an ex-convict to purchase an apartment with no problems at all." A day or so later a story also managed to find its way into the newspapers that another River House resident, who lived directly above Henry Kissinger, was "the greatest party giver since Caligula."

Breaking a stoic silence, the board of River House made a few disclosures of its own. Although Vanderbilt claimed in her board package to have assets of $7.6 million, an investigation of her finances showed that she really had only $215,000 "cash in banks" — practically broke for rich folk — and that most of her assets were "anticipated" from royalties for selling her jeans. Not only wasn't Vanderbilt a good financial risk, but the building residents didn't want to read about their home in "a ceaseless flow of gossip columns about Vanderbilt's comings and goings, where she eats and with whom, what parties she goes to." When Vanderbilt responded that River House residents Henry Kissinger and director Josh Logan also generated publicity, the building's spokesman retorted that they had "fame which attends public service and professional achievement," which is not the same as publicity "to promote commercial self-interest."

With that, the fight in Vanderbilt fizzled. On June 12, 1980, her attorneys agreed to drop the suit "on the merits with prejudice." "She knew she didn't have a case," a River House resident smugly told the *New York Post.* "Directors of a co-op can exclude anybody they want."

## III

THAT WAS NOT the way it was meant to be.

The original intent of the co-operative plan was actually quite utopian. It was the idea of a forty-nine-year-old architect named Philip Hubert, who first proposed it in a pamphlet he published in 1879 as a way to lift a million immigrants out of more than 20,000 tenement houses, the great shame of the city. These filthy tenements — so called because the first ones were originally single-family homes that had been subdivided into "tenant houses" by greedy landlords — had for the previous fifty years absorbed over 1.5 million hapless newcomers to America. They were located in greatest density on the Lower East

Side — incidentally on land owned by John Jacob Astor, who was the city's biggest slumlord of the nineteenth century — but eventually ran up the East Side of the city, with pockets on the West Side, too. They typically housed twenty different families who shared one toilet, and in winter influenza swept through the freezing rooms and thinned the population for the next year's wave of newcomers. For some, tenements were at least an improvement over housing for the poor prior to the 1850s, when 20,000 New Yorkers were literally submerged and lived in cellars or unheated shacks in and around Five Points (now Foley Square), New York's notorious first and worst slum. By 1890, when the police reporter and photographer Jacob Riis published his watershed book about the degradation of tenement life, *How the Other Half Lives*, there were over 32,000 tenement houses in New York with 1.25 million people living in them. The legacy of New York tenement life is so haunting that there is now the Lower East Side Tenement Museum, a tribute to the millions of immigrant Americans who escaped them.

Philip Hubert's initial idea was to replace the tenement houses with "fireproof buildings in lower class areas for the lower class." He believed it was possible for a group of tenement families to band together and build a fireproof house in which each family would have separate living space that they would pay for and be responsible for. Hubert envisioned the building as having other communal benefits, with the residents growing or buying food together or perhaps even sharing one kitchen. But land was expensive, and that approach was rejected as impractical by real estate speculators.

Philip Hubert was known mainly as an architect in New York, but he was in reality more of an inventor. Although he designed and built several noted apartment buildings and theaters in the city, he also held sixty-five patents for labor-saving or safety devices, including methods for fireproofing floors and walls, a "self-propelling" elevator, and a "cold air box" for rooms without refrigerators. Only later in life did he go into architecture, which led to his building the very first co-operative apartment building, the Rembrandt, at 152 West Fifty-seventh Street, just a hundred feet to the west of the newly built music hall that had been funded by Andrew Carnegie.

Hubert was a Frenchman, born Philip Gengembre, in Paris in 1830, to a French father and British mother, and he grew up speaking perfect English with a slight British inflection. At age fourteen he briefly ran away from home and worked as an ironworker, living on bread and water so he could buy schoolbooks to continue his education. When Hubert's father, an architect, moved the family from Paris to Cincinnati, Ohio, in 1846, no Americans could pronounce the family name, so Philip changed it to Hubert, his mother's maiden name. The name switch was just the beginning of Hubert's clever marketing strategies. His first job was teaching French in a local high school, a task the bilingualist accomplished with such aplomb that he wrote and published a textbook on teaching the language that was widely used in schools across the country. He also handily supported himself, and eventually a wife and son, as a prolific short story writer and successful creator of "serials," which were all the rage at the time. He wrote them under a pseudonym because he didn't like the attention paid to public success — or so he thought. In 1865, at the age of thirty-five, he took a position teaching French at Girard College in Philadelphia, where he got the notion that "manual training," or gym classes, should be added to the college curriculum, but his colleagues laughed at him. It was also while he was in Philadelphia that he invented the first "self-fastening" button and formed a company to manufacture it. He sold the patent to the U.S. Army for $120,000, a king's ransom at the time, and it was with this money that Hubert moved to New York and became an architect.

Hubert arrived just in time to witness an epochal kind of housing arrangement being introduced to the city — the first communal-living building for respectable middle-class families, an "apartment" building, after the French word *appartements,* as they were called at the Palace of Versailles, where members of court were given their own private suite of rooms in which to live. Communal living was unacceptable in the rigid formality of nineteenth-century Manhattan, where unrelated people did not live together under one roof, except in tenements. The rich lived in their own houses, always, and even the upper middle class owned or rented modest houses. Two families occasionally subdivided Manhattan brownstones, but it was looked down upon. At worst, if unmarried or from out of town, respectable people lived in a boardinghouse, of which there were 10,000 in 1869. Even some of the poorest New Yorkers chose to become squatters and run subsistence farms or live in tar-and-wood shacks rather than in a building that contained several families. Yet as the price of real estate rose and construction costs became prohibitive, the quickly growing middle class needed a new way to live. Newspapers were full of classified advertisements from people looking for housing: "Wanted by a family of five and a maid, a small dwelling . . ."

The solution was called "French Flats," named after the walk-up apartment buildings that were popular in Paris. These buildings were about seven stories tall, with a common hallway and a large central staircase. They were considered perfectly respectable for the middle class, with the building's owner and richer tenants living in large apartments on the ground floor so they didn't have to climb steps, while upstairs in smaller flats lived poorer, working-class people. Also on the premises generally lived a watchful concierge who ran the building. The idea that this mode of living was a fit for New York was first promoted in 1857 by a young British-born architect named Calvert Vaux, whose genius would later come to great renown as the designer of Central Park, along with landscape architect Frederick Law Olmsted. Vaux was less than five feet tall, yet he had a big influence over his colleagues. In a historic address to the American Institute of Architects just a year after moving to the United States, Vaux proposed the adaptation of "houses à la française" to the city. His presentation was accompanied by drawings of a building he designed that was fifty feet wide and four stories high, with a large central public staircase off which were individual apartments. Across the cornice in the sketch were written the words "Parisian Buildings." A photo and a story about the new idea appeared in *Putnam's Magazine* and attracted much debate about whether such an arrangement would ever work.

It was an ambitious friend of Vaux's with whom he had studied in Paris, the twenty-nine-year-old real estate speculator Rutherford Stuyvesant, who plunged in and built the first French Flats in 1869. They stood at 142 East Eighteenth Street, west of Third Avenue, on a plot of land that had once been a fruit orchard belonging to his ancestor Peter Stuyvesant, the city's first governor. A sharp promoter, Rutherford Stuyvesant was actually named Stuyvesant Rutherford, but he legally reversed the order of his name so he could satisfy a covenant in the will of his mother's childless great-uncle and thereby inherit his considerable real estate fortune, which included fifty-four pieces of property on Third Avenue between Tenth and Twentieth Streets. In announcing his intention to construct such a building, Stuyvesant gave his project credibility by securing the services of architect Richard Morris Hunt to design it for him, and Vaux himself signed on to lease one of the first apartments in support.

Stuyvesant and Hunt actually built two identical thick-walled brick buildings side by side, five stories tall, with duplicate entryways and steep mansard roofs, described as "grotesque but picturesque" by a contemporary critic, with tin bathtubs contained in wooden holders. Nevertheless, the twenty suites ranging in price from $1,200 to $1,800 a year rented out to a varied and free-spirited group of luminaries, including publisher George Putnam, the founder of G. P. Putnam's Sons; Elizabeth Custer, the widow of the unfortunate army general; and Lavinia Booth, the mother of the man who shot Abraham Lincoln. The building nearly burned to the ground in 1884 when someone threw a match down the airshaft and it landed on the rubbish outside of Mrs. Custer's apartment. The building managed to make it through the fire intact, only to be destroyed by progress when it was demolished to make way for a larger building in 1956. It never had a vacancy from the moment it opened its doors.

Apartment-house living got a literal boost when the first elevator — introduced by Otis in New York at the Crystal Palace of 1853 — was put into operation in the seven-story-tall Equitable Life Assurance Building. Suddenly it didn't make much difference if you lived on the fifth floor or the ninth, making the issue of climbing stairs in a tall multiple dwelling a moot point. In 1869 there was one rental apartment house; in 1872 there were two; and in 1874 the first apartment building to ever cost $1 million was built on Twenty-seventh Street and Fifth Avenue. By 1885 there were 300 apartment buildings. In 1901 the Tenement House Act was passed, permitting a residential fireproof building to be built twice the width of the street, ten stories on side streets, and twelve stories on avenues, allowing for much larger multiple dwellings. In the first ten years of the twentieth century, nearly five thousand apartment buildings were erected in New York. By 1914 the *New York Times* bragged that New York was "the greatest apartment house city in the world."

Philip Hubert's co-operative plan suddenly had a whole new audience, and in 1881 he unveiled a refreshed, more upscale co-operative format, a place for "like-minded men" to live, as he wrote in a pamphlet promoting the idea. In this plan each investor would buy an apartment in a building of great luxury maintained by a full staff of servants. Several apartments would be held aside and used as rentals to support the carrying costs of the building, so the owners would have to pay only a small maintenance fee. He called this scheme a "Hubert Home Club" because, he reasoned, it was just like owning your own home, except all the maintenance and care was done for you, so it was like staying at a club — an idea that had appeal to socially conscious New Yorkers. "Each owner has what amounts almost to a private dwelling, with no annoyance of tax bills, water bills, or insurance," an unsigned essay explained to the readers of *The Independent* newspaper, sounding as if Hubert had written it himself, which he was known to do.

The Rembrandt on West Fifty-seventh Street was a then-towering six-story building. Each apartment was designed on several floors with staircases between them so it would feel more like being in a house rather than a flat. The apartments also had graciously sized parlors, separate libraries, several master bedrooms, butler's pantries, and servants' bedrooms. The interiors were finished in fine woods, and fireplace mantels were made of carved marble. There was an elevator and an ash chute. In a typical Hubert co-operative detail, the building also offered the alternative of owners cooking together in a shared, large kitchen adjacent to a communal public room for entertaining. The building sold out, mostly to professional artists who were adventurous enough to try the co-operative system, and over the next few years Hubert and various partners built half a dozen spectacularly appointed co-operative buildings on the East Side, including the Hawthorne and the Hubert, both on Fifty-ninth Street, and the Sevilla on Madison Avenue. They were each eight to ten stories tall, with spacious apartments of ten to twenty rooms with snazzy spiral staircases connecting the floors. Hubert persisted in introducing his quality-of-life inventions in his buildings, such as "instant" hot water from the tap and a "fireless" cooker. One of his buildings had beds with hollow bed slats that could be connected to "steam heating" vents in the wall that kept the mattress warm at night. His buildings also pioneered such new safety features as the first so-called fireproof walls and roofs.

The co-operative template seemed to be working so well that Hubert expanded into a "theater club," for which he built his own theater, the Lyceum, on Fourth Avenue and Fourteenth Street, which still stands. In a "theater club" the investors "owned" a pair of permanent seats, which they could turn back to the box office to be sold for the night, and also benefited from the proceeds of hit shows. Hubert also built, at a then-staggering cost of $1.2 million, an eleven-story warehouse and storage facility for furniture and personal belonging that took up the entire block of Thirty-third Street between Lexington and what was then Fourth Avenue. It was completely fireproof, with honeycombed concrete walls and individual storage cells in self-contained fireproof bins and packing containers. There was also a ground-floor auction house where customers could sell off furniture when needed, as well as a bank/pawn shop for customers to borrow cash against stored belongings.

The most famous Hubert structure is the Hotel Chelsea, which was the tallest apartment house in New York when it was erected as a Hubert Home Club in 1884 on West Twenty-third Street, then a promising pocket of development in the city. Although it was reported that "fifty people of means" contributed to the $300,000 it cost to build the twelve-story building, it was also noted that many of the workmen on the project took apartments in the building in lieu of wages. As usual, fireproofing was a major concern, and Hubert built the Chelsea with concrete floors and fireproof partitions; and it has added to the bohemian legend of the hotel that the walls are so thick that you can't hear the screaming between apartments. Its facade is a forbidding rust-colored brick banded in horizontal lines of cast-iron balconies, and the building is topped with a Dickensian roofline of gables, dormer windows, and rectangular chimney stacks. Inside there are very wide and long hallways paved in marble. From the lobby rises a grand, swirling staircase with Victorian cast-iron railings and mahogany handrails, and at the center of the spiral was an open elevator car that ascended all the way to a private ballroom in the penthouse, which was available for rental. This particular Hubert Home Club lasted almost twenty years, until 1903, when hard times and the changing neighborhood caused it to go bankrupt and the original tenants were forced to move. The building was reopened as the Hotel Chelsea and became one of most famous hotels and artist asylums in the world. In 1907 the writer O. Henry lived and wrote at the Chelsea, and later came Arthur Miller, William S. Burroughs, and Arthur C. Clarke, who wrote *2001: A Space Odyssey* at the hotel and called the place his "spiritual home." It was also at the Chelsea that Dylan Thomas collapsed and was taken to a nearby hospital, where he died. Its infamy as a den of elite drug addicts was forged with the release of Andy Warhol's movie *The Chelsea Girls*, and the accompanying song by the singer Nico described the harrowing characters that could be found behind the numbered doors of each suite. It's no surprise that more than a fair share of people have been found dead or dying there, including the great American clothing designer Charles James and the artist Richard Bernstein. The Chelsea has also attracted plenty of artists who in lieu of paying their overdue rent gave the hotel owners the art collection that now hangs in its lobby. The Hotel Chelsea is the only extant tribute to Hubert, an architectural masterpiece of sheer melodrama, inside and out.

The Chelsea was barely off of Hubert's drawing board when he set out to create the most ambitious multiple-dwelling project ever conceived in the city, a vast complex of co-operative housing that would be built on Central Park South at a staggering cost of $4.2 million. Although its official name was the Central Park Apartments, it became famous in New York as the Spanish Flats, or the Navarro, after Juan de Navarro, the speculator who financed it, a former Spanish consul general to America and the father-in-law of one of the great stage stars of the day, Mary Anderson. The Navarro was actually eight buildings connected by parapet-like "sky sidewalks," and Navarro named them after his favorite childhood places in Spain — the Salamanca, Lisbon, Grenada, Valencia, Tolosa, Cordova, Madrid, and Barcelona. The building encircled a 40-by-300-foot landscaped courtyard with three burbling fountains. Carved out underneath the complex was an underground passageway and mezzanine where delivery and service vehicles could come and go unseen. The Navarro also had its own restaurant and a rooftop solarium with an isolation room for tenants who might be sick — infection from tuberculosis was a great concern. The corner apartments overlooking Central Park sold for $20,000 each — a fortune — but the *New York Times* noted that they were financially practical for people who "only need and really use some five or six bedrooms." The building soon attracted some contemporary celebrities, including Codman Potter, the Episcopal bishop of New York, and Mary Mapes Dodge, the author of *Hans Brinker, or the Silver Skates.* De Navarro was probably a better diplomat than he was a bookkeeper, and the building ran over budget by a great margin. Also, while Hubert's marketing skills might have been able to fill a six-story luxury building, he couldn't lure enough wealthy owners to occupy a building with 100 palatial apartments. That, compounded by legal problems from Hubert's somehow not conveying the deed properly, sank the building into bankruptcy.

The Navarro went into foreclosure in 1885 but managed to operate until 1927, when it was declared a loss and torn down.

The large-scale failure of the Navarro destroyed the momentum of the co-operative movement. "The sale of the Navarro Flats," gloated an editorial in the *New York Times* in 1885, "under foreclosure for only $200,000 more than the mortgages on them indicates unmistakably that the era of the palatial apartments in New York is already over. It has been a very short era. Ten years would cover the rise, progress, and decline of the movement to assimilate the social conditions of New York to those of Paris. . . . At one time the notion of cooperative dwellings, in which the cooperators should severally own their own dwellings under a single roof, and with many of the details of domestic service economized by cooperation, had taken possession of many intelligent men. . . . [Now] a prudent man will hesitate before committing himself and his money to circumstances that he can neither foresee nor control."

Hubert himself would later admit that his early version of the co-operative plan was not the most sensible. He related the story of friends who moved into one of his earlier buildings. They complained about the sound of the family above them walking on their ceiling and they were annoyed that two little boys who lived on the top floor tracked mud up the hall steps. Neighborhood children congregated around the entranceway; many tenants rented out their apartments in the summer, and instead of friendly neighbors, there always seemed to be strangers living there. Because of the proximity of apartments, Hubert's friends had neighbors "whose conduct, especially at night, made the center room unfit for a lady's occupancy." As the character of the building deteriorated with the quality of the tenants, Hubert's friends fled, calling the co-operative experience a "worthless, ill-planned, ill-built sham, unfit for human habitation."

Those words might have been the epitaph for co-operative housing if the idea had not been revived in 1903 by two plucky artists, Henry Ward Ranger, an impressionist whose paintings of smoke-shrouded city rooftops made him into one of the best known of his contemporaries, and Walter Russell, a Renaissance man who wrote children's books and enjoyed a career as a successful portrait painter and sculptor. Russell probably made most of his money as a real estate developer when, along with Henry Ward Ranger, he resurrected the co-operative plan as a housing solution for artists. The attention of the art world was shifting to New York from Paris, attracting artists from all over, and it was an impossible task to find affordable workspace. Artists preferred diffuse northern light and needed tall, open spaces to paint and display their canvases. In an interview he gave to a newspaper Ranger complained of paying $700 a year for his studio space and another $2,000 a year for his separate living quarters and a place to entertain clients. Ranger and Russell were joined by a dozen other artists, including Childe Hassam, Frank Dumond, and Charles C. Curran in forming a corporation that contracted to build a 12-story building built at 27 West Sixty-seventh Street, as "studio apartments,"* or "lofty studios." This was followed by five other buildings, including the famed Hotel des Artistes, at One West Sixty-seventh Street. The participating artists had a say in designing their own spaces, all of which were duplexes or triplexes with large lofts and tall windows for light. Some were much more elaborate, such as the fifty-four-foot-long wood-paneled studio built for philanthropist Aaron Naumburg. When one of the original owners sold his block of stock for $21,500 — an astonishing 40 percent gain over the $15,000 he paid for it — the success of

---

*In contemporary Manhattan real estate parlance, a "studio" apartment means one room, perhaps with an alcove for a bed.

the buildings began a rage in art circles, and several artists started organizing and owning co-operative buildings as a profitable avocation.* When portrait painter Robert Vonnoh bought property at Lexington Avenue and Sixty-seventh Street and announced the construction of an eleven-story co-operative for artists, several apartments were sold and resold at a $2,000 premium before the building was even completed. Other artists began to jump on the bandwagon, and over the next few years members of the group that built the Sixty-seventh Street buildings erected twenty-five other co-op buildings around the city, for nonartists as well, and they were soon joined in building co-operatives by a flurry of speculators flocking to the new market.

Yet in 1953 there were still only 162 co-operatives in New York City, with 5,797 apartments. It wasn't until the mid-1970s that rental buildings began to convert to co-ops in earnest, and there are now over 3,500 cooperative buildings in Manhattan and 10,000 in all five boroughs. It is the only city in the world where so much residential real estate is held in private hands.

As for Philip Hubert, after the failure of the Navarro he retired from the real estate business and dabbled in writing. In the 1890s he cowrote a hit Broadway play called *The Witch*, under the nom de plume Phillip Hamilton. He moved to Los Angeles in 1896, where he drove one of the first automobiles in that city, and devoted his remaining years to inventing labor-saving devices for housewives. He died at age eighty-one in 1911, never guessing what his "home club plan" hath wrought.

---

*Ironically, none of the new buildings would contain artists' studios, which had become the purlieu of prostitutes in the guise of artists' models, or as the *New York Times* put it in 1922, "those looking to cloak loose living by the glamour of art." An estimated 70 percent of artists' studios in New York were being occupied by "persons of questionable character."

# FOUR

# SUTTON
# PLACE

Betty Sherrill sprained her ankle the other day and was walking with a cane. She was seventy-eight years old and just that morning, her daughter, the author Ann Pyne, dragged her off to speak to an estate lawyer about writing a will. It was a chore Betty Sherrill had put off for years. "She killed me off twice in that book of hers," Sherrill said, referring to a collection of short stories, titled *In the Form of a Person,* that Pyne published in 1992, in which Sherill said two matriarchal figures are dispatched in the course of the narrative. In any event, Sherrill was not about to pop off and die, she assured a visitor to her apartment; she just wasn't as spry as she used to be, and with an injured ankle she didn't want to chance walking down the spiral stair-case between the ninth and tenth floors of her duplex apartment at One Sutton Place South.

Instead, a uniformed elevator man fetched her and her secretary from the tenth-floor landing in an elegant wood-paneled elevator, big enough for only three people, and gave her a lift down the one flight to the small entrance foyer of her apartment. If anyone else had done this — used the building's elevator to go between floors in a duplex — Sherrill would have been the first to have them admonished by the board. But since she *was* the board, practically, she just stepped into her own foyer with a smile on her face as sunny as the spring day outside.

She was a vision in yellow: her coiffed honey-blond hair, a cheery lemon-yellow Bill Blass suit with a large, inlaid ladybug brooch pinned to her left lapel, and matching yellow pumps, in which she hobbled into her cheerful living room, which was also, not by chance, yellow. There were pale lemon-colored walls and a yellow-and-green area rug and a yellow silk sofa and twelve upholstered chairs, some in stripes, some in prints. Every lamp in the room was turned on, even though it was daylight outside, and there were lots of glittering things to look at on the tabletops — cut-crystal objets and sterling-silver bibelots, along with framed photographs of her handsome family, her son and daughter with their respective spouses and children, posed like a Ralph Lauren ad, taken at the Sherrills' Southampton, New York, country home, Mayfair, built in 1899 for Secretary of War Elihu Root. Over the fireplace hung a formal portrait of her husband's late mother, painted when she was in her twenties, looking very much like the rest of the place — swank and elegant.

But even the handsomely appointed apartment has a hard time competing with the heart-stopping view from the windows — a panoramic swath of light blue sky and the choppy, ink blue surface of the East River, a majestic force of nature coursing so close by, with tankers and tourist ferries cutting through the foamy chop. In the background are the ruins of the abandoned insane asylums and prisons of Roosevelt Island, now overgrown with ivy, and just to the north, dominating the scene with its sheer size and majesty, are the iconic arcs of the eighty-year-old Queensboro Bridge, its massive stone pedestals anchoring the triple crescents joining Manhattan with the borough of Queens.* All of it is breathtaking — the spectacle of the view, the glamorous apartment, and certainly the grande dame of One Sutton Place South herself, Betty Sherrill, who lowered herself into a comfortable chair in her living room and asked a uniformed maid to bring two glasses of water for herself and a visitor.

For nearly half a century Betty Sherrill has been a social arbiter in New York City. Chairman of the co-op board of One Sutton Place South from 1972 to 1999, succeeding her husband, H. Virgil Sherrill, who was vice chairman of the board for nine years before that, she has for over forty years enjoyed absolute say over who can and cannot live in One Sutton Place South, the most important building in one of the most treasured enclaves in New York. However, Sherrill's clout extends far beyond the borders of Sutton Place South. She is also the éminence grise of the cabbage-rose-chintz world of interior decorating, the president and principal of the house of McMillen, Inc., the most revered, main-line decorating concern in the country, founded in 1923. Sherrill is such a fixture at the top end of the interior-decoration world and the very rich who are her customers that she has the honor of having a character based upon her, Cora Mandell, the influential society decorator in Dominick Dunne's perambulatory novel of society, *People Like Us.*

What all this means is that Betty Sherrill is not just rich herself, she understands rich people like an art form. She understands, because she is one, the way civilized and cultured people are expected to behave.

---

*F. Scott Fitzgerald wrote, "The city seen from the Queensboro Bridge is always the city seen for the first time, in its first wild promise of all the mystery and the beauty in the world. . . . Anything can happen now that we've slid over this bridge."

She understands the things they like to do and the way they like to do them, and that's how she creates environments for them, from the inside out. She has worked with a blue book of the American establishment; her company has decorated the bedrooms and bathrooms of three generations of Rockefellers and four generations of Hearsts. McMillen has primped a Parisian pied-à-terre for a wealthy American divorcée and supervised the interiors of a summer palace of a sheik and a yacht for a computer billionaire. Betty Sherrill was one of the first to learn that Lyndon Baines Johnson would not run for president in 1964 when Lady Bird Johnson called and asked her to ship their four-poster bed home to Texas from the private quarters of the White House, which Sherrill helped decorate.

The building in which Sherrill lives occupies the entire block from Fifty-sixth to Fifty-seventh Streets and is one of only sixteen luxury buildings on Sutton Place. One Sutton Place South is a thirteen-story, Georgian brick exterior design, with rows of many tall windows. It is the work of the architectural firm of Cross & Cross, which was active in New York in the 1920s, and the venerated Rosario Candela, the greatest name in apartment building design, a great craftsman in creating lush, beautifully laid out, palazzo-like apartments. Like many of New York's Good Buildings, the exterior of One Sutton Place South appears unremarkable to an untrained eye; the windows are closely spaced on a busy facade of brick and stone, and only its entranceway — a triple-arched recessed portico, with a crescent-shaped cobblestone-paved driveway that smartly cuts in and out of the front of the building — seems special. What sets One Sutton Place apart from other buildings is its location on the river and Candela's interior design. The forty-two apartments (there were originally only thirty-five, but a few were chopped up; the board has put a stop to that forever) are distributed in three wings of the U-shaped building. Most apartments are between nine and twelve rooms, and the center portion of the building has all duplexes, mostly with five bedrooms; the north and south sides have four-bedroom simplexes. Two of the building's most distinctive features are its marble-floored lobby and its wall of heavy glass doors leading to a gorgeously manicured 15,000-square-foot garden with wrought-iron benches, an Eden in the midst of a concrete-and-glass city. Naturally, to maintain the decorum of the building, tenants are discouraged from sitting on the benches in the garden, nor can they entertain guests in the garden without permission. Sherrill once returned to the building to discover twenty children at a birthday party for an eight-year-old in progress on the lawn and sent the building manager to ask the parents to move the party upstairs and out of sight. It is also in this garden that seven magnolia trees were planted along with a plaque in honor of Betty Sherrill's twenty-seven years of service as president of the board of One Sutton Place South.

"It looks like I'm dead," she chortled about the plaque, a good dollop of the honey-coated twang of her Louisiana upbringing coating her words. "I tried to pull the plaque up, but it was set in concrete."

Unfortunately, the state of New York is threatening to do the chore for her. In 2003, when the state needed to rehabilitate the seventy-year-old East River Drive, a six-lane highway that hangs off the eastern edge of Manhattan like a dirty ribbon, a stunning revelation came to public light: One Sutton Place South didn't own its fabulous garden. The building only owned 1,500 square feet, or just some 10 percent of the space. The rest was a ledge covered with two feet of planting soil that literally sat on the roof of the busy East River Drive and served as a buffer between the building and the traffic. When the drive was built in 1939 this ledge was leased to the building by the city for a nominal charge: initially, $1 a year and capping at $1.46 in 1980, when the lease ran out. When that happened, instead of trying to renew the lease, the board of directors of One Sutton Place South and its chairman, Betty Sherrill, decided to do a very naughty thing. They decided that if the lease was brought up for public review, the wealthy residents would be unjustly punished for the luxury of their garden and levied a costly increase that would have to be shared by everyone in the building. So they did nothing about the lease's expiration, and hoped nobody would notice. That the lease on the garden had expired in 1980 became the family secret of the building, the skeleton in the closet, only whispered about. New buyers were even asked to sign confidentiality pledges promising not to spill the beans, lest the authorities catch on.

But the state did catch on, nearly twenty-five years later, because of the reconstruction of the highway, and now is contemplating not returning the garden to One Sutton Place South at any price. Instead, there are plans to turn the garden into a public esplanade, like one of the "pocket parks" that exist to the north and south of it, some concrete and trees and landscaping and wooden benches, just a few feet away from the glass doors leading to One Sutton Place South. "That would be mean to all the people who live there," Sherrill told the *New York Times*. "It'd be right in front of their windows. They paid a lot of money for those apartments. The city doesn't even keep up the parks on the right and left of us, much less the one in front of us."

The threat of a public park has not helped the building's desirability; at the moment there were six apartments for sale, a large number for such a prestigious address. But the possibility of a public park does not affect the building's reputation as much as its daunting board of directors. Sherrill seemed surprised to hear that One Sutton Place South is thought of as one of the most difficult boards in the city — "total bastards," as one broker has called them. "Potential buyers into her Sutton Place South building are terrified to come in front of her," John Fairchild wrote of her in his 1989 book, *Chic Savages*. "In all the twenty-seven years I was board president," she said, now a wounded southern belle, her eyelashes fluttering over watery blue eyes, "I never turned anybody down. No! I wouldn't want to hurt anybody's feelings like that. If we think they won't make it, we ask them not to come [to meet with the board] because that's very embarrassing." How do they know who has a chance of making it or not in the first place? "We don't work with brokers who bring the wrong people," she explained. Her broker of choice, she said, is Edward Lee Cave, whom she trusts to offer up the right kind of people for consideration. "This is a family building," Sherrill said sweetly, and who could argue with that?

Except that by "family building" Sherrill doesn't mean that there are lots of children and nannies. Sutton Place has never been known as a neighborhood for couples starting families; it has an older, rather stuffy reputation. In particular, One Sutton Place South prefers more established people, such as David (Jim) Judelson, a cofounder of Gulf + Western; Brownlee and Agnetta Curry, billionaire horse breeders from Nashville ("Their children arrived beautifully," Sherrill noted); Shelby White and Leon Levy ("He's Oppenheimer. Have you ever seen their apartment? The art is like a museum"); or the actress Sigourney Weaver ("The tall one, her father was a friend of Virgil's, no problem at all").

What kind of person would Sherrill find a "problem"? Single people. "We don't have people who live with people outside of their family," Sherrill said. "No, no." Although, she admitted, she made exceptions, like for Carolyne Roehm, the tall, reed-thin former fashion designer whose business was backed by her billionaire husband, financier Henry Kravis. In 1994, when their marriage vaporized and Roehm fled their sixteen-room apartment with its $14 million Renoir, she tried to buy a bachelorette pad for $6 million at 131 East Sixty-sixth Street that was once owned by one of the Rothschilds, but she was turned down by the board because she was single. Wounded, she sought refuge in a $5 million, two-bedroom flat at One Sutton Place South.

"They said, 'Oh, she'll have too many boyfriends coming around,'" Sherrill said, without identifying the Greek chorus of "theys" that peppered her conversation. "And I said, 'Well! *Certainly* she can get in.' And she's been no problem at all."

Sherrill also made a special dispensation for the designer of the suit she was wearing, Bill Blass, even though he was a confirmed bachelor. When Blass sold his penthouse just around the corner at 444 East Fifty-seventh Street to European designer Wolfgang Joop, a real estate broker warned Blass that One Sutton Place South wouldn't let him in because he was single and might have "overnight guests." Word was that Blass was persuaded to write the board a letter promising never to have any sleepovers. Sherrill huffed at the thought. "Bill Blass is a very close personal friend of mine and a complete gentleman," she said. "Bill said to me, 'Betty, I don't want to apply if I'm not going to get in.' So I asked everybody on the board first and nobody objected and he wrote me a letter saying he would never embarrass us, and he never has. His apartment is bee-you-tiful," she crooned, even though Mica Ertegun, one of her rivals, decorated it. "It's not overdone and it doesn't even have curtains," she said sweetly. (When Abe Ribicoff, the former senator from Connecticut, and his wife, Casey, were about to appear before Sherrill and the board in their quest to buy an apartment at One Sutton Place South, Bill Blass advised Casey, "Just shut up and wear a WASPy bow in your hair." The Ribicoffs passed Sherrill's scrutiny and became Blass's neighbors.) Blass passed away in 2001, and his apartment was up for sale.

The "unmarried" rule did, however, scuttle the hopes of the diminutive society fashion designer Arnold Scaasi, seventy-one, and his genteel life partner of twenty-five years, Parker Ladd, seventy-five, who is a director of Literacy Partners of New York. Technically, Sherrill said, "Arnold and Parker never applied," but only because she told them not to. "Arnold used to call me and call me and call me," she said, rolling her eyes. "He's fun, and I love Parker Ladd, but Arnold said to me" — and here Sherrill imitated Scaasi's nasal voice — "'Betty, I want to live in One Sutton Place South.' I said to him, 'Arnold, they won't let you in, and I don't want to embarrass you. I don't want to hurt your feelings, but you live with Parker, and that's not allowed in the building.' And Scaasi said to me, 'I don't live with him except in the summer.'" Sherrill had a hearty laugh at the suggestion.

Scaasi bought instead an apartment in another luxurious riverfront building, 2 Beekman Place, also by Rosario Candela, where he paid about $5 million for twelve rooms with a river view. Unfortunately, he had lived there only a month or so when the broker who sold it to him, Robby Browne, of the Douglas Elliman company, was quoted in a *New York* magazine article, boasting about being able to pull off difficult co-op board acceptances. "I took Arnold Scaasi to Two Beekman Place," Browne bragged to the magazine, "and he's a garmento, a Jew and a gay." Browne denied ever saying those words, but Scaasi was livid beyond consolation, and the designer enlisted the aid of his chum the newspaper columnist Liz Smith to get retribution. Smith lambasted the broker in several of her columns, defending Scaasi for being a fashion designer, a Jew, and a gay and suggested that if Robby Browne never said those words, she expected he would *sue New York* magazine to clear his name, wouldn't he? A few days later the owners of 2 Beekman Place fired Douglas Elliman as its property-management company and the matter was put to rest. Scaasi can console himself about the purchase in that he recently put the apartment up for sale at nearly $12 million. And Robby Browne can console himself in that not only did he retain his reputation as one of the top brokers in the business, he shattered all sales records in July 2003 when he sold a condominium at the Time Warner building for $45 million.

Sherrill herself had no problem getting into One Sutton Place South when she applied in 1960. "It was a good thing there were no financial requirements back then," she chuckled, "because we wouldn't have gotten in, either." She was born in New Orleans, the daughter of an architect, and as a young girl satisfied her creative bent by decorating the third floor of her parents' gracious country home. She met Virgil at a Queen's Supper after a Mardi Gras ball. "After we were married, we moved to New York," she said, "where he worked on Wall Street for Shields and Co." They lived uptown in a rent-controlled apartment on upper Park Avenue, and one day in 1951, because she "needed to pay for Nanny MacKenzie," she literally knocked on the door of McMillen's offices and talked her way into an apprentice job as an interior designer. She loved her work, but because McMillen was located on East Fifty-fifth Street, "it was a pain in the neck because I had two children and couldn't go home to have lunch with them because taxis were a dollar." One of her clients at McMillen was Adams Ashforth, the city's most prominent real estate broker at the time. Ashforth was grateful to Sherrill for the decorating work she had done for him on three of his residences, and one day he asked her, "What can I do to thank you, Betty?"

"I laughed and I said, 'Oh, I don't want anything, I just want to have an apartment in One Sutton Place South,'" she said, thinking it was a next-to-impossible request. Ashforth called her back a few minutes later and said that there had just been a turndown at One Sutton Place South and that she and Virgil should make an offer. "So I bid. Virgil was in California, and it was a rubber check, and yet now here I am, forty years later."

# I I

A FEW HUNDRED years before Betty Sherrill presided over Sutton
Place, it was a high river bluff called Cannon Point that extended into
the river at Fifty-second Street and was where the Indians once speared
fish and gathered oysters and shellfish from the rocky shores below. Cannon Point was surrounded inland by a lush forest, dense with native
walnut groves to which the early Dutch settlers added peach, cherry, cur-
rant, and apricot trees, creating what one long-ago chronicler called the
"perfumed air of the island." By the early 1800s the forests and bluffs of
the Upper East Side remained pure and distant enough from the city
center four miles south that the area first developed as a sleepy summer
retreat. It took a day to get to there from downtown, traveling by horse
and carriage along the Boston Post Road, which ran up the East Side
about where Second Avenue is today. Off the road were country lanes
that meandered toward the river and the "country seats" of the richest
Manhattanites, including John Jacob Astor Sr.; Archibald Gracie, a
wealthy merchant who, far north on an idyllic bluff facing Hell Gate,
built his clapboard house in 1799, which since 1942 has been the residence of the mayor of the city of New York; the Schermerhorns, who
built a house on the river at the edge of Jones Woods; and the infamous
Captain Kidd, who owned a farm at East Sixty-eighth Street that was
turned over to the state when he was hanged in England (New York–
Presbyterian Hospital and the Rockefeller University stand on that
property today). Perhaps the best known of these country estates belonged to James Beekman, who built the picturesque white mansion
he named Mount Pleasant in 1763. This is where the well-meaning
Mrs. Beekman inadvertently helped a convict escape from a jail for

"disreputable adults" on Blackwell's Island when he swam ashore on her property. Mrs. Beekman thought he was drowning and helped him recover. Years later the British commandeered the Beekman house and used it as their military headquarters during the Revolutionary War, and the treason trial of Nathan Hale was held in the greenhouse, where he was convicted of espionage. Hale was hanged from a tree nearby, at a now forgotten location but where today there is probably a dry-cleaning establishment on some street corner along lower Third Avenue.

The Beekman family was eventually chased away from Mount Pleasant in 1854 by a cholera epidemic triggered by the polluted groundwater. All the other owners of country estates along the shoreline gradually fled the pollution brought by the encroaching industry that began to fill up the East River waterfront after the Civil War. As luxury residential housing entrenched itself farther and farther up the backbone of the island, all the undesirable aspects of big-city life — tenements, slums, and large industry — were pushed outward to its shores. Real estate speculators predicted that if luxury housing developed anywhere along the thirty-three-mile waterfront circumference of Manhattan island, it would develop along the West Side, where the elevations were higher and it was believed that the towering cliffs of New Jersey were prettier to look at than the bleakness of the low-lying land in what would become the borough of Queens across the East River. As it would turn out, the West Side shoreline would soon be lined with huge commercial piers of transatlantic vessels that preferred the more easily navigable Hudson River, while the East Side shoreline remained a craggy landscape of slums and industrial development. Where the United Nations stands today was a neighborhood almost entirely of cattle yards, slaughterhouses, and fat-rendering plants known as Blood Alley because so many animals were dispatched and packaged there, and just south of Fifty-ninth Street was a Quaker Oats factory.

At Fifty-second Street the Cremo "Cream of the Islands" cigar factory stood alongside the Consumers Brewing Company of New York,
which contributed the fragrant scent of hops roasting to the ambience
of the neighborhood. All of these businesses used the East River to
dump their raw sewage.

The first dramatic change in terms of luxury housing along the waterfront came in 1924, when a developer named Joseph Thomas bought
a group of ramshackle buildings from Fifty-first to Fifty-second Streets
and began to build apartment houses with a Venetian theme that would
have their own boat basins moored with gondolas to take the residents up and down the East River. This was one of Thomas's many promotional ideas for the development of real estate. Thomas had earlier
been responsible for turning Nineteenth Street, on which he lived with
his wife, Clara Fargo Thomas, a noted muralist, into New York's "Block
Beautiful." "It is natural that we should have taken the theme of Venice
as our inspiration," wrote his wife in *Arts and Decoration* in 1933. "Let not
all of these places be on narrow streets or even Fifth or Park Avenue, but
let us remember that the most beautiful buildings in the world in Venice,
in Paris, London, Budapest, and Vienna, have water as a foreground."
Thomas's first Venetian-themed building, Beekman Terrace, at Fifty-first
Street, a six-story brick apartment house with its own pier and bas-reliefs
of Saint Mark, the patron saint of Venice, was followed by the luxurious
Campanile, finished in 1930, whose tenants included Noël Coward, Clare
Booth Luce, Greta Garbo, and theater critic Alexander Woollcott.*

---

*Every Sunday Woollcott served breakfast in his pajamas in his third-floor apartment to
his friends from the Algonquin Round Table. Because of the building's seeming remote-
ness, Franklin P. Adams, the newspaper columnist, suggested that Woollcott name his
apartment after the Indian word *ocowoica,* "the Little Apartment on the East River That
It Is Difficult to Find a Taxicab Near." But it was Dorothy Parker's suggestion that
stuck. Parker said that the building was "far enough east to plant tea" and that it should
henceforth be known as Wit's End.

The Campanile shares a cul-de-sac with River House, the building that caused such an uproar in the life of Gloria Vanderbilt. River House was the most expensive luxury building ever built in the city in 1930, at the cost of $10.63 million, just as the nation was sinking into the pit of the Great Depression. At the moment the massive foundation was being poured, the nation had 4 million unemployed and a quarter of New York's population was jobless, including as many as ten thousand who lived in makeshift huts in Central Park. One of the worst pockets of poverty in the city was at the eastern tip of East Fifty-third Street, just where River House was being built. Across the street stood a row of decrepit tenement houses abutting a gravel yard. A rotting wooden dock built out into the river, graced by an occasional forlorn-looking seagull, became the neighborhood hangout for a bunch of "dead-end kids." The fact that the building's "rear" door and service entrance opened directly onto the rabble on East Fifty-third Street facilitated many uncomfortable encounters for the River House residents, who lived in splendor seemingly untouched by the Depression. This brutal juxtaposition came to the attention of writer Sidney Kingsley, who had already won the Pulitzer Prize in drama for *Men in White* about the medical profession. Kingsley wrote a play called *Dead End*, which went on to become a popular movie starring Humphrey Bogart and Sylvia Sidney. The play opened on Broadway in 1935, with a set that included the back door of River House and a dock that went out into the audience where the East River would be. The original cast of juvenile delinquents included Huntz Hall and Leo Gorcey, two actors who were spun off into the popular Dead End Kids movie series. Today, there is a small plot of grass and a park where the real Dead End Kids used to hang out.

Ironically, River House itself sank into poverty and misfortune. After the Depression the price of luxury apartments fell so drastically that apartments that had sold for $50,000 were now on the market for $500. Although River House was a succès d'estime, there were simply not enough people rich enough to fill it. Eventually the owners forfeited on the building's $4.2 million in mortgages, and in 1941 it was sold at auction in the Vesey Street salesrooms to a succession of realty corporations, including the powerful Tishman Realty & Construction Company, which in 1948 announced that it was "reconstructing" the luxury building — carving the 79 apartments into 170 smaller units and that all tenants were to be paid off and had to move out. With this threat hanging over their heads, the residents banded together and bought the mortgages to the building themselves, and it has been owned by the people who live there ever since.

Yet none of the other luxury enclaves and neighborhoods made living on the East River chic the way Sutton Place did. In the early 1800s a farmer named Thomas Pearsall tilled the few acres that would become Sutton Place, land that would later temporarily pass through the hands of politician William "Boss" Tweed. By the end of the Civil War the mansions and farms were all gone, the streets had been graded, and noxious industry lined the short six-block stretch in the East Fifties that would become Sutton Place, then called Avenue A. Towering above the neighborhood, at Fifty-third Street, was the George Youle brick "shot tower," where molten lead was molded into bullets during World War I. The tower stood belching rancid smoke over the neighborhood, which seemed forever cloudy, even on the sunniest day.

In 1875, after Central Park opened and prices for real estate on Fifth Avenue began to soar, an entrepreneurial New Yorker named Effingham B. Sutton observed the social migration of the rich directly up that street and tried to divine where else the wealthy might live when all the land on Fifth Avenue was spoken for. Sutton had founded the California Clipper Shipline in 1840 and made a small fortune shipping dry goods during the California gold rush. He was persuaded that when the wealthy ran out of developable building plots on Fifth Avenue they would branch out east on Fifty-seventh Street, eventually ending up on the East River, despite the ugliness of the neighborhood. He assembled a small group of investors, including James Stokes, the banker, to build a blocklong row of three- and four-story, one-family brick town houses on the south side of the street from Fifty-sixth to Fifty-fifth Streets, next to the Peter Doelger brewery. So certain was Sutton that his new enterprise would turn the neighborhood around, he sold his own house at Fifth Avenue and Sixteenth Street and built for himself a large brick town house on the corner of Fifty-seventh Street and Avenue A, which he called Sutton Manor, and waited for the rich to show up. They didn't. The row of town houses that Sutton hoped would spark a housing revolution were soon divided into one- and two-room cold-water flats and became run-down like the rest of the walk-ups that dotted the neighborhood. Near the end of the century, Effingham B. Sutton went bankrupt and lost everything — except the honor of having the street officially renamed after him, albeit posthumously, in 1897, as Sutton Place.

The string of ramshackle town houses was eventually bought by the real estate development company of Henry Phipps, the man who was Andrew Carnegie's so-called silent partner. Like Carnegie, Phipps was the son of an immigrant cobbler, raised in a Pittsburgh slum, and by some accounts made even more money than his partner. Phipps sold out to Carnegie in 1901 and moved to New York, where he built a great mansion for himself on Fifth Avenue and Eighty-seventh Street. Ironically, it was from this great château of a house that he became one of the nation's leading pioneers of affordable housing for the poor. Phipps built the first "model tenements" on East Thirty-first Street, and the Phipps Company later built half a dozen early housing developments in and around New York City, and today the company continues to own and run over 4,000 apartments.

By the time the Phipps Company bought the row of cold-water flats on Sutton Place, they had collectively become known as "The Arc" by their hardy residents, a bohemian mix of writers, artists, and oddballs who enjoyed the $15-a-month rent and being able to hunt for game and fish from their apartment windows, if they so desired. As luck would have it, one of the tenants, William L. Laurance, was a friend of Mrs. George Tuckerman Draper, better known as Dorothy Draper, the society interior decorator. Interior decoration for the very rich had emerged as an influential profession with the luxury housing boom of the late nineteenth and early twentieth centuries, and Draper was a predecessor of Betty Sherrill's. (It was Draper's sister, Ruth, who became a famous monologist.) One day Draper visited her friend Mr. Laurance and was struck by how similar the Arc was to a neat little group of buildings she admired along the Thames in London, designed by a famous London town house architect named Paul Nash. She was also impressed by how ingeniously her friend Laurance had painted and decorated his small flat, improving it by adding a hot-water heater and a bathtub. Inspired by the houses and the collection of people who lived there, Draper appealed to the Phipps Company to let her experiment with the aging buildings and give them a cosmetic renovation into "English flats." With the Phipps Company's blessing, Draper painted the brick black, the fire escapes white, and the doors in bright blue, scarlet, and yellow. She installed window boxes of flowers and planted gardens and a lawn that reached to the East River. In no time The Arc became quite a fashionable place to live, and the bohemian bunch who had lived there happily for years was elbowed out by more upscale newcomers, including Bradley Martin, a grandson of Henry Phipps; Clarence Francis, the head of

General Foods; and Mrs. Goodhue Livingston, whose little flat was so admired that *Vogue* magazine ran a two-page spread on it. The new group banded together and formed an Arc Tenants Association and hired their own concierge and a "doorman" to do chores, which included serving cocktails on the communal lawn behind the houses. The Arc lasted until 1958, when the charming buildings were reduced to dust by a wrecking ball and replaced with a nineteen-story luxury apartment building called Cannon Point North.

In the end, it was three unusually free-spirited women who established Sutton Place as an enclave for the rich. The spiritual pioneer of Sutton Place was Elisabeth "Bessy" Marbury, a onetime literary agent whose clients included Oscar Wilde. An author herself, of *Manners: A Handbook of Social Customs*, a bestselling book that in its time defined good manners in society, Bessy Marbury was perhaps best known as the longtime companion and lover of Elsie de Wolfe, the petite, blond, slightly pixilated stage actress turned interior designer who had become the darling of café society. Marbury and de Wolfe had for many years divided their time between Trianon, a villa they owned on the grounds of the Palace of Versailles, where they entertained movie stars and royalty, and a town house on Irving Place in Manhattan, where they held weekly salons with such guests from the artistic and literary worlds as Ethel Barrymore and Wilde. In 1921, as the twenty-year relationship between the two women was winding down (four years later de Wolfe would surprise everyone by marrying Sir Charles Mendl, a British press attaché six years her junior), Marbury bought a small, run-down house at 13 Sutton Place South and hired de Wolfe's protégé, architect Mott B. Schmidt, to renovate it, attic to wine cellar. Marbury later wrote that she made the move to Sutton Place because she was drawn to the waterfront views that she nostalgically remembered from trips to that area with her grandfather when she was a child. "It's all so peaceful," she wrote about her house on Sutton Place, "that one might as well be living miles away."

Before long Marbury was able to entice two of her closest friends to follow, who, as the legend goes, inaugurated an absolute pilgrimage of the rich to the east, what one writer called a "*drang nach osten.*" The second Sutton Place convert was another single woman, thirty-eight-year-old Anne Morgan, the daughter of J. Pierpont Morgan, who happened to be one of the richest women in the world. Anne Morgan bought 3 and 5 Sutton Place and again hired Mott B. Schmidt to combine and renovate them. Schmidt became so fond of the area himself that he, too, eventually moved to Sutton Place. The last and most significant of the immigrants to the neighborhood was Anne Harriman Vanderbilt, the second wife of William Kissam Vanderbilt. Anne Vanderbilt's move to Sutton Place shocked New York society. The *New York Times* social columnist was so outraged that he took her to task for moving into "the heart of the slums." Anne Vanderbilt was a tall, slender woman with white hair and gentle blue eyes. She was twice widowed and had lost both her sons in tragic automobile accidents. In 1886 she married Vanderbilt on the rebound from his divorce from the profligate Alva Vanderbilt, who had commissioned Richard Morris Hunt to build for her a lavish limestone mansion on Fifth Avenue and Fifty-second Street that was too big and too garish for her successor's more gentle sensibilities. After W. K. Vanderbilt died in 1920, Anne gladly sold the mansion to the Empire Trust Company for $3 million and paid only $50,000 for Effingham B. Sutton's decrepit old house. She too hired Mott B. Schmidt to renovate the house into a four-story, thirteen-room town house with one hundred feet of terraced gardens overlooking the East River, which "descended to the water's edge like billowing ruffles on the hem of a women's frock," wrote a reporter from the *New York Times* in 1926. (The house, which was later owned by

Mrs. Drue Heinz, the widow of the 57 Varieties man, is now the property of the United Nations and is used by the sitting secretary-general as a New York residence.)

By the mid-1920s the private home splurge along Fifth Avenue was over and just as Effingham B. Sutton had predicted fifty years before, there was a flurry of new construction of luxury housing centered on the intersection of Fifty-seventh Street and Sutton Place. "When Mrs. William K. Vanderbilt established her residence in Sutton Place about six years ago," the *New York Times* of 1929 noted in an article about the luxury housing boom, "it was little dreamed that within so short a time such a marked migration from mid-Midtown to the East River district would occur as is now in full swing. In the unbroken line of new towering apartment houses . . . those who doubted the wisdom of Mrs. Vanderbilt's move have found a convincing answer to their conjecture as to the ultimate success of the Sutton Place movement." Said a New York guide of the era about Sutton Place: "Here drying winter flannels are within fishpole reach of a Wall Street tycoon's windows and the society woman in her boudoir may be separated only by a wall from the family on relief in a cold water flat."

The final phase of the "Sutton Place movement" began in 1924, when the Phipps Company, now keenly interested in developing the neighborhood, spent more than $3 million financing the construction of the street's first luxury apartment building, One Sutton Place South, on what was then the site of a coal-storage company. Rosario Candela and his collaborators, Cross & Cross, designed the redbrick building to "harmonize" with Mrs. Vanderbilt's brick house across the street. Original plans for the thirteen-story building show a deepwater dock for yachts along the East River and an indoor tennis court under the garden, but neither was built. It had some unusual amenities, such as the private laundry rooms for each apartment in the basement with giant mangles to wring out the wash, and tall gas-fired drying ovens with racks upon which to hang bedsheets to dry flat.

Most of all, everyone marveled at the baronial, 6,400-square-foot penthouse that Henry Phipps built for his beloved daughter, Amy, so extravagant that it was called a "roofhouse" because it was like having a house that sat on top of the building. It was surrounded on all four sides by an additional 6,000 square feet of terrace landscaped into a lush lawn with voluptuous sky gardens and brick-and-tile patios. When Mrs. Vincent Astor saw it for the first time she said, "Why, this apartment makes mine look like a pigsty." Actually, the "roofhouse" was more like two fantasy apartments, because it had two wings, north and south, which shared a vast central dining hall, twenty-nine by twenty-two feet, with Queen Anne antique pink boiserie on the walls and one wall of French doors overlooking the river. Each wing had its own elliptically shaped "parlor," which was more like a ballroom or small concert hall, each forty feet long and twenty-two feet wide. The parlors had marble floors, carved doorways inlaid with gold and ivory, and matching six-foot-tall white marble fireplaces that were saved from Phipps's mansion on Fifth Avenue before it was demolished. The northern parlor also had a twenty-two-foot-high coffered ceiling with an oval-shaped, frosted skylight from which dangled a six-foot crystal chandelier. According to the fashion of the day, as spacious as the entertaining areas were, the four bedrooms — two in each wing — were small, the largest only eleven by eighteen feet, and there was limited closet space, since civilized people were expected to use armoires.

The penthouse has had only three owners. The first was Amy Phipps, an adventuresome woman who financially backed Amelia Earhart's first transatlantic flight in 1928 and begged to be taken along with her. She was even measured to see if she could fit into the fuselage somewhere but was dissuaded by her family. She also showed spirit when she married Fredrick E. Guest, the dashing first cousin of Winston Churchill and former British secretary of state for air. The Guests' son, Winston, who became an internationally known polo player and sportsman, grew up in the apartment, and when the Guests moved to a gracious mansion on Long Island's Gold Coast, they passed the city "roofhouse" down to him. Young Winston gave his family some pause in 1947 when he announced his intention to marry a rebellious debutante from Boston named Lucy Cochrane, a former Ziegfeld showgirl and onetime nude model for artist Diego Rivera. It was Rivera's portraits of her in the buff that gave her some notoriety and led to a movie contract with Louis B. Mayer. The elder Guests eventually gave Winston their permission to marry Lucy, but only after buying and destroying the most revealing of the paintings that hung over a bar in Mexico City.

The young Mrs. Guest, who was known to her family as C.Z., shook off her past. With her husband's pedigree and some good taste and common sense, she managed to transform herself into a great social lioness, admired for her elegant parties and charitable work on the Palm Beach–New York–Long Island circuit. She also became a well-known gardening expert and writer, whose horticultural columns were syndicated in more than eighty newspapers. C.Z. Guest called the roofhouse "the most magnificent apartment in New York City. . . . It was not for a normal family. We lived on one side and my son, Alexander, lived with Nanny on the other side." They found it necessary to divide one of the living rooms into three furniture groups, with seating for forty, where she entertained the Rockefellers on the night of the 1960 Nixon-Kennedy presidential debate on TV. "I wanted it comfortable, so guests didn't feel that the room is a museum." Still, it was decorated like a museum, with seventeenth-century rugs, English and French antiques, and J. P. Morgan's porcelain collection. "It should be cozy and attractive," Guest said. "That's the charm of having nice things."

In 1963, about the time their daughter, Cornelia, was born, the Guests sold the roofhouse to Janet Annenberg Hooker, one of the seven daughters of Moses L. Annenberg, the wealthy Jewish publisher whose empire included *TV Guide, Seventeen* magazine, and the *Daily Racing Form*, who closed the apartment down for an entire year to renovate and restore it. Hooker married thrice, the last time to a publishing executive at one of the Annenberg companies. She dedicated virtually her whole life to philanthropy and became one of the country's great supporters of culture and the arts. Her beneficence included the redecoration of several rooms in the White House, the construction of the Metropolitan Opera House at Lincoln Center, and support for the New York Philharmonic for over twenty years. She gave many elegant parties in the apartment, including an eightieth-birthday party for Elmer Bobst, the chairman of Warner-Lambert Pharmaceutical, attended by eighty guests, including Richard Nixon. The last great party she gave before retiring to Palm Beach was for Prince Michael of Kent. When Hooker died at age ninety-three in December of 1997, it had been thirty years since the last extensive renovation of the apartment. Her estate put it on the market with a $15 million "as is" price tag and with Betty Sherrill standing guard at the gates below.

# I I I

THAT'S WHEN ONE of the new people, J. Shelby Bryan, showed up at One Sutton Place South and made an offer. "What's his name?" Sherrill asked when Bryan's name came up, as if she didn't remember. "The guy with the cell phones?" she asked innocently. "The guy who just went broke and ran off with the editor of *Vogue?*"*

Indeed. But back when J. Shelby Bryan appeared on Betty Sherrill's doorstep, wanting to buy the penthouse apartment, he was still a happily married, fifty-four-year-old businessman and the CEO of a high-flying, Colorado-based cell phone company with nearly a billion dollars in financing. The handsome blue-eyed telecom executive lived with his wife, Katherine, and their two children in a twelve-room, six-bedroom town house at 134 East Seventy-first Street. The $7.3 million house was decorated with the help of society hostess Susan Gutfreund and was so splendidly appointed that President Bill Clinton, attending a Democratic fund-raiser there in 1997, said that it made the White House "look like public housing."

"Yes, he applied," Sherrill said, "but he didn't even bring his plans to his meeting with the board." Sherrill was referring to Bryan's architectural plans for the renovation he intended for the apartment. "See, you have to present your plans, what you're going to do," Sherrill explained. "Because we have building restrictions. We don't want to tear up the old building. . . . People would say they didn't like it this way or that, and I would say, 'It was good enough for Mrs. Phipps and C.Z. Guest, it's good enough for you.'"

What happened with "what's his name," Sherrill said, was that at his meeting with the board "he looked at me — very attractive, he is — and he said, 'I hear you don't allow parties in this building.' I said, 'Oh, that's ridiculous. What we don't allow is *fund-raising*. We don't want it. No, we don't like fund-raising because everybody here gives as much money as they can. They give a lot, as a matter of fact,

---

*Contrary to what Mrs. Sherrill believes, Mr. Bryan did not "go broke" and he sued the *New York Post* when they printed that he had lost all his money.

and we don't want to have political things going on in the building and we don't like people coming to the building who aren't known. And we have to hire an extra man to run the elevator.' And what's-his-name looked at me and said, 'How would you know if it was fund-raising or a private party?'"

Sherrill was exasperated at the memory of this temerity. "Fresh!" she cried. "Don't you think that was fresh?" she implored. She blinked her watery blue eyes. "*'How would I know?'* Well, *naturally* I would know. And I said, 'The meeting is over.'"

A few weeks later it was reported that Shelby had been given the runaround for six months by the board at One Sutton Place South and that ultimately he was turned down because he was a financial supporter of Bill Clinton and the Democratic Party — a notion that incensed Sherrill. "Why, Patricia Lawford lives just below me," Sherrill pleaded. "I got her *into* this building. They wouldn't let her into a building on Seventy-second Street, and I was in Paris when I heard, and I was so *mad* because she was the sister of the president of the United States. Well," Sherrill said indignantly, "being a Democrat doesn't qualify as a reason for rejection. So we called up Steve Smith, her brother-in-law, and we said, 'She's going to get into our building' — and she did. She's got the prettiest apartment in here. It once belonged to Madame Balsan, you know, the duchess of Marlborough? Who married Jacques Balsan? And it's beautiful, a duplex like this."

However, admitting Patricia Lawford didn't stop the board from instituting some peculiar rules, including one that prohibited more than one Kennedy brother with his entourage from being in the building at the same time, which would cause mayhem with security and the elevators. Rose Kennedy frequently stayed with her daughter in the building, and residents claimed they could set their watches by the punctuality with which mother and daughter left for church each morning.

Shelby Bryan walked away from the deal before he could be officially rejected by the board, and just as well. In a few months his life would explode onto the pages of America's gossip columns after he began an affair with *Vogue* fashion editor Anna Wintour, which ended both their marriages. More recently, Bryan's communications kingdom, ICG, went broke and filed for bankruptcy. Bryan divorced his wife, and the East Seventy-first Street town house sold for $11 million.

In the end, the roofhouse apartment was sold to Richard Perry, the president of an international hedge fund whom the *New York Observer* gleefully described as "famous for . . . being rich!" (The combined assets of Mr. Perry's funds total around $1 billion.) Perry bought the apartment for a steal — only $10.9 million, down almost a third from its original $15 million asking price. A few months later he sold his previous digs, a sixteen-room, 6,000-square-foot apartment at 117 East Seventy-second Street, for $9.8 million — so he was only out of pocket a little over a million. Many observers believe that Perry got the apartment for such a bargain because of the difficulty of anybody getting past Sherrill and the board and that perhaps Sherrill's immutability has hurt the price of apartments in her building. "It could have gone for fifteen million," Sherrill sniffed, "but it's a difficult apartment. I don't really know Richard Perry," she added. "Charlotte Ford tells me they're very nice and gave a nice recommendation and the Perrys appeared nice at the interview and they agreed to all the stipulations of the building."

What those stipulations were is not exactly clear. It was originally reported that the Perrys were restricted to only $200,000 worth of plumbing and partition work to the aging apartment, mostly in the kitchen. But lo and behold, in September 2002 there appeared in *Vogue* magazine an article and photo layout of the transformed penthouse of which Mrs. Sherrill couldn't possibly have approved. Under the direction of high-profile architect David Piscuskas and interior designer

Tony Ingrao, the famed apartment was stripped and reconfigured. The inner hallways were demolished, and the warren of maids' rooms near the front entrance and the coffered ceiling were removed. "The apartment's illustriously provenanced features were stripped away and sent to auction," it said, noting that the last of the original architectural elements, the ballroom's fireplace, was removed to make way for a Lichtenstein painting.

As it would turn out, the roofhouse apartment wasn't the only apartment in the building whose price had to be lowered to help promote its sale. The price of Bill Blass's apartment was lowered three times by the executors of his estate, who wanted a quick sale so they could give the money away to a cancer charity Blass had chosen, and there have been as many as five apartments for sale at one time at One Sutton Place South, too many for an allegedly desirable building.

Indeed, Sutton Place itself is suddenly less desirable than it once was. Statistics compiled from real estate companies show that prices for Sutton Place apartments remained flat or didn't rise as quickly as other areas of the city and that the small, old-fashioned enclave, so far away from the city center, has lost some of its luster.

Sherill would not listen to the notion that Sutton Place has become a relic of another era. "This is a family building," Sherrill repeated, smiling pleasantly, slowly lifting herself up from her chair with the aid of her cane and bringing her chat to a close. "Everybody *loves* the building. It's a nice building and everybody gets along well."

# FIVE

# BROKER
# TO THE STARS

But *Ru-pert*," Linda Stein purred huskily into her cell phone, enjoying the double entendre she was about to make, "in New York City, town houses aren't about *height*, they're about length and width."

Stein stopped pacing and strained to hear the voice on the other end as it faded in and out. "Look," she said more briskly, "you're not going to have much of a view from a Greenwich Village town house, no matter what. If what you want is sparkle value, then you should look with me on Central Park West, not in the Village. But, *Ru-pert*, you want *where the boys are*."

It was a crisp, clear autumn morning, and bright sun flooded through the wraparound windows of Stein's comfy Fifth Avenue penthouse, illuminating it with the brilliance of a stage set. Outside the windows there was a sweeping panorama of building tops, the low jumble of East Side town houses and the spires of apartment towers, dominated by the majestic tower of the Carlyle Hotel, only one avenue away. Inside her apartment there was gold-leaf nineteenth-century furniture upholstered in rose velvet, built-in cabinetry, hand-burnished putty-colored walls, and an antique Chinese desk piled with neatly stacked file folders. Stein, fifty-four, Manhattan's "broker to the stars," had been gathering the provisions she needed to leave her apartment for a busy day — a change of comfortable shoes, a leather appointment calendar littered with yellow Post-it reminders, her cell phone — and packing them into a red leather Prada shopping bag. But like Penelope's weaving, the more she packed, the more it seemed to come undone. Mostly she fielded phone calls from friends and clients while wandering around the sisal-covered floor of her living room in her stocking feet, worrying aloud about the "ten-million-dollar Donna Karan deal," about the "mumble" that could kill it, and about the "bad phone call" yesterday afternoon that might ruin everything.

At that moment the openly gay British movie star Rupert Everett was on the phone, calling from a film set in Chicago. Everett was explaining rather naively about his requirements for a town house he hoped to buy in Greenwich Village. Stein listened impatiently to his stipulations about height and location as her right eyebrow cocked into a skeptical boomerang and her lips simultaneously formed into a bow with the remarkable fluidity of an animated character. She is a small woman — only five feet tall — but a large presence. She has a brash, husky voice with the delivery of a red-hot mama, and her expressive face telegraphs the subtlest of emotions, even with her dark brown eyes cloaked behind the tinted lenses of tortoiseshell frames. She was fashionably dressed in a soft, caramel-colored wool Zoran dress. A sterling-silver Tiffany watch hung around her right wrist with just the right amount of looseness. Still tanned from long weekends at a friend's estate in Montauk, Long Island, Stein wore little makeup, except for her trademark fire-engine-red lipstick, traces of which were left everywhere — on coffee cups, napkins, cigarettes.

"Rupert, single-family town houses have no views," she said curtly. "They are at the *most* five stories tall and they face *other* town houses, usually. What you want, ideally, is a town house that's at least twenty-five feet wide with a south-facing garden to make the best of the daylight. And let me tell you *this*, Rupert," she said, her voice rising, *"two million dollars is not a lot of money for a town house in Greenwich Village."* She paused to let that sink in. "I've got something for you to see on West Twelfth Street. It's two point six-five. It's not big but it's got original eighteen-fifties wide-plank floors and central air."

Although she was forcing herself to concentrate on the matter at hand, Stein was clearly in no mood to explain the subtleties of buying a private home in Manhattan to a movie star in Chicago. The "bad phone call" yesterday had come from her soft-spoken cancer specialist from Memorial Sloan-Kettering Cancer Center, Dr. Jeanne Petrek, who had called her at the office to report that her recent CAT scan showed a small "shadow" on the left side of her chest. Dr. Petrek reassured her that the shadow could easily turn out to be harmless scar tissue left by the radical mastectomy Stein had of her left breast in 1996, or it could turn out to be harmless scar tissue caused by the removal of her reconstructed breast when it, too, was discovered to have malignant lymph nodes in 1998, and she had a second radical mastectomy. Whatever it was, they would need to find out right away.

So, after this bit of news she went into the office of her boss and mentor, Edward Lee Cave, and told him about the shadow on the CAT scan, and they both cried a little. Then she went to a friend's apartment on the Upper West Side, drank a couple of bottles of red wine, and slept fitfully on the sofa. She woke at dawn and took a taxi to her apartment, where she showered and dressed and tried to pull herself together to face a long and complicated day of showing apartments, culminating at Memorial Sloan-Kettering with a needle biopsy — after which she was determined to go out to dinner at Harry Cipriani with a friend and put on a good face.

Stein ended her conversation with the actor by promising to preview properties for him later that week and flipped her cell phone shut with an emphatic snap. "Fuck," she said, looking annoyed. "Two million and change for a town house. I can see there is only twenty-five thousand dollars' commission in this for me."*

Stein looked resigned as she repacked the cell phone into the leather shopping bag. "Sometimes this broker-to-the-stars thing is not all it's cracked up to be," she said. "Sometimes I think I have more hype than I have commissions. People are impressed that my clients are movie stars, but what they don't realize is that *in the long run it doesn't matter if your client is a movie star or a dog.* What matters is *closing the deal.*" Stein worries all the time about closing the deal. It is the leitmotif of her life. No dog has ever gnawed a bone more intently than Stein worries her deals together, networking, coaxing, finessing her buyer and seller to terms, and then threading her clients through the eye of the needle of the co-op board.

In Stein's rarefied end of the business, where the competition is cutthroat and big-dollar clients are as scarce as the high-end inventory, things can go cold very quickly. Twice in her career she's had to work her way back to financial solvency from near bankruptcy. "There were times when I sold furniture or a bracelet to get by," she told *New York* magazine in 1991. "It's hard to be talking big numbers with a customer while you're searching for a twenty to pay the taxi."

There were also many good years. She's sold real estate to some of the biggest names in pop culture — Bruce Willis, Steven Spielberg,

---

*As it would turn out, there would be no commission for Stein. Everett rented a West Village townhouse through another broker and later bought it, for $3.7 million, direct from the seller, paying a commission to no one.

Andrew Lloyd Webber — and pulled off something of a real estate hat trick when she sold newlyweds Billy Joel and Christie Brinkley two apartments at 88 Central Park West, one on top of the other, which they joined into a 7,000-square-foot, eighteen-room duplex, and then several years later sold the apartment for the couple when they were divorcing, this time to the rock star Sting, for $4.8 million, and simultaneously found both Joel and Brinkley separate places to live. In the 1990s Stein broke records three years in a row with $25 million a year in sales, "when twenty-five million dollars was a lot of money," she said. Now $100 million a year in sales barely gets a broker into the top echelon.

Yet she frets that her big sales were years ago and that the younger celebrity crowd isn't coming to her. "I didn't sell to Uma and I didn't sell to Gwyneth," she said, half smiling despite herself at how silly it all sounded. She also couldn't help but smile while admitting that she consciously networked with newly rich rap impresarios such as multi-millionaire Rock-A-Fella Records owners Jay-Z and Dame Dash, who have money to throw around on expensive condominium apartments and town houses where there are no co-op boards to turn them away. She was even learning a new vocabulary to accommodate them. "If they say an apartment is 'dope, phat,' or 'large,'" Stein ticked off, "it's all positive. I wear my mink coat and big diamond earrings when I take them out to see apartments so they think I've 'got it going.'"

Part of Stein's appeal is that she's funny and quick and also a straight shooter who tells it the way she sees it. This can be good and bad. Sometimes even she doesn't know exactly what's going to come spilling out of her mouth. Once, she was growing weary of showing Warren Beatty apartments that "I knew he would never buy," she said, "and in every apartment he kept wanting to know 'Who lives upstairs? Who lives downstairs? Whose windows do the living room face?'" On

Alice Mason (*right*), the doyenne of carriage-trade brokers, with her friend Sosette Bross. Mason's exclusive dinner parties not only were her best marketing tool but were tax-deductible, too.

The elegant and understated entrance of 820 Fifth Avenue, the holy of
holies of all Manhattan buildings—until the board allowed the hip-hop
clothing designer Tommy Hilfiger to buy an apartment.

Social arbiter and philanthropist Jayne Wrightsman (*left*, with Annette de la Renta) wasn't on the board of 820 Fifth, but she had a say over everything, down to the color of the paint in the elevator.

Elegant, expert, and the soul of discretion, top-end broker Edward Lee Cave enjoyed selling expensive things to very rich people, from Monet paintings to the walls to hang them on.

Hidden away on a dead-end street on the East River is the gated entranceway to River House. The co-op board unleashed a publicity tempest by rejecting Gloria Vanderbilt's bid to buy the tower apartment that once belonged to department store heir Marshall Field.

For over forty years the high society couple Betty and Virgil Sherrill ruled the co-op board at One Sutton Place South. Virgil worked on Wall Street, and Betty was the queen of the cabbage-rose-chintz world of interior decorating.

The facade of One Sutton Place South is austere and unrevealing of the treasured apartments it contains inside. Its residents are locked in a dispute with the city over plans to build a public park overlooking the East River just below their windows.

The inimitable "Broker to the Stars," Linda Stein became as famous as the people to whom she sold apartments.

Donna Karan's new home is the art deco 55 Central Park West, recognizable to the public as the building in the movie *Ghostbusters*. The brick exterior is said to be forty different shades, getting lighter toward the top, so it looks as if the sun is always shining on the building.

Donna Karan and her husband, Stephan Weiss, were famous for their dedication to each other. Weiss died of lung cancer before they were able to move into their dream apartment at 55 Central Park West.

The twin-towered San Remo is architect Emery Roth's greatest masterpiece and one of the city's best-known residential silhouettes. Its celebrity residents include Steven Spielberg, Bruce Willis, Steven Jobs, and Steve Martin.

Jerry Seinfeld, John McEnroe, and Helen Gurley Brown live in the San Remo's sister building on Central Park West, the Beresford. The small park across Eighty-second Street from the building makes a perfect spot to inflate the giant Macy's Thanksgiving Day Parade balloons, and every November the building's residents hold viewing parties as the giant balloons rise past their windows.

When Vincent Joyce arrived in New York, he didn't want to be the doorman in the same building in which he lived. That was nearly forty years ago, and now he's as much a part of the Ansonia Hotel's rich lore as any other tenant.

A weary and wounded gem, the Ansonia Hotel as it looks today—stripped, its gargoyles toppled, the archways cemented up. Yet it still dominates the gritty urban crossroads of West Seventy-second Street and Broadway a block south.

Although the Ansonia had its own elevator system invented by its owner, W. E. D. Stokes, many of the residents and especially the children loved to use the vertiginous staircase with the polished banister. The hallways and interiors of the Ansonia were used in the movie *Single White Female*, with Bridget Fonda.

Fanciful, energetic, and despicable in equal measure, W. E. D. Stokes built the Ansonia and filled it with the greatest cast of characters a New York multiple dwelling has ever known, including spies, gamblers, opera singers, and Babe Ruth, who made the Ansonia his home for nine years.

*Giovanni Boldini, c. 1911*

W. E. D. Stokes was so smitten when he spotted a photograph of Rita Hernandez de Acosta in a store window that he decided to marry the fifteen-year-old without even knowing her name. The teenager later rued the day she agreed to Stokes's proposition of matrimony and divorced him after giving birth to his son.

Stokes's son, known as Weddie, was presented with the Ansonia Hotel as a fourteenth-birthday gift. He built a wireless station on the top of the hotel that broadcast over three states. Weddie later wrote a book called *Planetary Configurations and Stock Market Sentiment* about the connection between astrology and stocks and real estate.

The grand Ansonia Hotel in her prime in 1913, a terra-cotta curio cabinet where every other apartment held an extraordinary story.

GRILL FOUNTAIN

THE ANSONIA, BROADWAY AND 73D STREET, NEW YORK. N. Y.    SOUVENIR POST CARD CO. N. Y.    MOST SUPERBLY EQUIPPED HOUSE IN THE WORLD.

An orchestra played from the balcony of the Ansonia's Louis XIV–style ballroom, where the chandeliers were festooned with ropes of crystal. When all the ballrooms and restaurants were at capacity, the hotel could accommodate 1,300 dinner guests.

© Rob Rich

Dolly Lenz, the powerhouse broker of New York real estate, with over $3 billion worth of sales, and her boss Howard Lorber, who owns Prudential Douglas Elliman. In 2005 Lenz shattered price records in the Northeast for a private residence, with the sale of the mansion Burnt Point in East Hampton for $45 million.

The towers of mammon rise against the western skyline as the Time Warner Center reaches skyward, six months before its completion date. The dark monolith of Trump International Hotel & Tower stands to its right, blocking the Time Warner view of Central Park.

Three titans of real estate sales and development: the idealistic yet tough
Dottie Herman, CEO of Prudential Douglas Elliman, who is mother
confessor and disciplinarian of 2,500 employees; Howard Lorber (*left*), her
partner, who also owns Nathan's Hot Dogs; and their pal Donald Trump,
who calls the residential real estate business "brutal."

the second day, they were in a $6 million, four-bedroom Fifth Avenue apartment, peering out the windows of the master bedroom at the building across the street, when Beatty asked, "Did you say it was Robert Redford who lived across the street?"

Stein said quietly, "Robert Redford. Warren Beatty. What difference does it make? It's all the same."

Beatty didn't buy in New York.

And once, riding around Manhattan in the backseat of a limousine with Sylvester Stallone, looking at apartments, the action star wondered aloud if he would be happy living in Connecticut. Stein sneered at the idea. "Rambo in Connecticut just isn't happening," she told him. Stallone didn't buy from her, either. (Or from anybody else, for that matter; he stayed in L.A.)

Stein sat down for a moment on a rose-colored sofa with her back to the New York skyline and curled her legs up underneath her. She lit a forbidden Virginia Slims Light cigarette and exhaled a plume of smoke into the sunlight. She bought her jewel-box one-bedroom aerie for only $250,000 in "as-is" condition from an estate, the booty of being a real estate broker in the know. Elegant and feminine, it was a modest three-room flat with the bedroom located beyond a set of mahogany pocket doors just off the living room. Throughout the apartment, on tabletops or tucked in bookshelves, were photographs in a variety of sterling-silver frames of Stein with her family and celebrated friends. On her art deco bedroom dressing table was a picture of Stein with her pretty daughters, Mandy, twenty-one, and Samantha, twenty-four; in the living-room bookcase was a black-and-white photograph of her taken in a Hollywood restaurant next to Elton John, who is her daughter Mandy's godfather; on the nineteenth-century Chinese inlaid wooden desk in the living room there was a shot of Stein grinning shyly as she is being hugged by Sly Stallone at her fiftieth-birthday party at Le Cirque; tucked away next to a CD player is a grainy paparazzi shot from the front page of the *New York Post* of Stein and Madonna, both in sunglasses, emerging from under the shadows of the canopied portals of the San Remo on Central Park West.

Stein's favorite photograph of herself, which sat in a bookshelf in the living room, is a paparazzi shot of her sitting courtside at Madison Square Garden in her spike-heeled Manolo Blahniks, engrossed in a Knicks game with Richard Johnson, the handsome editor of "Page Six," the *New York Post*'s much-read gossip column. In the early nineties Stein made no bones about having a giggly sort of crush on the younger, married newspaper columnist. Eventually, her friend and fan, writer Billy Norwich, then the *New York Observer*'s Style columnist, printed a tongue-in-cheek item implying that Stein and Johnson were having a romance. It backfired on Stein by infuriating the powerful *Post* editor, and Johnson remanded her to what he called "publicity rehab," restricting her mentions in "Page Six" and leaving her in a public relations exile.

Stein was grateful. She herself realized she needed to keep a lower profile. There was a time when Stein had so much publicity that it seemed as if a whole Linda Stein cottage industry had sprung up. Although there had been many well-known brokers in Manhattan before Stein, she was the first to harness the press and market herself as the New York City show business specialist. Her name and pithy quotes peppered the gossip columns, and she had feature articles written about her in *Vanity Fair* ("Hot Property") and *New York* ("The Rap on Linda") magazine. She also had the distinction of having two movie characters based on her: the name-dropping real estate agent in the movie *Wall Street*, played by actress Sylvia Miles, who goes on about "Sean and Madonna," and the predatory record-company executive in the Miramax movie *54*, played by actress Sela Ward, who beds all the hot younger boys in her Fifth Avenue penthouse apartment. Although she told the *New York Post,* "I don't name names," she did. Sometimes she talked too much, and it got her into trouble: Patrick McCarthy, the feared editorial director at Fairchild Publications, which includes *W* magazine and *Women's Wear Daily,* demanded she return a commission after he read in a 1991 *New York* magazine article that Stein had discussed the details of his co-op negotiations with him on her cell phone in the presence of a reporter in the backseat of a limousine. In another incident, in January 1996, when the "Home" section of the *New York Times* ran an article about rich men who buy houses in Manhattan and never move into them, including billionaires David Geffen and Ronald Perelman, Stein was quoted as saying "It's amazing these guys can ever make a business decision." The following morning she was fired from Sotheby's International Realty, where she then worked, and was told to clear out her desk and leave the building within fifteen minutes. She stood on the street corner in the snow with her files and Rolodex in a corrugated box and cried as she tried to hail a cab.

Stein doesn't talk to the press anymore. The problem is, she's about the only broker who doesn't. These days all the big brokers feed the press real estate items promoting themselves, and there are lots of "brokers to the stars." There are lots of brokers, period.

Over 40,000 brokers and salespeople in the greater New York area alone.

Residential real estate in New York City has turned into a $3-billion-a-year breeding ground for type A personalities. Attracted by the barrage of media stories of how the real estate market is burgeoning, applicants for real estate licenses stand in line at 6:00 A.M. at the real estate examining board offices in downtown Manhattan. Years ago if someone at a cocktail party said she was in "real estate," you'd excuse yourself and rush off to get another drink; today, people latch onto real estate brokers as if they're the prettiest girl at the ball.

Indeed, real estate has become a voyeuristic preoccupation in America. Rich men read the "City Residences" section of the *Wall Street Journal* the way their grandfathers used to leer at girlie books while waiting to get their hair cut at the corner barbershop. Journalist Carl Swanson knew what he was talking about when he fingered the once-serious journal *Architectural Digest* as "an interior design stroke book." The *New York Observer*'s "Manhattan Transfers" column, the scoop on who's buying what co-op from whom, is the second-most-read section of that newspaper, and a similar column called "Hot Properties" in the *Los Angeles Times* was so popular that it went into worldwide syndication in 1998. The *New York Times* spruced up its Sunday real estate section with a gossip column in 2004, and the *New York Post* upped its Saturday circulation by 40,000 with the addition of a citywide real estate section. Even the buttoned-down *Wall Street Journal* began to run a weekly gossip column called "Private Properties," highlighting the manses of the financially famous.

When Stein first started in the business twenty years ago, the residential sales force was mostly women, with a few notable exceptions. Men with college degrees went into commercial real estate, where the money was made brokering long-term business leases that paid off year after year, like annuities. Residential brokers were mostly rich widows or divorcées who wore white gloves to showings and sold real estate to their friends from the club, "bedroom brokers," they were sometimes called because they set up offices in a spare bedroom after their grown children had flown the coop. But as residential prices rose, so did the skill and education of brokers, and today entrance-level applicants to the bigger brokerages commonly have MBAs.

Today in New York, knowing the right residential broker is as important as knowing the best plastic surgeon or getting your child into an elite preschool. One reason residential brokers have such clout is that not only is real estate a particular fetish of New York City, but unlike most other cities in the world, there are no "open listings" — a centralized listing of all the apartments or homes for sale available to all brokers.* In New York one broker, who represents the seller of the apartment, holds a listing "exclusively," which means he is solely responsible for the apartment's marketing and sale, and only he can show the apartment to interested buyers. Ninety-five percent of all co-operative apartments in New York City are sold on an "exclusive" basis. In a complicated mating dance, a second broker represents the buyer, and brokers for both the seller and buyer have to be present whenever the apartment is shown. Sometimes the exclusive broker hits the jackpot and finds his own buyer for the apartment and keeps the whole 6 percent industry-standard commission. Although brokers deny it, they frequently "shave" commission points to persuade sellers to give them high-dollar exclusive listings; since most of those listings are $5 million and above, it's worth it to them to lose a point in commissions to get a listing.

The top-earning brokers, known in the business as "producers," account for 80 percent of the revenues of the companies they work for. They invariably specialize in the sliver of the market that accounts for only about 5 percent of all sales, the high end, where the big money is. These apartments start around $3 million and escalate as high as $50 million. (As of 2002, an estimated 30 percent of all co-operative

---

*In 2003 the Real Estate Board of New York, a self-governing creation of the industry, made it mandatory that all brokerages share listings with one another electronically seventy-two hours after getting them, a largely unenforceable decree.

apartments for sale in Manhattan cost $1 million or more, according to research done by real estate brokerages.) Most of the top producers are paid between $250,000 to $1 million a year in salary against their commissions, and a handful earn as much as $2 million a year in advances. Roger Erickson, a former CBS Records marketing flack who is now an executive at Sotheby's and was once known as the "$125 Million Man" in honor of his biggest year so far in gross sales, complained to *New York* magazine that in 2002 he clocked in at only $64 million.

It's no coincidence that a former rock-and-roll marketing executive is one of the city's most successful brokers. "This is an arena," said Barbara Corcoran, who started her business in 1978 when her boyfriend ran off with his secretary and told her she'd never amount to anything, "where if you can't get yourself noticed, you're dead." Corcoran got attention by always featuring herself, smiling warmly, in every Corcoran ad, branding her preppy good looks and cheerful persona as the company. Corcoran's high-end experts include the coiffed and tailored Sharon Baum, sixty-two, who has a master's degree from Harvard Business School and takes her clients to showings in a chauffeur-driven, butter-colored Bentley that bears the license plate SOLD 1, which is also spelled out in diamonds in a pin that she always wears on her left lapel. (Baum keeps a bottle of Grey Poupon mustard in the back of her car for the many people who pull up next to her car and ask for it.) There is also the elegant A. Laurance Kaiser IV, who runs Key Ventures, a petite boutique for high-end real estate, and has literally memorized the floor plans of every apartment in every Good Building on Fifth and Park Avenues as well as which closets hold what skeletons. Dominick Dunne spent an afternoon in Kaiser's library listening to his tales of the tribulations of high society before writing *People Like Us.* Downtown, there are specialty brokers who command entire segments of the city, such as Helene Luchnick, the "Loft

Queen of TriBeCa," who has sold more giant lofts in TriBeCa than any other single broker and twenty years ago helped convert half of SoHo's lofts into co-operatives.

And then there is the broker whose fame became so great that it began to obscure her purpose in being a broker in the first place, the original "broker to the stars," Linda Stein.

## II

"YOU SEE THAT building across the park?" Stein asked, gesturing toward the handsome silhouette of skyscrapers on Central Park West in the distance, beyond the Sheep Meadow and the swaying treetops of Central Park. She pointed out one of them: a corn-yellow building that seemed to shimmer in the bright sunlight. "That's the building, Fifty-five Central Park West, where the ten-and-a-half-million-dollar Donna Karan deal is in contract," she said. She peered intently at it, compressing her lips as though she were making a silent wish. "Can you see where the building steps back at the sixteenth floor?" she asked, pointing out a series of architectural setbacks toward the top. "It forms a wraparound terrace — *a one-thousand-square-foot terrace* — the fifth-largest terrace on Central Park West," she said, and without thinking, went on autopilot and began to rattle off the merits of the apartments, the possible flow, the enormous windows. She couldn't help herself, giving this sales pitch to a court of no recourse. The pending sale of the apartments consumed her. Two weeks before, Donna Karan and her husband, Stephan Weiss, had signed papers to buy adjacent apartments 16 D and F at 55 Central Park West. Joined together, the nine- and seven-room apartments would constitute the entire front and sides of the sixteenth floor, 6,000 square feet of space with thirty-six giant single-paned windows and sweeping views of Central Park and the skyscrapers of midtown Manhattan.

Just getting Karan to sign a contract was something of a coup in the real estate business, let alone for a deal over $10 million. The saga of Karan and her husband's search for a place to lay down their mattress had become something of a public soap opera in New York. For over a decade the couple had enlisted what the *New York Times* described as a "platoon" of real estate brokers, only to skittishly back out or change their minds every time they came close to making a deal. Among their flirtations, they considered buying three separate apartments that they intended to join together at 279 Central Park West, for about $6 million; a $5.75 triplex penthouse condominium at the Alfred, a modern high-rise located on the inauspiciously urban corner of Sixty-first Street and Columbus Avenue; and Woody Allen's duplex penthouse at 930 Fifth Avenue, which was for sale for $14 million. For a time they unpacked their bags in a $25,000-a-month sublet in the San Remo that belonged to Texas natural gas heiress Adelaide de Menil, and more recently they had been biding their time in a 5,000-square-foot duplex loft with a rooftop swimming pool on Wooster Street in SoHo — swank digs but social purgatory for middle-aged baby boomers like Karan and Weiss.

What the platoon of brokers didn't know was that Stephan Weiss and Donna Karan's restless search for a place to live had its own ebb and flow because Weiss was dying of lung cancer, and this new apartment, wherever it was, would probably be their last together. A former heavy smoker, Weiss was diagnosed with the disease in 1995. The couple was famously in love and dedicated to each other, and even though they insisted that Weiss had the cancer in remission, it somehow kept coming back. Weiss had quietly been in and out of the hospital in recent months for various radiation and chemotherapy treatments. Still, they were determined to find a new place to live together, although some observers believed that the unfulfilled search for an apartment was more of a wistful kind of denial than a desire to find a new home. "What we want most," Karan told brokers, "is a terrace where we can sit outside and have our morning coffee."

Karan was looking for more than just a terrace: an apartment that would in some way be a unique manifestation of her self. The street on which Donna Karan and Stephan Weiss felt they most belonged was Central Park West. After a century of being denigrated as the bourgeois, Jewish aunt of the WASPy, blond, patrician Fifth Avenue, Central Park West exploded in the 1980s and 1990s as one of the most furiously desirable places to live in Manhattan, the "Glammiest Address," as Christopher Mason dubbed it in a 1996 *New York* magazine article about the street's wild popularity. Hip, cosmopolitan, and sexy, CPW, as locals call it, had become so trendy that by 1995 it even had its own television series named after it, the ill-fated *Central Park West*, created by *Sex and the City*'s Darren Starr. The show starred Mariel Hemingway as a tough magazine editor with a terrace overlooking the park, one of the typical denizens of this glammiest street. "The reality goes and you become a character in a play," *60 Minutes* producer Don Hewitt, who lives at the San Remo on Central Park West, told the *New York Times*.

Central Park West does feel unreal, if only because it is such an enchanting thoroughfare, a wide, six-lane boulevard, flanked on its western side by a display of unique and fanciful architecture from some of the city's finest architects; its eastern side is buttressed by a charming cobblestone sidewalk and green slat benches on which to sit and watch the world go by, and behind them a low stone parapet, a runway and perch for squirrels, that hems in the vast, verdant park beyond. "Central Park West is not a street," Pulitzer Prize–winning architectural critic Paul Goldberger wrote in his book *The City Observed*, "it is a place. It has a sense of style, an aura. [It is] New York's finest street at large scale . . . it is better by far than Fifth Avenue . . . it is better than Park Avenue."

Denizens of Park and Fifth Avenues across Central Park might choke on Mr. Goldberger's opinion, but they are used to it. There are no two streets in New York more frequently pitted against each other than Fifth Avenue and Central Park West. A sniping match as old and wide as the park itself exists between *la vie bohème* on the left side of upper Manhattan island and *l'ancien régime* to the East. West Side residents like to characterize the East Side as repressive and populated with Republicans, closet cases, and dinosaurs of social protocol. Central Park West residents snipe that Fifth Avenue apartments are less spacious because Fifth Avenue buildings were cobbled together from the lots of private homes, and save a few exceptions, most Fifth Avenue apartments are only two or three plots wide and only twelve or thirteen stories high. (The narrowest building on Fifth Avenue is 969 Fifth, a mere twenty-four feet.) On Central Park West, where land was mostly undeveloped when the first apartment hotels appeared in the 1890s, large vacant lots were easier to come by for developers, and the more important apartment buildings, some thirty stories tall, cover entire blockfronts. And if the view is better from Fifth Avenue, it's because the people who live on Fifth Avenue get to look at the glamorous skyline of the four twin-towered buildings of Central Park West, in particular the romantically majestic peaks of the San Remo, while people who live on Central Park West are greeted each day with the stolid, sober silhouettes of Fifth Avenue's fortresses of propriety. Critics point out that Fifth Avenue is a one-way street downtown; Central Park West is sixty feet wider and has the convenience of being two-way, making it easier to find taxis. And for a distinction that only New Yorkers would appreciate, the residents of Central Park West have only one parade down their street each year, not seven, like the people who live on Fifth Avenue — and that one parade is considered the best of them all, Macy's Thanksgiving Day parade, during which the giant helium balloon characters float by just outside the windows of Central Park West's apartments.

Linda Stein gave *New York* magazine her own spin on the benefits of Central Park West: "At co-ops on Fifth Avenue and Park new money is frowned upon. On the West Side it is worshipped." If money be the judge, apartments on Central Park West are certainly as expensive as those on Fifth Avenue, particularly if you take into account the prices being asked at the Trump International Hotel & Tower, a luxury hotel and condominium at the intersection where Central Park West meets Columbus Circle, with takeout available to residents from Jean Georges, the four-star restaurant of Jean-Georges Vongerichten. Up the street at some of the more traditional buildings, prices are just as choice, for instance, the $9 million actor Robin Williams got for his relatively modest-size, 2,850-square-foot apartment at 271 Central Park West, or the $26 million Oracle CEO Larry Ellison asked for his 6,000-square-foot apartment at 50 Central Park West. Hotelier Ian Schrager originally wanted $23 million for his 6,000-square-foot tower apartment in the Majestic at 115 Central Park West, with an oval tub in the master bath carved out of a boulder of marble. Dustin Hoffman's 8,000-square-foot San Remo triplex, a combination of one half of the fifteenth floor and all of the sixteenth and seventeenth floors, was on the market for $25 million (with a monthly maintenance fee of $11,000) — even though it faces the back of the building.

Yet the age-old jeering between the approximately 250,000 people who live on the Upper East Side and the 250,000 who live on the

Upper West is more than just xenophobic rivalry. Hard-core East Siders truly despise the West Side as being vulgar and lower-class. Census numbers from 1997 show that the families on the Upper West Side are bigger and younger; the families on the Upper East Side are smaller, better educated, and much richer — double the income of their West Side counterparts. It is said that no real society lives on the West Side, and the people who live there care nothing about real society, who live across the park. For East Siders, the West Side is a place that people drive through on their way to Connecticut. One nanny told the *New York Times* that nannies were treated better by East Siders, who had more experience with domestics, than by West Siders, who regarded them as "help." As for the much-vaunted intellectualism of the West Side, Gay Talese told the *New York Times*, "The men, though carrying books you may want to read, are all in need of dental work." He said of the doormen, "On the West Side they're wearing Yankee jackets and listening to the baseball game while double-parking cars in front of lobbies where the paint is flaking and there is a playpen full of kids running wild."

As for the cliché that Central Park West is the "Jewish side" of Central Park and that Fifth Avenue is the bastion of eastern establishment, it's partially true; although there are many Jews living on Fifth and Park Avenues, there are probably not quite as many as on Central Park West. The West Side of New York has always been considered the "Jewish" side since Jews began to move there in the 1880s. Thousands of Jewish families, many of them refugees from czarist Russia, managed to scrimp and save and lift themselves out of Lower East Side tenements to the comparatively bucolic Upper West Side. These refugee families mostly bought single-family brownstones from land speculators, who, like themselves, were Jewish. The great city planner chief engineer of Central Park Egbert Viele predicted one day that the

West Side would house "the great and prosperous class of our Hebrew fellow-citizens."

Some of the earliest apartment buildings on Central Park West were built specifically for wealthy Jews who were not welcomed in buildings on the East Side. For example, 101 Central Park West, which to this day is still considered the premium white-glove building on the street, was built to attract Jewish tenants and was intentionally left unnamed to make it sound as if it could be located on the East Side. (This is where Harrison Ford, Peter Jennings, and Rick Moranis make their home.) The twin-towered, twenty-nine-story Majestic two blocks north, at 115 Central Park West — developed by Irwin Chanin, who got his start building two-family houses in the Bensonhurst section of Brooklyn — was known among the tenants of Central Park West as the "Jewish building," even though it was better known as where Walter Winchell lived and wrote his columns from a room overlooking Central Park, and the gangster Frank Costello had a seventeen-room penthouse suite there, and Bruno Hauptmann, the kidnapper of Charles Lindbergh's baby, had worked there as a carpenter.

Of course, the Majestic was no more Jewish than the San Remo, where Philip Roth's fictional Jewish kvetch, Portnoy, played with kosher liver in his bedroom, or the El Dorado, where Herman Wouk's quintessential fictional Jewish American Princess, Marjorie Morning-star, the daughter of a Garment District manufacturer who changed her name from Morgenstern, gazed out over the treetops at the reservoir and dreamed of her prince, Noel Airman. Only today it is Bono, the Irish rock star and humanitarian, and his family, who gazes out over the park and the renamed Jacqueline Kennedy Onassis Reservoir from his apartment at the El Dorado.

In 1939, when such stereotyping was still very much acceptable, *Fortune* magazine characterized the West Side as being "inhabited chiefly, though by no means exclusively, by New York–born Jews who have standards of their own but whose interest in social prestige is practically nil." These West Side Jews, *Fortune's* writer opined, were "not only wedded to the city, but they know how to get the most out of it for their money. They take more pleasure than the Ivy Leaguers in cultural activities; their theater is a necessity; and they habitually cultivate a wide variety of tastes, from food to music." The article also postulated that a West Side Jew's "maid (probably a Negro) gets $60 a month wages and has no style."

After World War II the Upper West Side went into devastating decline. The first generation of Jewish residents — by then one-third of all the people who populated the Upper West Side — were aging and began moving to Florida or the suburbs, except for the very oldest Jews, who continued to sun themselves on the concrete median along Broadway and patronized the last few kosher butchers and restaurants left around Seventy-second Street. But many also felt chased away by the large influx of Caribbean immigrants that poured into the plentiful rent-controlled apartments on the Upper West Side. Between 1950 and 1955, 250,000 men, women, and children from Puerto Rico moved to New York and the Upper West Side and became the city's newest immigrant villains, with the West Side as their turf. While the movie and play *West Side Story* romanticized the racial problems and living conditions of the slums, the danger and squalor of the Upper West Side were bleak and real. The neat blocks of town-house rows between Central Park West and Riverside Drive were transformed into boardinghouses or multiple dwellings with one- or two-room apartments, which, much like tenement houses a hundred years before, were home to families of ten people or more. The secondary apartment buildings on the back streets in the Eighties and Nineties were chopped up into small units as well and quickly decayed into slums. The rats literally took over the streets at night, and the once-lovely little Verdi Square at the intersection of Broadway and Seventy-second Street was now known as Needle Park because of all the heroin addicts who congregated there. It was estimated that 25 percent of all drug addicts in the city lived on the Upper West Side. Gang warfare among whites and Puerto Ricans was common, and in 1961, when lye was thrown into the face of a black woman who lived on West Eighty-first Street, a street fight erupted into a full-scale race riot.

The Upper West Side was resurrected in part by city planner Robert Moses's policy for urban renewal and also by a huge influx of investment from both government and private development — in particular, by the building of Lincoln Center, which rose from the rubble of the buildings where the movie *West Side Story* was filmed. In the end it was a mixture of fashion and Mother Nature that revived the allure of Central Park West. In the eighties and nineties, fires, floods, mud slides, and earthquakes sent a great influx of celebrities hightailing it from the Los Angeles area, many of them originally New Yorkers who had moved to the West Coast two decades before. They returned in droves to the luxury buildings of Central Park West with their romantic charm and generous spaces, and relatively liberal boards, turning it into the most dazzling strip in town.

It's been said that the problem with Central Park West isn't who lives there but that it doesn't have the right neighborhood behind it. Central Park West is only a front, like a Hollywood set, one building thick. While Fifth and Park Avenues are surrounded by exclusive "service streets" with upscale shops, expensive restaurants, and other amenities of civilized living (most of the important private schools are on the Upper East Side), Central Park West has Amsterdam and Columbus Avenues and Broadway, a seething multicultural and honky-tonk world, filled with fruit stands, bars, burger joints, an occasional shiny new apartment building, giant movie multiplexes, chain bookstores, and expensive gyms. The ballyhooed resurgence of Columbus Avenue in the 1980s with trendy restaurants and boutique clothing stores was only a middling success; it couldn't shake the Tenderloin feel of the West Side. The street has settled back into a comfortable seediness. Devotees may romanticize the West Side's multiculturalism, its colorful residents, and its reputation for a liberal constituency, but the Upper West Side is also raw and urban, with dramatic displays of wealth and poverty everywhere, including many homeless and emotionally ill people on the streets. It's guerrilla theater on every block.

## III

IRONICALLY, THE BUILDING in which Donna Karan was finally buying two apartments was considered "second tier" by real estate insiders, despite its distinctive 1929 art deco exterior designed by architects Simon I. Schwartz and Arthur Gross, a prolific team who met in school. Schwartz and Gross designed more than two hundred buildings in New York, including 912 and 920 Fifth Avenue, two rather luxe co-ops. Yet there is nothing luxe about most of the apartments at 55 Central Park West. Except for the highly prized half a dozen apartments on the top five floors, where a series of dramatic architectural setbacks create cascading terraces, the units have low ceilings and prosaic layouts. Most of the building's pizzazz is on the outside; the tinted brick that forms its shell is said to comprise forty different shades, beginning with a tan color at the street level and fading to a whitish corn yellow at top, so, it is claimed, it looks as if the sun is always shining on the building. Most strikingly, the building is adorned with elongated art deco fluting as it rises skyward like a spaceship from a Flash Gordon serial, topped by a majestic water tank enclosure accentuated with art deco cornices that look like modernistic stalactites. One of the first tenants was the crooner Rudy Vallée, a superstar of his time, who earned $20,000 a week in the 1920s. The penthouse apartment, in which the master bedroom is in the old water tower with a giant picture window overlooking the city, was once owned by composer Jerry Herman, who wrote *Mame* there, and later fashion designer Calvin Klein liked the apartment so much that he bought and sold it twice — three years apart — and tripled his original investment. The building is probably best known to the public as the *Ghostbusters* building, after the 1984 movie that featured the real exterior of the building with its metal deco canopy as the "home of all supernatural evil in Manhattan," as one character puts it. "In other words, it's spook central!"

One detail that made Donna Karan's purchase of the apartment at 55 Central Park West particularly complicated — and unusual — was that the seller was Linda Stein's former husband, Seymour Stein, the legendary music business impresario and founder of Sire Records. Linda met Stein on a blind date, set up by one of the students at the Bronx high school where she taught, not far from where she grew up and where her father owned a kosher catering hall. Her nine-year marriage to Seymour Stein was as exciting and voluble as a roller-coaster ride. He discovered and nurtured some of the most enduring and prestigious acts in pop music history, including Madonna, the Talking Heads, and k.d. lang. Indeed, part of Linda Stein's pedigree as "broker to the stars" is that before she got into real estate, she comanaged the seminal punk rock band the Ramones and signed them to a deal on her former husband's record label. Although the Steins divorced over twenty years ago, they are still joined in some sort of symbiotic relationship, and not just because of the interest they share in their two grown daughters and certainly not because of the modest $1,700 alimony check Linda Stein receives each month. (Seymour Stein's personal wealth is estimated at $60 million.) If Linda and Seymour Stein have a lingering connection, it is real estate. Seymour Stein is a peripatetic buyer and seller of luxury real estate and owns homes in London, Miami, Hawaii, Paris, Southampton, and New York, where Linda Stein has been the broker for four different transactions of her ex-husband's.

It was Linda Stein who convinced her ex-husband that a portal needed to be opened in the wall between the bedroom of one apartment and the living room of the other in 55 Central Park West, to show the unusually good flow between the layouts, which is often not the case with conjoined apartments. But instead of creating a graceful archway, as she expected, her former husband hired a man with a sledgehammer to whack a hole in the wall big enough to step through and never bothered to have the plaster and rubble carted away.

Yet another peculiarity of the apartment was that Seymour Stein's lifelong acquisitiveness for museum-quality furniture and objets d'art had created a storage problem. Thirty-five years ago his precious collectibles had been few enough to be contained in four curio cabinets in his living room; now all sixteen rooms of both adjoining apartments were brimming with great treasures, all crated and stored. It looked like the last scene in the movie *Citizen Kane*, when the camera pulls back to reveal the great castle called Xanadu filled with packing crates. "There were stacks of pre-Raphaelite paintings," Linda Stein said, "and crates of rare porcelain, half a dozen jukeboxes from the forties, museum-quality art deco furniture, rolled-up Persian rugs, and crated crystal chandeliers. The packing crates were piled so high that it blocked the views from the windows."* But there were also rooms filled with less than treasures. There was a room stacked with dozens of cartons of unpacked Ralph Lauren sheets, and another room piled thigh-high with boxes of brand-new shoes. Although Seymour Stein owned over 100 valuable antique and vintage beds, visitors noted that his mattress lay on the floor of the master bedroom.

Linda Stein brought a parade of celebrity clients to see the apartments, all of whom had their reservations about it. Actor Harrison Ford and his wife at the time, *E.T.* screenwriter Melissa Mathison, were so put off by the dusty cartons and crates that they gingerly avoided touching the walls. The multimillionaire illusionist David Copperfield and his then-girlfriend Claudia Schiffer came to see it, but "he didn't want an apartment," Stein said. "He wanted a stage set." She also showed the paired apartments to former Sony Records president Tommy Mottola, but he was disturbed by the halo effect of the thousands of tiny white lights that were wrapped around the thousands of branches of trees that gave the popular tourist restaurant Tavern on the Green its fairy-tale-like luster sixteen stories below.

At first Donna Karan refused to visit the apartment because the ceilings were only nine feet high — a big problem in a city where a measure of one's status is the distance between one's head and the ceiling. But Stein was determined that Karan see it and she patiently showed the apartment over and over again to Karan's minions, working her way up the food chain, first giving a tour to Karan's assistant, then to her interior designer, Michael Gabellini, and penultimately to Stephan Weiss, before finally getting an audience with the fashion designer herself.

---

*In November 2003, just one-sixth of Seymour Stein's remarkable collection of objets was auctioned off at Sotheby's for over $4 million.

Stein did her entire sales pitch for Karan, touring the apartments from room to room, cupboard to closet, pretending it didn't look like a storage warehouse, discoursing instead on the inlaid floors, the single-pane windows, the original moldings, the twenty-three closets, the butler's pantry, the bathtubs, and the magnificent wraparound terraces.

Karan walked around the apartment in silence, and visibly appalled after literally crawling over packing crates and then discovering the rubble from the hole in the wall, she turned to Stein and demanded, "Does the asking price include all the debris?"

Stein said it did, and after a tiny bit of haggling, things happened fast for a big deal. There was a signed contract and a deposit within just a few days, and the board package was assembled surprisingly easily, except that the financial section of the application listing the couple's assets was initially left practically "blank," Stein said. Stephan Weiss was reluctant to reveal their liquidity to strangers. "His feeling was, 'We're *Donna Karan*,'" Stein said. "'We don't need to show how rich we are.'" Stein convinced them it was necessary to add real figures, and Weiss finally named a minimum amount they had in assets, along with bank documents attesting that the figures were accurate. Letters of recommendation were gathered and a board interview quickly arranged. It wasn't helpful that Donna Karan showed up to the meeting thirty minutes late, casually dressed, wearing sandals. She apologized to the board members, saying that she was tardy because of a harried business schedule, but actually she was at the hospital all day with her husband, who had suffered another relapse and was back on chemotherapy, an issue she didn't want to discuss with the board.

Stein was so nervous about someone leaking the deal to the press that she snuck Donna Karan in and out of the building, unceremoniously whisking Karan past the doorman with their heads down. The board of 55 Central Park was finicky about celebrities. It had just spurned one of

New York's most admired couples, Diane Sawyer and Mike Nichols, who tried to buy the penthouse duplex from designer Calvin Klein. When Sawyer and Nichols's astute attorney noticed that the rights to the rooftop, with its mullioned greenhouse and brick terrace, weren't mentioned in the contract, the board decided that the rooftop was never actually part of the apartment to begin with, and demanded an extra $1 million for it. As soon as Sawyer and Nichols balked at coughing up the additional dough, they were informed that — oops — they couldn't have the apartment anyway, because it was sold by "right of first refusal" to a resident, Steve Gottlieb, the owner of TVT Records, who lived on the floor just below it and paid $8.6 million, including the outdoor space.

Stein's greatest worry at the moment was "mumble." That was the euphemism du jour that Stein and her employer, Edward Lee Cave, were using to describe the kind of destructive chatter that goes on in the real estate business. Jealous or vengeful competitors can easily ruin a deal by purposely leaking the details to the press ahead of time, a practice jocularly (and in this case, ironically) called "DKNY" in the trade, for "deal killers of New York." Building boards, buyers, and sellers all hated to see the details of their business transactions announced in the gossip columns. Stein also knew that, unable to think or talk of little else, she could be the possible source of mumble about the Karan deal. "I might banish myself to Montauk until this deal is closed to save myself from myself," she said.

# I V

STEIN STEPPED INTO a pair of mahogany-colored Christian Louboutin heels with flame-red soles that matched her crimson nails and lipstick and took one final look at herself in the mirror. She saw reflected an impeccably dressed and groomed Upper East Side businesswoman, save for the protrusion of a flesh-colored elastic bandage from the sleeve of her dress that she wore to control the swelling caused by her chronic lymphedema. She opened her apartment door and stepped into her small private landing and rang for the elevator man. While she waited she found a brown shahtoosh shawl, made from an endangered Tibetan animal and an illegal luxury in the United States, and threw it over her left shoulder to hide the bandage. "Today," she said, "I am completely endangered."

She burst through the doors of her apartment building out into the golden sunlight on Fifth Avenue. The street was bustling with people leaning into a surprisingly brisk autumn wind that whipped around the corners and tossed the branches of the trees across the way in the park. The road was tangled with traffic, most of it taxicabs, in a midday standstill, despite a green light. One of Stein's doormen, in a dark navy uniform and cap, rushed ahead to open the rear door of a Lincoln Town Car that Stein had rented for the day with a driver, as she sometimes does when she has a busy schedule with a lot of stops. Behind the wheel sat a white-haired African American man dressed in a Stars and Stripes necktie and a brown sport jacket with a large GOP elephant pin on his lapel. "Oh my," Stein whispered when she saw the driver, "he's a black Republican." She handed him a list of addresses, and they inched their way into the molasses-like flow of traffic. She powered her way through a busy day, starting with four open houses, which are a way for listing brokers to show off their exclusive apartments to brokers invited from other agencies. To avoid the embarrassing moment of having rival brokers show up at the same time, brokers are booked in solo segments, fifteen minutes apart. The exclusive broker usually stands in the entrance hall and hands out flyers describing the apartment while the visiting broker roams around the apartment. The first two apartments Stein saw were coincidentally in the same building, 4 East Seventy-second Street, a good but not top-notch address just off Fifth Avenue that nevertheless had a very fussy board. The apartments were both duplexes, listed for about $4.5 million each, with monthly maintenance fees pushing $5,000. The staircases between the apartments weren't grand enough for Stein, and neither were the layouts of public rooms on the lower floor, with three bedrooms on the upper. Wandering through a stranger's apartment when he's not at home is an oddly disconcerting experience tinged with a guilty thrill. Each apartment told a brief tale. One apartment had only novels in the bookshelves, none newer than twenty years old; the second apartment had stacks of expensive coffee-table books about architecture and interior design. In one there were the artifacts of an empty nest, the long-ago vacated bedrooms of children with their private-school decals still affixed to the dresser mirror, children who had grown up and married, from the looks of the framed photographs on the dresser in the master bedroom, leaving behind an apartment either too filled with memories or too valuable for the parents not to cash in. In the other apartment, although there was a lot of expensive electronic equipment and flat-screen TVs, it was easy to guess from the extra safety handrails in the shower and next to the toilet that perhaps they were the toys of a rich man who was ill or aged and motivated to sell. In the elevator on her way out, Stein judged the two apartments "okay but *vin ordinaire*" and criticized the way one of the brokers showed "too much cleavage for an apartment that price."

Then Stein was back in the car and made a quick stop at 33 East Seventieth Street, where she viewed a nine-room apartment for just shy of $7 million with a lot of glamorous touches and expensive furniture that "showed better than most" and "had possibilities," and then dropped in on an eleven-room duplex at 784 Park Avenue (asking price: $6.25 million) that had rather humdrum views up and down the side street. Finally, the tastiest of all, an estate sale at 969 Fifth, the street's narrowest building, on the third and fourth floors, for $8.6 million, with a $6,300 monthly maintenance fee, which Stein assessed as "pricey but worth it."

Through all this, wherever she went, she was at the beck and call of the birdlike chirp of her cell phone, fielding calls from buyers and sellers and brokers about deals and possible deals, calls filled with details that melded into one another, the square footage, the previous price, the kind of windows, the cabinetry in the kitchen, the president of the co-op board. There were phone calls from Rock-A-Fella Records rap impresario Dame Dash, who wanted to look at a $12 million town house, and a call from Jane Wenner, the estranged wife of *Rolling Stone* publisher Jann Wenner, who said she was bored with living in the five-story town house on West Seventieth Street that Stein sold her in 1987 for $4.2 million. "Don't even *think* of selling that house," Stein scolded Wenner. "Where are you going to go if you sell it? Even if I got you eight million dollars for your place, *there is nothing out there for less than ten million* that's comparable." Stein paused for a moment to let that thought sink in, but she could tell from Wenner's quick protestations that she wasn't really listening and politely got off the phone.

At 1:30 P.M., while the car and driver waited at the curb, Stein made a pit stop at the first floor of Barneys department store on Madison Avenue to buy a new lipstick in hopes of keeping her spirits up. ("Do you have a color called Prozac?" she asked the salesman. He looked at her and said, "Lady, you have so much spunk, you don't need Prozac.") Then she ate a quick salad with a glass of red wine upstairs at Fred's, the trendy lunch restaurant that draws a fashion and real estate crowd, and she was back in her car in less than an hour.

It was then, while she was stuck in midtown traffic on Fifth Avenue, on her way to the West Village to preview town houses for Rupert Everett, that she got the call she dreaded. It was Allison Utsch, her cobroker at Edward Lee Cave's office on the Donna Karan deal at 55 Central Park West. "We've got trouble at the building," Utsch said. She said that the board of 55 Central Park West had been told that Donna Karan was a "serial renovator" and that she would strip the apartment down to its bones if she got her hands on it. It seemed that a chatty doorman at the San Remo — the building in which Karan had recently sublet an apartment — had tattled to a member of the board of 55 Central Park West about a major renovation Karan had undertaken in her sublet at the San Remo without permission of the board or the owner of the apartment — a cardinal sin in the co-op world and justification to blackball her.

Considering that Donna Karan had only a two-year lease on her sublet at the San Remo, some might consider her renovation there a tad obsessive. With the aid of a creative team that included a TV production designer, a lighting designer, an interior designer, and a group from her fashion design studio, she cleverly transformed the three-bedroom apartment into a peaceful Zen landscape, with dark floors, Etruscan gold and black walls, slabs of upholstery on pedestals for seating, and fountains on the wall illuminated by dim pools of light. It turned out that this wasn't the first time her renovation plans got her into trouble with a co-op board. Two years previously she made a deposit on a $5 million apartment at the posh 10 Gracie Square along the East River, but word leaked to the board that she planned to gut the fifteen-room apartment and build an open "loft in the sky," as one shareholder described it, and the board suggested to the seller that Karan be given back her $500,000 deposit.

It wasn't just design-conscious types such as Donna Karan who were caught up in making apartments over into a personal architectural statement. The soup-to-nuts, floor-to-ceiling renovation craze had become the bane of the co-op world. To be sure, a lot of the top-end apartments had changed hands only one or two times in eighty years, and some — gingerly described as in "estate condition" — were in need of serious renovations,* but the kind of renovations that were pandemic in Manhattan and caused neighbors so much anguish were motivated more by the desire to see the new apartment get six pages in the *New York Times* "Living" section than to update ancient plumbing.

Fifty-five Central Park West and the San Remo were both battle-scarred victims of the renovation obsession. At the San Remo, which is packed with the rich and famous who are used to having their own way,** Bruce Willis and Demi Moore went through three contrac-

---

*Perhaps the most famous of these "estate condition" apartments was the 810 Fifth Avenue apartment of Mary "Tod" Rockefeller, Nelson Rockefeller's first wife, who died in 1999 at the age of ninety-one. The apartment hadn't been touched since her divorce in 1962, and it had a tiny twelve-by-eleven-foot kitchen and appliances from the 1960s. The *New York Observer* quoted a broker describing the apartment as "moldy." And yet, within a month, the historic apartment had a signed contract for $16.5 million from fifty-one-year-old Gary Winnick, a telecommunications multibillionaire from California, who hired architect Charles Gwathmey to draw up plans. When the co-op board, which included art patron Maureen Cogan, the wife of high-rolling investment banker Marshall Cogan, and Elizabeth Rohatyn, the wife of financier Felix Rohatyn, was presented with Gwathmey's ambitious architectural plans, it returned Mr. Winnick's deposit to him.
**The San Remo's formidable list of famous residents, as subletters, renters, or owners, includes songwriter Peter Allen, whose apartment had a music composing room with walls covered in tonga bark from New Hebrides; singer Barry Manilow, who sublet his apartment to actress Raquel Welch, who gave him a hard time about leaving when the lease ran out; Diane Keaton, who was a member of the board; concert pianists Misha and Cipa Dichter, whose apartment has a soundproofed practice studio designed around their two pianos; Zero Mostel, who lived at the San Remo when he starred on Broadway in *A Funny Thing Happened on the Way to the Forum*; actress Mary Tyler Moore, who

tors and two years of disruption to the building before they finished their renovation of the triplex south tower — which once belonged to the entertainer Eddie Cantor — and ripped out the screening room/ discotheque (complete with mirrored ball) of the previous owner, *Saturday Night Fever* producer Robert Stigwood. Steven Spielberg's renovation of a 6,000-square-foot, thirteen-room apartment on the sixteenth floor of the San Remo (for which he paid $7.3 million) was designed by architect to the stars Charles Gwathmey. It took three years to accomplish, which included two years of nonstop jackhammering to remove all the marble floors installed by the previous tenants. The noise became so intolerable to the people who lived below him, screenwriter Marshall Brickman and magazine editor Jackie Leo, that Spielberg felt obligated to offer to rent offices for them elsewhere in the building so they could get some peace and quiet during the day. When the renovation was complete, the director allegedly then asked to renovate his view; he was unhappy with the dilapidated water tower on the roof of the Kenilworth Building, 151 Central Park West, just across from his sixteenth-floor windows, so he offered to pay the building to have the wooden tank covered with a more attractive shell.

---

took refuge at the San Remo when she first retired from her TV series; the Princess Yasmin Aga Kahn, whose mother, actress Rita Hayworth, died of Alzheimer's disease in the building; actor Steve Martin, who bought two apartments, 11D and E, and joined them together when he married actress Victoria Tennant, then separated them again with a soundproofed wall after a bitter divorce. Tennant remarried and continues to live side by side with her ex-husband, sharing the tiny elevator landing, not speaking; prizefighter Jack Dempsey, who lived in a fourteen-room tower apartment for thirty years; and Diane Arbus, the great photographer of freaks and oddities, who once stood on the window ledge of her twenty-second-floor apartment to flirt with her own mortality. Many Americans recognize the exterior of the San Remo as the home to Neil Simon's fictional characters from *The Odd Couple*, Oscar Madison and Felix Unger, who was portrayed by Tony Randall, who did once live in the San Remo, selling his apartment there for $1.5 million in 1984 and moving ten blocks north to the Beresford.

Spielberg's renovation was simple compared with the seven-year saga of Apple Computer founder Steven Jobs's complete refurbishment, including windows, of the north tower of the San Remo — an apartment he never lived in. Jobs bought the triplex from Jacob Rothschild, of the French banking family, along with unexecuted plans by Robert A. M. Stern, the dean of the Yale School of Architecture. But Jobs didn't care for Stern's ideas, so he hired world-renowned architect I. M. Pei for his only known apartment-renovation job. Over the next seven years the tower apartment and the neighbors endured a renovation said to have cost $15 million. The results are striking but not very pretty — a study in grim, gray granite, with granite floors imported from Europe, and twelve-foot-tall nickel and bronze doors that weigh eight hundred pounds each but are so precisely balanced that they can be opened and shut with a fingertip. In the master bedroom, at the very top of the tower, there are six pivoting, single-pane windows that cost $80,000 each to fabricate. By the time the apartment was finished, Jobs had lost interest and he never moved in. It was uninhabited for a decade. In 2002 Jobs quietly put it on the market for $26.5 million, but with no takers interested in living in a granite quarry, he eventually dropped the price to $18 million, and sold it to Bono, the Irish rock star, who moved from the El Dorado just down the street.

Over the past ten years co-op boards in the better buildings have adopted stringent rules pertaining to renovations. In some buildings a tenant can't even change a toilet bowl without first having the appliance approved by the board and then paying a security deposit in case accidental damages occur to the building during the installation. There are buildings where construction of new bookcases can trigger a charge or a "renovation fee" of several thousand dollars. In some buildings the use of power tools (such as jackhammers) during renovation is prohibited because of noise and possible damage to the structure, and workmen are obligated to work with old-fashioned hand tools. Some buildings have dicta that not more than one renovation can be taking place at one time, and tenants have to wait their turn. More commonly there are "summer work rules" that permit renovations only during June, July, and August, when neighbors are presumably away at their summer homes. Even sticking to summer months, residents in some buildings are bound to a total of six months of work time, which really puts the whip to contractors and raises everyone's fees. The San Remo now has an architectural overseer of all renovations who twice-monthly administers a "flow chart" of the work so service elevators will not be tied up and the building's work crews inconvenienced.

If a resident goes over the allotted time limit, there are stiff fines, from $250 to $500 per day. However, many people are just so rich that they calculate the fines into the cost of renovation, the way Jerry Seinfeld did at the San Remo's sister building, the Beresford. Seinfeld bought his duplex apartment in April of 1998 from violinist Isaac Stern for $4.35 million, and he didn't even move into the building for two years while it underwent a guts-to-glamour renovation by Charles Gwathmey. Seinfeld had promised the board when it approved his plans that his renovations would be finished in four months, even though they included demolishing the existing staircase, sealing it up, and then carving a huge hole between the floors elsewhere in the apartment to create a glamorous new staircase of imported marble. When the four-month time limit passed, work was hardly finished, and Seinfeld very apologetically disregarded the board's insistence that his contractors finish up, and continued to apologize even when the board began to fine him $500 a day.

No sooner was the Seinfelds' apartment finished than he bought a second one, next door: his wife had a baby girl and evidently the three-bedroom duplex wasn't enough space. He bought the apartment of

Broadway producer Edgar Lansbury for $8.6 million, and the board at the Beresford quickly made more stringent rules — all renovations had to be completed within ninety working days, excluding weekends, when no work at all was allowed in the building. If the renovation exceeded ninety days, penalties started at $1,000 a day for the first thirty days, and $2,000 a day beyond that. By the time Seinfeld was finished, the Beresford ended up with a huge bonus in the building fund, which greatly helped dispel his neighbors' ire at the noise and inconvenience. He's also charmed his neighbors by being warm and chatty in the elevator or when he's working out with his trainer in the building's private gym in the basement, and he acted as the auctioneer in a lobby fund-raiser on the first anniversary of the attack on the World Trade Center, at which he auctioned off, among other things, the services of fellow resident Tony Randall as a butler for an evening.

But it didn't seem as though the people at 55 Central Park West were inclined to allow the largesse of a two-year renovation to Donna Karan. Still stuck in traffic on Fifth Avenue, Linda Stein contorted her lips into one of her rubbery frowns in the backseat of the car while she listened intently on her cell phone to Utsch despair that the Karan deal was dead. "Well, I'm not going to let that happen," Stein said, exasperated. She began to dig around in her bag for a pen and pad and started to map out a plan of defense. "I'm not going to let this go down the drain because of what a doorman said. That's *ridiculous*. If the issue is Donna Karan's renovation at the San Remo, then we've got to find out what she did or didn't do and we've got to get a letter from the person she sublet from, or maybe even the building management. I know people in the building and I'll call and ask them what really went on." Stein flipped her cell phone closed and stared out the window of the car in agitated silence.

## V

BUT BEFORE LINDA STEIN could mount a defense on behalf of Donna Karan, fate intervened.

That Sunday a seven-page article ran in the magazine section of Sunday's *New York Times* about the interior decoration of Donna Karan's sublet at the San Remo. The article, which had been prepared months before and serendipitously ran that weekend, was headlined GIMME SHELTER and subtitled "Even on a short-term lease, Donna Karan proves you can take it with you." The text explained that mindful of being a good tenant at the San Remo, Karan did not really renovate the sublet but instead had the interior built like a stage set, and every design detail was built to be removable. The *Times* article almost went out of its way to say that she left the apartment just the way she found it and that she had used removable interiors in her most recent sublet in SoHo as well. The article also noted that Karan and her husband wanted to stop wandering from rental to rental and settle down in an apartment on Central Park West for good. "This one," she told the *New York Times*, "will be permanent."

It couldn't have sent a clearer message to the board members of 55 Central Park West about Donna Karan's responsibility as a neighbor, and her dedication to making a home in their building, if Linda Stein had written it herself.

One day later more good news. The spot on the X-ray was, as hoped, just a shadow from scar tissue, but her doctors wanted her to increase her check-ups to every three months and to monitor her medication more closely. "When I hung up with the doctor I made the phone calls I always make, good news or bad," Stein said. "I called my daughters, my father, my sister, and my ex-husband."

On October 25, two weeks after the deal was put into motion and one week after the *Times* article ran, the board of 55 Central Park West approved Donna Karan and Stephan Weiss's application to become owners, and the deal closed.

Nine months after purchasing the sixteenth floor of 55 Central Park West, Stephan Weiss died of cancer at New York Hospital–Cornell Medical Center. A few months later, Donna Karan became romantically involved with her interior decorator, Michael Gabellini. It hasn't quickened the pace of her renovation. The board at 55 Central Park West already has its regrets. Donna Karan knocked down every single wall in both apartments except for load-bearing ones, and the other tenants endured over three years of inconvenience before the renovation was finished.

Linda Stein was paid her six-figure commission and decided to treat herself to a few days in Paris to celebrate. She knows Paris well because she has been a frequent visitor there, and as a young woman, after getting a graduate degree in education, she adventurously moved to the XVI arrondissement for a year and worked as a shopgirl in a chic men's clothing shop on the Right Bank. Thirty years later she checked into a deluxe room at the Hôtel Ritz and spent the weekend by herself, wandering the city, window-shopping along Faubourg Saint-Honoré. But even with the six-figure commission check sitting in her savings account in New York, she couldn't bring herself to buy anything. She needed to make the money last, she told herself, she had to put some away for taxes and savings, and, most of all, she worried about where the next deal would come from and why she didn't have enough business.

On her last morning in Paris before returning to New York, she took a long stroll from her hotel to the Basilique du Sacré Coeur, and went inside the cool, dark cathedral and took a seat in a pew, where she sat quietly and meditated. Ten minutes or so went by before the silence of the church was cut by the startling chirping of her cell phone coming from deep inside her purse. It had been days since her phone rang, and as shrill as it sounded in the basilica, it was somehow a familiar relief. The caller was a lawyer in New York who represented a client whom Stein had shown an $11 million town house on East Seventy-seventh Street over a month before. She never heard from the man again after showing him the house and assumed the deal was dead, but the lawyer wanted to know if the seller would accept $10 million. Stein told him to hold tight, she'd get right back to him.

Before she left Sacré Coeur that day, she closed the deal at $10.2 million.

Her cell phone bill that month was $1,700.

# SIX

# THE CONCIERGE
# AND THE LANDLORD

The more that people come to the Ansonia Hotel and try to change it, the more the building remains the same," Vincent Joyce said, his lilting Irish brogue making it sound as though he had just uttered some great Gaelic aphorism. "People don't change the Ansonia," he said. "The Ansonia changes the people. That is, of course, if the people *stay* long enough. See, *that's* the part that's changed, you know?" Vincent paused for emphasis and blinked his gray eyes behind his gold-framed eyeglasses. "People don't *stay* anymore. It used to be that if you moved into the Ansonia, you stayed a long, long time."

Vincent Joyce knows whereof he speaks. He has lived in the Ansonia for thirty-six years. He was standing behind the counter of the concierge desk, dressed in an immaculate navy blue uniform with gold piping around the lapels and the words *The Ansonia Condominium* embroidered in gold script over his breast pocket. He wore a crisp white shirt with a spread collar and a dark tie. His hair, silver-gray, was neatly parted and combed. Behind him was a wall of tenants' cubbyhole mailboxes, each with numbered brass tags and stuffed with the morning's mail. Vincent — nobody calls him Mr. Joyce or Vinnie except the Federal Express deliverymen — is the senior of the building's five doormen. He has worked the prized ten-to-four daytime shift and lived upstairs in a twelfth-floor, one-bedroom apartment almost since he first arrived in America from Galway, Ireland, in 1964. He is a social historian of this big New York apartment building, and he knows almost every one of the 414 tenants by name, with the exception perhaps of the transient people he hasn't quite figured out yet, like the actress Jennifer Tilly, who stops by the desk to pick up her dry cleaning. "I think she's some television actress," Vincent said dismissively as Tilly walked off down the hallway. "Anyway, she's only a sublet."

Vincent was dubious when he was first offered his doorman job, which included the rental of a cheap apartment upstairs. "I said I would do it only briefly because I don't want to get to know the people in the building where I live. Now thirty-five years have gone by. I never expected it to turn out like this. I expected to have a wife, two kids, and a dog," he said wistfully, "but I got distracted by other things."

The other thing was drinking. Vincent took his first drink the day he arrived in the United States at his welcoming party in Brooklyn. "I asked for tea and they made me a highball," he said. "That highball lasted for twenty-two years. Of course, once I moved to the Ansonia, it became very convenient for me to be drinking and living upstairs and going to work downstairs. But when you're drinking, it takes you on a hayride."

His boozing got him into all sorts of trouble, but it was the incident with Mr. Singer in 1510 that put an end to it. "Mr. Singer was a retired businessman," Vincent said. "His son paid me fifty dollars a week to look in on the old man. One day, he needed a bath, but he was very heavy, and I had to struggle to get him into the bathtub."

Vincent decided that while Mr. Singer soaked in the tub he would run down to the corner bar for a drink. "I forgot about him, of course," Vincent said. "I was at Donohue's bar, busy having a drink, staring at the TV when I saw something that reminded me of the old man and I said, 'Oh Jesus.' I was afraid he had died, because that water was cold by then. So I ran back to the Ansonia and I went up to his apartment and I opened the door a crack and there wasn't a sound. Then I heard a voice, 'Vincent! You son of a bitch! Come in here!' I was so glad to hear him, I could have kissed him." Soon after that, Vincent went to Smithers, an alcohol-rehabilitation clinic in Manhattan, and sobered up for good.

"When I first moved into the Ansonia I wanted to move out the same day," Vincent remembered. "It was awful. The hallways were dank. They were covered in linoleum and all the ceiling lights were those long fluorescent bulbs and half of them were blinking away. Old man Starr owned the place back then, and it was a neglected building. The best you could expect was a polish of the linoleum floors once a month. There was no security and they stole the rugs right off the floor. Some of the tenants formed a vigilante group and roamed the hallways with baseball bats. But you know why I stayed? I stayed because of the music. On every floor, there was nothing but music, up and down the hallways, sometimes late into the night."

The hallways were filled with music because among its many distinctions, the Ansonia Hotel has been the home to some of the world's greatest opera stars, conductors, and musicians of the past century. Part of the building's legend is that the right to make music was once written into every lease. The sounds of music still drift up and down the wide hallways all day long: a pianist practicing a difficult passage over and over, an oboist who plays in the orchestra pit of a hit Broadway show rehearsing for that evening's performance, an opera singer being put through her scales by one of the many voice teachers who live in the building. There are times in the late afternoon when it seems like an opera or concerto is being performed behind every other door.

The building was, famously, soundproofed between apartments,* which is one reason so many musicians and opera singers have been drawn to it over the years, although nobody knows for certain how it became the residential muse of the opera world. The Ansonia is unpredictable like that. Through its many incarnations it has been a magnet for all sorts of unexplainable things, a sort of Beaux Arts curio cabinet. German spies plotted to blow it up during World War I. The 1919 Chicago "Black Sox" scandal was concocted in one of its suites. Babe Ruth wandered the halls in a red silk bathrobe, and he was so inspired by the beauty of the music that surrounded him, he took up playing the saxophone. At its nadir the Ansonia was the home of the world's most famous swingers' sex club, Plato's Retreat, as well as a hotbed of spiritualism and the occult. They say that more séances have been conducted in the Ansonia than in any other building in New York, and stories persist of the ghosts of children roaming the halls and men buried within its soundproofed walls.

The Ansonia's physical presence in the city is as formidable as its social history. Known as the "wedding cake" of the Upper West Side because of its abundant terra-cotta ornamentation, it looks as if it were lifted whole from the XVI arrondissement and dropped intact onto a bend in the road at Broadway and Seventy-third Street. It is a city block long and nearly 500 feet deep, seventeen stories of Beaux Arts overkill, with row upon row of pediments, wrought-iron balconies,

---

*Unfortunately, this is no longer true. The apartments have been divided and reconfigured and new walls built so many times that it is only slightly less noisy than an ordinary apartment building.

terra-cotta bas-reliefs, hissing demon gargoyles, and fleurs-de-lis, the Ansonia's insignia. Its elegant green mansard roof is peppered with round and elliptical windows, and its four corners are capped with circular towers. It is so startling and unusual that it practically dominates the gritty urban crossroads a block to its south, where Broadway and Columbus Avenue and Seventy-second Street all intersect at a small park, with the French-inspired glass kiosk of the Seventy-second Street Subway station, the fourth-busiest stop in all of Manhattan, in the middle.

Yet, on close inspection, the Ansonia appears less like a gussied-up Parisian whore than it does a Manhattan bag lady stripped of her costume jewelry. Its facade is pockmarked where its original ornamental iron work has been stripped away and sold off for scrap, and the glorious cartouches that once crowned its towers are also gone. The towers themselves have been stripped of their copper domes and tarred over. On the street level what was once the gala arched Broadway entrance is now the storefront of a defunct supermarket, whose elevator pit stands in what was one of the first indoor pools in New York City. The cobblestoned porte cochere with the vaulted roof and hanging lanterns on Seventy-third Street now has an electric-eye door, and the arches next to it are cemented up with concrete blocks, like a face with its features erased. Big gray ventilation flues that pull carbon monoxide fumes from the underground parking garage protrude from the sidewalk.

Even the Ansonia's immediate surroundings are inelegant. To the south is a Chemical Bank building, and its northern neighbor is a low commercial structure with a jujitsu parlor on the third floor, a ballet school on the second, and the Fairway Market on street level — a block-long, neon-lit supermarket with outdoor stands of fruit and vegetables piled as high as a man. It's a colorful New York street scene, but gritty.

The Ansonia Hotel is a New York hybrid. Despite its name, the Ansonia hasn't been a hotel since it was declassified as one in 1983, and it had long since stopped renting rooms anyway. Instead, the bottom three floors — 22 percent of the building — have been converted to commercial use and are owned by the landlords. The upper fourteen floors of the building, with their own separate bank of elevators and a security guard, are solely residential. Thirty percent of these apartments are rent-stabilized or rent-frozen, and 70 percent are condominiums. The rent for the stabilized apartments, which is regulated by the city, will either stay frozen forever or increase only slightly over the years, until the tenant moves out — or dies.

That's one reason there are so many old people living in the Ansonia, clinging to their roomy, low-priced apartments. It also means that some tenants are paying as little as $177 a month for the same spacious, 1,000-square-foot, one-bedroom apartment that sells for about $800,000 on the open market and whose owner pays an additional $822 a month in common charges toward the support of the building. The sooner the old people depart, the sooner the landlords can sell the last 30 percent of the apartments and turn a tidy profit. So far, the highest price paid for an apartment in the Ansonia is $4.2 million, and one is presently on the market for $4.5 million. Because the building is partly a condominium there is no board to turn away buyers, and that egalitarian paradigm maintains what is euphemistically known in the trade as a "rich mixture," meaning many professionals who are European, Asian, and people of color are tenants. There are also many voice and opera teachers, lawyers, movie stars, doctors, people on welfare, and professional psychics. One of the city's most successful restaurateurs, Steve Hanson, who owns the Ruby Foo chain of restaurants featured so prominently in the TV show *Sex and the City*, owns several apartments in the building, as does Conal O'Brien, the Emmy

Award–winning director of the soap opera *All My Children*, who resides in a suite in the western tower with a view of the Hudson River and a circular living room that is on the market for $3 million. On the ninth floor there lives a man who was born in his apartment sixty-one years ago and has lived there his whole life. Michel Madie, a transplanted Corsican who speculates in Ansonia real estate, claims he has owned, rented, or renovated fifty-one apartments in the building, including one he sold to an international jewelry manufacturer from Bali, Indonesia, who bought drummer Baba Olatunji's seven-room apartment for $2.65 million. There is also a Japanese doctor who owns six apartments but lives in Tokyo and rents out all his units to tenants at a great profit. Then there's an apartment with an angry hand-lettered sign on the door that says, in part, "You are your ego and you know it and act it." It is the quintessential New York mix.

From where Vincent is stationed at the concierge desk he can see up and down the Ansonia's block-long lobby, with its black-and-white checkerboard marble floor and creamy white and gray-stippled walls and rows of tall mirrors framed with painted moldings. The lobby runs through the middle of the building from Seventy-third to Seventy-fourth Street. It's a long, tall corridor, and it is as much a busy city thoroughfare as it is a vestibule, frequently filled with exuberant young students who attend the American Musical and Dramatic Academy that is located off the lobby floor of the Ansonia, including one young girl with a backpack who whizzed across the smooth marble floors on Rollerblades while one of the security guards barked at her to take them off.

Vincent can also see reflected in a mirror the small, frumpy sitting area opposite the elevator bank, where a security guard is calling upstairs to announce visitors and making them sign in first. The seating area is strikingly ugly. It is furnished with two semicircular sofas upholstered in a purple fabric, several purple-brocade armchairs, and a cheap purple hassock with a torn skirt in the middle. There is a long sideboard with a vase and an overly large display of dusty artificial flowers. The walls are lit by silver-painted seashell sconces, fabricated of composite material, reminiscent of foam-sprayed molds from a window display. To add to the slightly surreal quality of the setting, an old man in a windbreaker was sitting on one of the sofas intently doing a crossword puzzle while nearby a young Latino man sat with headphones on and his eyes closed, mind-numbed by the pounding music that was apparently blasting in his ears. Three gay Asian men in short fur jackets were draped over the circular hassock, chattering like magpies in their mother tongue.

Sitting by herself in one corner was a woman in her early seventies with her shopping cart strategically positioned so no one could sit too close to her. Looped through the handle of the cart were half a dozen crinkled plastic bags, and in the top bag there was a small sprig of seven green grapes. She wore a putty-colored raincoat, buttoned to the top, which pulled tightly against her ample girth, and her red hair was covered with a tattered kerchief of blue tulle tied in a knot under her chin. In her hands was a single piece of mail Vincent had just given her — an advertising circular — that she turned over and over again, reading and re-reading, for a half an hour or so.

"I can't hear you," she said loudly to a stranger who asked her if she had lived in the building for a long time. She couldn't hear because she was wearing wax earplugs, which she popped out and put into the pocket of her raincoat. "I help serve lunch at a senior citizens center," she said, "and I don't like to hear the chatter of the old people." She said she doesn't like to talk to strangers in the Ansonia's lobby "because they might be one of the watchers."

She looks around suspiciously. "I had a fire in my apartment," she confided, even though she kept a "five foot path" through her "antiques" so they wouldn't become a fire hazard, just as the landlord warned, but her extension cords somehow ignited and there was a fire anyway. ("The only antique in her apartment is her," Vincent said.) Fortunately, the building is to a great degree fireproof, so the fire didn't spread. But now the landlord is suing her for over $52,000 in damages. "That's only because they're just trying to get rid of me," she said. "But I'm not afraid. The landlord can't scare me. Other people tried to scare me once and it didn't work." She used to be a singer, she said, years ago, and she's lived in her apartment for over thirty years, before the lobby looked like a "funeral parlor." She stopped talking and looked angrily at a man sitting on the opposite sofa who paid no attention to her. "He's one of the watchers," she said with conviction. "They watch and report on you."

Who watches? Where do they report? "They work for the landlord," she said. "They watch to see what you do because they want me out of here. They want *all* of us out of here. But they will not get me out. The landlord tries to frighten me, but I won't be frightened. That's all I'm saying."

The man the woman in the lobby was talking about is Jesse Krasnow, fifty-three. He is the head of a company that is a "converter" of distressed buildings, a carrion end of the real estate business in which buildings in financial collapse are bought up on the cheap, efficiently renovated, and turned into co-ops or condos, reaping a huge profit. In the twenty-odd years under Krasnow's stewardship, the building has been embroiled in "the most bitterly fought landlord-tenant battles in the history of New York State," according to New York judge Arthur Birnbaum, who tried more than forty of the lawsuits in which tenants sued Krasnow or Krasnow sued them.

But why should today's incarnation of the heartless proprietor be any different? The landlord as villain is a leitmotif of the Ansonia that goes back 100 years, to W. E. D. Stokes, the building's creator, who was one of the most notorious men of his age. Among other quirks, he was known as the most litigious man in New York, who sued almost everyone he ever knew or worked with — and that was the gentle side of his personality. Everyone who lives in the Ansonia knows that there was some dark secret about him, something nefarious — perhaps that he liked very young girls, or perhaps even worse.

## I I

ONE WINTER'S DAY in late 1894, William Earl Dodge Stokes was striding along Fifth Avenue on his way to one of the many men's clubs to which he belonged, when he spied a framed photograph of a beautiful young girl in the window of a photographer's studio. Stokes, forty-two, a millionaire real estate developer and notorious roué, stopped in his tracks and let out a long, low whistle beneath his waxed handlebar mustache. "What's this?" he whispered.

The girl in the black-and-white photograph had small rosebud lips, a pert, upturned nose, and long dark hair piled dramatically on top of her head. She was smiling coquettishly at the camera over her right shoulder, with the décolleté of a Spanish lace dress revealing her naked back. While he stood there, fascinated with her beauty, the notion came to him that perhaps she might turn out to be the very girl he should marry, and he hurried inside the photographer's studio to find out who she was.

Her name was Rita Hernandez de Acosta de Alba, and she was only fifteen years old, a fact that hardly cooled his ardor. Her picture was in the window of the photographer's shop because she was already quite celebrated in fin de siècle New York for her exquisite beauty, as well as for her "rare charm and intellectual brilliance," as a *New York Times* social column of that year described it. Paul Helleu, the *en vogue* portrait painter of the day, called her "the most nearly perfectly beautiful woman in the world." Even at her tender age she was noted for her wit and poise, and when she rode her own horse in the Madison Square Garden horse show, the newspaper of record heralded her as one of society's "stars in a beauty show who shone more brilliantly than others."

She was, in fact, the pampered daughter of a Spanish heiress and an impoverished Cuban poet, an exotic flower, moody and vivacious by turns. She lived with her parents and seven brothers and sisters in a town house just off Fifth Avenue on West Forty-seventh Street, which was then a fashionable part of town. Her mother, also named Rita, was a xenophobic Spanish nationalist and devout Catholic who insisted that the family speak only Spanish at home and hired only Spanish maids. The de Acosta family strove for social acceptance, but their proud Spanish heritage would forever keep them on the cusp of society.

Aside from their mutual interest in horses, Stokes and young Rita de Acosta had not one whit in common. She was small, delicate, and fashionable; he was a big, rawboned oaf who wore clothing that was frayed at the sleeves and whose pockets were always bulging with papers and notes. She was an aesthete who had such delicate sensibilities that she could have only white flowers in her room. He was as happy in a hotel as he was in a house. She was extravagant, romantic. He was a tightfisted realist. And he was a man who knew what he wanted.

As the legend goes, that day he first saw her photograph in the store window, he decided he would meet, woo, and marry her.

## I I I

TO HIS FAMILY and friends, "Wild Bill" Stokes's plan to marry a teenage girl whose photograph he had barely glimpsed in a store window seemed only slightly more eccentric than any of his other oddball schemes or peccadilloes — for instance, his financing of Dr. Friedman's Turtle Vaccine for tuberculosis, a cure that he planned to have distributed for free to the poor, or his insistence on writing exclusively in red ink. There was also his widely promoted scheme to build an underground tunnel between Riverside Park and midtown Manhattan, and his predilection for litigation involved him in literally hundreds of lawsuits, including contesting his father's estate, from which he received $1 million. There was, of course, his biggest folly: his plan to build the grandest hotel in New York on the Upper West Side of Manhattan, which he intended to name the Ansonia Hotel, after his paternal grandfather, Anson, who had founded the small town of Ansonia, Connecticut, where Stokes had spent many idyllic childhood summers.

Stokes's eccentricities, average looks, and careless dress didn't seem to hurt his appeal with women. As the *New York Times* pointed out in 1894, "his indifference to fads and fashion have made him always attractive to women who, after all, find a man with good family and lots of money, who is not a slave to conventionalities, a very refreshing individual."

He certainly was refreshing — exuberant, enthusiastic, full of energy and "wild charm," but his "not being a slave to conventionalities" might have been something of an understatement. Stokes had a dark reputation and was known for carrying a gun, or two, which he laid out on the table in front of him in whatever club he was eating at that day. He also liked his women young, and it was said that his spécialité was taking barely pubescent girls to Patchen Wilkes, his 300-acre stud farm in Lexington, Kentucky, and tying them naked to a post in the barn, where they were forced to watch a stud horse mounting a mare as a preliminary event to his own brutal night of lovemaking.

It was no wonder why Will Stokes was "the all-time black sheep" of his prominent family. He was one of nine children of Caroline Phelps, the heiress to the Connecticut Anaconda Copper fortune, and James Stokes, a wealthy merchant turned banker. After Will received a law degree from Yale, he reluctantly became a clerk in the family banking firm, Phelps, Stokes & Company, where he locked horns with his eldest brother, Anson, a prominent member of New York society who abhorred his outlaw sibling. When James Stokes died in August 1881, Will contested his father's will, sued his brother Anson for conspiring to throw him out of the family business, and walked away with $1 million — but only one-tenth the amount of his eldest brother's legacy.

Anson Stokes turned his $10 million into $75 million. He bought real estate on the East Side of Manhattan, developed office buildings on Fifth Avenue, and built a legendary one-hundred-room vacation house with fifty bedrooms in Lenox, Massachusetts. His younger brother Will went into real estate as well, but ever the contrarian, he began buying up lots on the déclassé side of town, the West Side, where he started building row houses of brownstones for the emerging middle class. Will Stokes believed that the Boulevard, as Broadway was then called, a long-ago Indian trail that the Dutch had renamed Bloomingdale (Bloemendael) Road because of the "vale of flowers" that grew there, would eventually become one of the most important streets in Manhattan, eclipsing Fifth Avenue, he predicted, to become the Champs-Elysées of New York. He and other developers were instrumental in influencing the city to pave the Boulevard with asphalt in 1889, five years before Fifth Avenue was paved. Still, the West Side above Fifty-seventh Street was a hard sell when Stokes began building his first brownstones in 1885. It was only two square miles — half the size of its eastern counterpart, and it seemed psychologically cut off from the rest of the city by the strange angle it took at Fifty-ninth Street. According to a *Harper's Weekly* from the 1880s, the Upper West Side was a "desert of rocks and shanties, half-opened and unimproved streets," the air pungent with the smell of wet wood burning from the stoves that heated the communities of "shanty principalities," as *Harper's* described them, the nucleus of which was usually a saloon. Seventy-ninth Street was known as Shantyhill, and nearby Seventieth Street was called Dutchtown. Harsenville was a community around the site of the old Astor mansion. Interspersed were blocks of undeveloped land straight to the Hudson, or an odd antebellum mansion, or an orphanage or home for unwed mothers or the insane, the kind of bleak institutional buildings that were usually found on the desolate outskirts of the city. At mid-century the main means of transportation above Forty-second Street on the West Side was a horse car/trolley line that ran on a single track up the Boulevard to Eighty-fourth Street and then turned back around again on the same track to take passengers downtown. The other choice for public transportation was the Bloomingdale stage, a horse-drawn vehicle that came by only once an hour, with luck. While trolleys and trains were operating all along the Upper West Side by the end of the century, only Central Park West was developing as a residential street, with the streets behind evolving into commercial neighborhoods with low business buildings instead of housing. In 1866 the West Side Association was formed, which included influential architects and developers who felt the time was ripe for the development of what was then thought of as the "plateau."

Eventually Eighth Avenue was renamed Central Park West and Eleventh Avenue became West End Avenue in an effort to attract a higher-class resident. An act was passed to create a riverside park along the Hudson, where another luxury neighborhood was being promoted.

The apartment building that uncorked the residential development of the Upper West Side was the Dakota,* which opened in October 1884. It was the creation of Edward Severin Clark, a pioneer in the development of the Upper West Side who, like Stokes, was an heir to a large inheritance — in Clark's case, the Singer sewing machine fortune — and who also believed that the future of residential New York lay in the Upper West Side. The Dakota was an extravagant affair, with sixty-five apartments, some with as many as twenty rooms, centered on an elegant courtyard and fountain. There was a dining room for tenants on the first floor, and tucked under the eaves of its mansard roof were rooms for domestic help. It become the most famous private residence in the world, the subject of countless magazine articles, as well as the subject of its very own biography, written by social historian Stephen Birmingham. In 1968 it gained international notoriety when it was used as the setting for the home of a coven of witches trying to create the Antichrist in Ira Levin's book *Rosemary's Baby,* which was made into an indelible horror film starring Mia Farrow, using the real exterior of the Dakota. Twenty years later, the building added much greater and darker notoriety to its reputation when former Beatle John Lennon was slain under the shadows of its gated archway by a mentally ill fan.

---

*The tale that Clark chose the name Dakota because the Upper West Side was so distant and untamed is probably apocryphal, claims *New York Times* architectural historian Christopher Gray, who notes that although it was fashionable to name buildings after new states, Dakota was not a state at the time but a territory, and Clark had long held that Central Park West should have been called Montana Place and that Ninth Avenue should have been Wyoming Place, etc.

As impressive a structure as the Dakota might have been when it was first built, it was still an Antaeus, built like the Pyramids, with floors three feet thick and load-bearing walls over two feet wide. It stood only a stubby seven stories tall because that was all the weight its base could support. With the new hotel that Stokes intended to build, he would be able to dwarf the Dakota in size. Stokes planned to use the steel-skeleton construction that had recently been introduced in Chicago, where they were erecting buildings so tall that the newspapers were calling them "sky buildings." With the use of the steel skeleton, the bearing load was carried down into the foundation and the walls were only a veneer. A building could be much taller and more elegant, and the costly square footage of the building's footprint be put to better use. Stokes imagined a creation that would be twenty stories tall, the tallest building in Manhattan, and on its roof he would erect a magnificent brick tower, like the Eiffel Tower, soaring another nine stories into the air and visible from all over the city. In 1887 Stokes began piecing together twenty-two parcels of land on the site of the old New York Orphan Asylum, at Seventy-third Street and the Boulevard, on which to build his Ansonia.

In the interim, he contented himself with building brownstone houses that he sold for about $25,000 each. His customers were primarily newly middle-class Jewish families, refugees from czarist Russia who had lifted themselves out of the squalor of the Lower East Side to the comparatively bucolic Upper West Side. For his part, Stokes was quite content that his buyers were mainly Jews. He spoke of his admiration for what he perceived as a Jewish gift for accumulating money. He respected the Jews, he said, for protecting their ancestry and gene pool by marrying within their race. Stokes had proof that genetic planning paid off with his stud farm in Kentucky; he had produced two of the fastest horses in the world, the legendary Thoroughbreds Lexington and Peter the Great. Stokes realized that by applying much the same breeding techniques, he could probably develop a superior chicken that had more breast meat. And if people could breed a faster horse or a fatter chicken, he conjectured, why couldn't you also breed people better suited to their jobs? It was Stokes's experience in building all those brownstones that half the construction time was spent with plasterers putting up scaffolding and taking it down. Why not just breed plasterers who are taller so it's easier for them to reach the ceilings? And if people could be bred for labor, why couldn't they be bred to be leaders or surgeons? Stokes was so passionate about eugenics, as it's called, that he wrote a book about it called *The Right to Be Well Born,* in which he advocated that a national law be passed requiring the registration of human pedigrees and that immigration be monitored so as not to dilute American bloodlines. The book caused such an outrage and sold so poorly that his publishers sued him for his $5,000 advance.

"Some people try to raise children," Stokes wrote in his book. "Others who know their business, breed them. They carefully select the cross to mate with what they lack in their own make-up."

And that's where Rita Hernandez de Acosta came in.


# I V


SHE WAS SIXTEEN years old when they married, on January 4, 1895. They were wed in the backyard of her home under a bower of orange blossoms intertwined with violets and American Beauty roses, and one thousand guests watched the teenage bride descend the petal-strewn staircase of the town house, wearing an ivory-white satin gown with lily of the valley sprays on the skirt, around her neck a choker of pearls, one of many wedding gifts to her from the groom.

It is lost to time and memory exactly what else it was that Stokes gave or promised Rita in that one year from the time he first saw her photograph to the day they married, but he managed to persuade not only young Rita to consent to the marriage, who was easily impressed by the promise of the life his money could bring, but also her protective mother. Perhaps it was purely mercenary motivations that convinced Rita Sr., since Stokes reputedly paid off all of the Acosta family's debts, although it's hard to conceive. Whatever the incentive, Rita's mother so loathed her new son-in-law that for the rest of her life she could never bring herself to call him Will and referred to him only as Stokes. Rita's youngest sister, Mercedes de Acosta, who grew up to become a talented writer (as well as the lover of Greta Garbo and Marlene Dietrich), wrote in her memoir *Here Lies the Heart* that "when Rita finally decided to marry Will Stokes it was, I believe, because she felt his wealth could open doors to certain ambitions she undoubtedly possessed. But she paid a high price for any material gain she obtained from him."

Rita got her first glimpse of that high price on her wedding night at the old Waldorf-Astoria, on Thirty-fourth Street and Fifth Avenue. According to an account given in a family history, *Tales of the Phelps-Dodge Family*, written by Phyllis B. Dodge, "thanks to the brutality of the groom and the outraged innocence of the bride, before morning numerous members of the hotel's staff had to intervene." Rita's honeymoon continued at the Jekyll Island Club off the coast of Georgia, the membership club known as the resort of 100 Million-aires. According to an account in Cleveland Amory's book *Last Resorts*, Rita appeared in the doorway of the dining room one night, looking terrified, desperately clutching a stray puppy she had found on the train station platform earlier that day, both of them appearing pathetic and lost. The group of powerful men who happened to be in the dining room, including the publisher Joseph Pulitzer and Henry B. Hyde, the founder of the Equitable Life Assurance Society, felt so sorry for her that they immediately arranged for her to have her own secret room as a refuge from her husband. Stokes was later expelled from the club.

Just a year and a day after their marriage, on January 5, 1896, Rita gave Stokes what he wanted: his first child, a son, named William Earl Dodge Stokes Jr., whom they called Weddie. Rita hated him and could hardly bring herself to hold him in her arms. "When she gave birth to her son," Mercedes de Acosta wrote, "she could not disassociate him from the dislike she felt for his father and never felt in any way maternal toward him." The child was turned over to a nanny and nursemaid, and Rita went about her life, trying to make the best of the deal she had made by spending Stokes's money lavishly. In the first years of their marriage they traveled restlessly, to Paris and Russia, where Stokes presented the czar with a number of his American trotting horses for the Household Guards and Grand Duke Dimitri gave Rita two Orloff Trotters for breeding purposes. Back in the States they took summer "cottages" in Newport and Bar Harbor, where Rita gave unusual parties that were reported in the New York newspapers. In Bar Harbor she gave a dinner for seventy at which there was a small basket at every place setting with a yellow ribbon that extended from under the cover and was attached to a fourteen-karat-gold safety pin. At a certain point during the dinner, Rita instructed the men to pin the safety pins to the tablecloth and open the boxes. Out from each basket jumped a large, frenzied bullfrog with the ribbon tied around its middle, desperate to get away but held fast to the tablecloth by the ribbon and safety pin. The frogs jumped into the soup and knocked down wineglasses while Rita laughed deliriously as pandemonium reigned and several of her women guests fainted. On another occasion, at their horse farm in Kentucky, Rita gave a lavish party celebrating the opening of a new brick barn, which had been rebuilt after a fire, to which she shocked everyone by inviting only black people to celebrate. The *New York Times* reported in detail on this "Negro Ball" and "How the New York Woman Entertains the Colored People on Her Kentucky Farm" at a lavishly set 110-foot-long table with dance music supplied by "Jones's colored band." Alas, although her parties were the talk of the town, the *New York Times* society column reported that "socially during their recent married life Mr. and Mrs. Stokes hardly made the headway they desired. A season at Newport was not a success, but later at Bar Harbor was more of a success."

Even less of a success was their life back in New York, where Rita expected to live in luxurious grandeur. Instead, she found herself and the baby in one of the gloomy Upper West Side brownstones her husband had built, at the distinctly unfashionable address of 262 West Seventy-second Street. She was so unhappy living on the West Side that eventually, in June 1898, three years after their marriage, Stokes broke down and bought several properties at 4–6 East Fifty-fourth Street, just off Fifth Avenue, for a total of $100,000 and began to build a mansion in which to install Rita and the baby. No doubt to satisfy the aspirations of his young wife, it was going to have marble floors and columns and herringbone-patterned oak floors in a grand ballroom, with burbling fountains recessed into the walls of a conservatory. But it was going to take years to complete, and Rita was becoming as frantic as the frogs tied to the ribbons.

In the meantime, Stokes was obsessed with the monumental undertaking of building the Ansonia Hotel. By then he had decided upon a style of architecture. The inspiration came to him while he was in Paris with Rita, pushing Weddie in a perambulator in the Bois de

Bologne and admiring all the fussy Beaux Arts–style buildings. Stokes began to collect and study the floor plans of Parisian apartment buildings as well and hired a French architect named Paul Emile Duboy, who had studied at the Ecole des Beaux-Arts. Duboy managed to render one set of original drawings for the hotel before Stokes reduced him to little more than a draftsman, although he is officially cited as the Ansonia's architect. Duboy was paid only $5,000 for his efforts and sent back to France, where he had a nervous breakdown and ended up in a mental hospital.

Stokes opened a construction office in the basement of his Seventy-second Street town house and formed his own construction company, Onward Construction, named after one of his champion trotting horses. He also formed his own terra-cotta company, the New York Architectural Terra Cotta Company, to manufacture the durable, cheap, hard-baked clay that was going to be one of the primary ingredients of his confection. "I would say offhand," wrote Weddie Stokes to the Landmarks Preservation Commission some sixty years after the Ansonia was built, "that the fellow who brought the terra cotta molds from France was probably the one who should share the credit for designing the Ansonia Hotel along with my father." It was also terra-cotta that helped make the building fireproof, a major concern to Stokes, who was just as passionate in his hatred of the big insurance companies as he was concerned about the safety of his patrons. Stokes wanted to fireproof the building to avoid carrying fire insurance, which wasn't mandated by law at the time. He consulted with the former fire chief of New York City, Hugh Bonner, about how to construct a building that would contain fire within individual units, and together they came up with a system of walls that were 12½ inches thick, made of concrete and terra-cotta on wire mesh fixed in place to the girders and beams.

As the time grew nearer to breaking ground in the summer of 1899, Stokes tried to involve Rita by setting up a large spyglass through which she could watch construction and see the building rise a block away, which was hardly any consolation to a girl of Rita's sensibilities, and in August 1899 she fled to a beach house in Quogue, Long Island, with her mother and sued Stokes for divorce after four years of marriage. At that time New York State Supreme Court granted divorces only on grounds of adultery, and the court kept the papers sealed, but it was widely rumored that Stokes paid Rita $2 million in cash, the largest divorce settlement ever granted, in addition to $36,000 a year in support.

In return, Stokes wanted Weddie.

She gave up the child easily, and it would turn out that she would not see her son again for sixteen years, when "he returned of his own volition," as Rita put it.

Once Stokes got custody of Weddie, the boy was shipped off to the Fifth Avenue home of Stokes's maiden sisters, Caroline and Olivia Stokes, where he would get a proper childhood and education, and his father could be left alone to create the Ansonia.

Rita remarried two years later, to Major Phillip M. Lydig, a wealthy and socially prominent man with whom she was able to live the life of elegance she had hoped possible with Stokes. Rita's reputation as a legendary beauty only grew as she aged, and many of the great artists of the day, including Sargent, Boldini, Madrazo, and Zuloaga, asked her to sit for them, and Rodin sculpted her. Boldini's portrait of her in a chair was so popular that it was reproduced and sold, much like the famous poster of Farrah Fawcett in 1977. Now known as Rita Lydig, she sponsored much philanthropy and worked in the women's suffrage movement and campaigned against narcotics. When she discovered that her husband was keeping a mistress, she sent the girl to her own dressmaker, telling her husband, "I can't have you going around with a girl who looks like that." They divorced in Paris, in 1918.

In the end, her great extravagance would bring her down. In 1927 she declared bankruptcy, with liabilities of $94,352. One of her largest creditors was Elsie de Wolfe, the society interior decorator, whom she owed over $12,732. Rita appeared before the bankruptcy referee on lower Broadway, wearing a black costume with a tricornered hat with drooping plumes and a long coat wrapped around her like a cape. "You have been told by the newspapers," she told the referee, "that I once received two million dollars from the late W. E. D. Stokes after my divorce from him, for giving him back his son, and the implication is that I probably still have these millions hidden somewhere. I did not receive a penny from Mr. Stokes for surrendering his son to him. I gave the boy back to his father so that he might inherit his father's estate, which he has inherited. The story that I sold the boy is a lie which I have been too proud to contradict in the past."

She lived the rest of her life in hotels. In the early 1920s Rita tried her hand at writing and produced a novel, *Tragic Mansions*, about how the very wealthy lead secretly unhappy lives behind the doors of their fancy homes. In June 1928 she had a nervous breakdown and recovered in a sanitarium. The following October, with her sister at her side, she died from "pernicious anemia," according to newspaper reports, in a room at the Gotham Hotel.

She was only fifty years old.

# SEVEN

# THE
# ANSONIA HOTEL

The Ansonia took four years to build and cost $6 million dollars — 800 percent over budget. Typically, its cantankerous creator became embroiled in myriad lawsuits with laborers and suppliers, including a dispute with the plasterers, who went out on strike for six months. Yet, just as he had promised, when it officially opened, on April 19, 1904,* there was nothing quite like it in the world. Larger than an ocean liner, grander than any luxury hotel, the Ansonia was the "monster" of all residential buildings, according to the *World* newspaper.** It stood only seventeen stories tall — not the promised twenty with the ten-story tower that Stokes had originally envisioned. His son Weddie later explained its height in a letter to the Landmarks Preservation Commission: "They just put one floor on top of another and they got up to the seventeenth floor, and they decided they wouldn't build any more."

*The Ansonia started accepting guests in 1903, but Stokes didn't consider its opening official until the finishing touches were on the hotel in April 1904.
**Over twenty years later, the Ansonia was the fifth-largest hotel in New York.

Nevertheless, it was a statistical blockbuster. It had 50,000 square feet of interior space — 1,400 rooms and 340 suites connected by four and a half miles of hallways. Seventy thousand electric bulbs lit its suites, ballrooms, lobbies, and shops, powered by its own coal-fueled electrical generators.* There were 400 bathrooms and 600 hundred toilets — more bathrooms and toilets than in any other residential structure in the city — and 125 miles of pipes and wiring snaked within its walls, as well as a maze of pneumatic tubing that delivered capsules containing messages between the staff and tenants. Hot, cold, and ice water were available at the turn of a spigot, and in the summer freezing brine was pumped through a series of galvanized steel flues buried in the walls, thereby, Stokes claimed, keeping the building a uniform seventy degrees despite the heat.

Stokes billed the Ansonia as "the most perfectly equipped house in the world." Each suite had double-width mahogany entrance doors, and the rooms had playful shapes, such as ovals or that of a church apse, and the corner apartments were laid out on a whimsical bias. Some parlor rooms were designed with dramatic domes in which were hung cascading crystal chandeliers, and the hardwood parquet floors were carpeted with Persian rugs, woven to size for the Ansonia. There were original paintings on the walls in all the suites, and in the hallways too, because the Ansonia had its own curator, Joseph Gilmartin, who collected 600 paintings for the hotel to display. Year-round tenants had a choice of using their own furniture or the appointments of the hotel, and in one of Stokes's outrageous touches, each suite had an inventory of eighteen face and bath towels and eighteen dinner

---

*The building's original generators are still in the subbasement, two stories below street level, because it would be too costly to disassemble and remove them. The coal furnaces that powered the generators are still underground as well, with remarkable four-foot-thick brick walls to contain the enormous heat they generated.

napkins, which were refreshed, along with the table linen, soap, and stationery, three times a day.

Every day thousands of visitors passed through the arched entrance-ways of the hotel to gawk at the mahogany-paneled lobbies and watch the live seals barking in the lobby fountain. At night there was a constant flow of people to and from the restaurants and ballrooms, the women fashionably dressed in long gowns and plumed hats, the men in cutaways and top hats. The hum of the lobby was punctuated by the cries of young bellhops paging guests; there was a corps of several dozen black youths, all dressed in trim navy uniforms, carrying silver trays with messages. The Ansonia's ornate main dining room seated 550 people and was decorated in a grand Louis XIV style, with hand-painted panels depicting the "Pageantry of Summer" and chandeliers garlanded with crystal ropes. Every night an orchestra played from the balcony. Off the main lobby, in the late-night English Grill, there was a burbling mosaic fountain in which live trout swam while a Hungarian string quartet provided background music. In addition, during the summer months there was a roof garden for dancing under the stars, with a view in all directions, the rest of the Upper West Side dark below. Altogether, when the ballrooms and the dining rooms were at full capacity, the hotel could accommodate 1,300 dinner guests in one night.

In the basement were more wonders of the day. There was the world's largest indoor swimming pool, tiled in blue, and down a flight of stairs from the lobby Stokes built an elaborate shopping arcade that included a liquor store, a florist, and a barbershop, where many of the male residents would get a daily shave by the mustachioed barber, Mr. Fred. B. Mockel. The arcade also had a ladies' millinery shop run by Mme. Estelle, a tall fashionable blonde to whom Stokes gave the money to start her business. In addition, there was a valet, a tailor, and a laundry with automatic washing machines in which, it was boasted, clothes were exposed to 650 degrees of steam heat, "sufficient to ensure the destruction of any possible microbes."

One of the Ansonia's most astonishing conveniences was in the center of the main lobby: two banks of open-faced elevators, each manned by an operator in starched white shirt and dark uniform who slid the filigreed gate closed and rotated a brass lever to make the floors drop away. It was a bold move for Stokes to have so many elevators in a time when about fifty people a year died in elevator accidents in Manhattan, caused mostly by cars that moved while people were getting in and out. Stokes was outraged over the price that Elisha Graves Otis, the man who had invented the elevator in 1852, demanded to install elevators in the Ansonia, so Stokes belligerently formed his own elevator company, the Standard Plunger Elevator Company. Stokes even invented his own elevator, a "long-run plunger elevator" that operated at the then unheard-of speed of 400 feet per minute, controlled, he claimed, by a plunger "resting upon an incompressible body of water [that] affords ample protection against danger of the car falling." His design worked without much incident for many years until the elevators were replaced with more modern models.

While the adults marveled at the ease with which the elevators glided to a stop, the many children who lived in the building with their families were much more mesmerized by the dizzying cascade of the white marble staircase with its dark mahogany banister and ornate iron railings, seventeen stories of it, snaking round and round, getting smaller and smaller until it vanished into a clear glass skylight 500 feet above, where the clouds passed by overhead during the day, and at night, if you were lucky, you could glimpse the stars.

The hotel's most curious addition wasn't open to the public — it was a farm in the sky. This was part of Stokes's utopian vision for the Ansonia — that it could be self-sufficient, or at least contribute to its own support by raising enough animals on the roof to supply milk, eggs, and fowl to feed the entire building below. Every day a bellhop with a large basket under his arm delivered free fresh eggs to all of the tenants, and any surplus was sold cheaply to the public in the basement arcade. "The farm on the roof," Weddie Stokes wrote to the Landmarks Preservation Commission years later, "included about 500 chickens, many ducks, about six goats and a small bear." Some of the ducks were the product of Stokes's genetic experimentation, "mule ducks," they were called, a sterile hybrid of an Egyptian goose with a wild duck from Winnipeg that had been bred at the Cold Spring Harbor Experimental Station on Long Island, which was partially supported by Stokes. Two of these mule ducks flew off the Ansonia rooftop one day and made their way to the Lake in Central Park, where they were spotted by naturalists and proclaimed rare snow geese from Labrador, and as "Artic Geese" in an article in the *New York Times.* Stokes poked fun at the scientific community by writing "grave notes of scientific inquiry about the [birds] to various scientists," reported the newspapers, before gleefully revealing the ducks as his own and having a good laugh at the experts' expense. None of this charmed the city fathers, however, and in 1907 the Department of Health shut down the farm in the sky and the animals went to Central Park and lived happily ever after.

## I I

THE ANSONIA MIGHT have been considered luxurious, but it was never thought chic. In spirit as well as in location, it was part of the bohemian stepchild of the city — the Upper West Side — and would always have a risqué reputation. It was a reputation that W. E. D. Stokes, who was drawn to gamblers, sportsmen, and whores, couldn't help but engender.

The hotel first became indelibly linked with gambling and shady characters just two years after it opened when, with Stokes's encouragement, Al Adams, the notorious millionaire "Policy King" of the New York numbers racket, moved into the Ansonia straight from a stint in Sing Sing. After his incarceration, Adams, who it turned out had invested in Stokes's Standard Plunger Elevator Company, lived in the Ansonia for two years, badgered by police and reporters, before Stokes found him dead of a self-inflicted bullet wound to the head in suite 1579. Adams had arranged his death very considerately so as not to leave a messy aftermath in the room. He positioned his head over a cuspidor so his blood "would not leave a stain on the carpet," reported the *New York Times.* There was immediate conjecture that Stokes had shot him over a gambling debt, but the coroner ruled it a suicide.

It was also Stokes who welcomed to the hotel one of the great villains of Mexican history, General Victoriano Huerta, the deposed dictator who had briefly seized power from "the liberator" of Mexico, Francisco Madero, in February 1913, and summarily had Madero executed. Woodrow Wilson refused to recognize Huerta's "government by assassination," and his reign of terror lasted little over a year, until he was run out of Mexico. After a stop in Europe he moved to a suite at the Ansonia and began plotting to overthrow the Mexican government just as America became involved in World War I. Huerta found co-conspirators in the former German diplomatic attaché to Mexico, Franz von Papen, and his colleague Karl Boy-Ed, who were both agents of the imperial German government. In a far-fetched scheme, von Papen and Boy-Ed were going to fund Huerta's efforts to regain control of Mexico, from where he would open a southern front and help the Germans defeat the United States in World War I. Huerta, however, was being followed and monitored by American counteragents, who were eavesdropping on his phone conversations at the Ansonia. After being discovered, Huerta fled and was later captured in New Mexico and drank himself to death in 1916.

Meanwhile, his presence at the Ansonia was just coincidental to von Papen's plot to blow up the second-floor ballroom of the hotel a year later. Von Papen and Boy-Ed had developed an expertise in explosives, and their handiwork became evident to the public in 1916 when a storage pier known as Black Tom, piled high with ammunition destined to be used against the German army, caught fire and exploded with such force that shrapnel scarred the Statue of Liberty three miles south. Von Papen had in mind a similar fate for the grand ballroom of the Ansonia, hoping to demolish it on the night of a grand dinner dance that was going to be attended by almost the entire U.S. Navy leadership on the East Coast, plus the navy brass from sixty-four battleships that were moored in New York Harbor. Von Papen's scheme was to explode a massive bomb of TNT under the Ansonia's main staircase, causing the ballroom to collapse into the busy lobby below. The plot was foiled by federal agents working with the New York City police, who staked out the Ansonia basement and lobbies for days before the naval ball to prevent von Papen and his men from planting the explosives.

It was the Ansonia's racy reputation as a home to gamblers and spies and deposed dictators that made it attractive to the world of professional sports. Jack Dempsey trained for the heavyweight championship of 1919 against Jess Willard while living in the hotel, and after World War I the Ansonia became the preferred lodging of professional baseball players in New York. It was the full-time home of many New York Yankees, including Wally Schang, Lefty O'Doul, and Bob Meusel, as well as Babe Ruth, who moved there with his wife after being traded from Boston in 1919. There wasn't a fitness regimen to follow in those days, and the ballplayers spent a lot of their free time sitting around the bars and lobbies of the hotel, smoking cigarettes and watching the women come and go, or at night wandering up to the Babe's suite, where there was always some sort of party or card game. Ruth, who liked to drink and eat and thought of the entire hotel as an extension of his apartment, would sometimes wear his scarlet silk bathrobe down in the elevator to the basement-arcade barbershop for his morning shave, where Mr. Mockel kept a shaving mug with THE BABE hand-painted on it. The squeaky bleatings of Ruth's saxophone were familiar sounds up and down the wide hallways on his floor. He was making over $50,000 a year during the years he lived in the Ansonia, a king's ransom at the time, but was such a spendthrift that he had hardly a nickel to his name. An ambitious young lawyer named Christy Walsh asked to meet with Ruth and talk to him about increasing the value of his marketing and income, as well as putting him on a financial plan that would provide for his later years, but the hard-partying slugger didn't want to hear about it and refused to grant Walsh an appointment. One day a delicatessen delivery-man appeared at Ruth's Ansonia apartment with a case of beer, and by the time the deliveryman carried the case into the kitchen, he had revealed himself as the lawyer Christy Walsh. Before Ruth could throw him out, Walsh began to spin some of his ideas, promising Ruth to make him $1,000 within sixty days. Walsh had to borrow the thousand dollars, but Ruth signed with the young lawyer, who became baseball's first official sports agent. Walsh earned hundreds of thousands of dollars for Ruth and made him a wealthy man.

The September of the year that Babe Ruth arrived at the building, the nexus of bad guys, gambling, and baseball met with bitter results. On September 21, 1919, eight players of the pennant-winning Chicago

White Sox made a pact to throw the 1919 World Series, an incident that F. Scott Fitzgerald said tampered "with the faith of fifty million people." The White Sox were one of the most esteemed organizations in baseball, an unbeatable club whose games were avidly followed by millions of fans across the nation. Every player on the team had his own legion of admirers, and the club's most famous player, Shoeless Joe Jackson, the illiterate son of a tenant farmer, had become an idol to rival Babe Ruth. Chicago was the heavy favorite in the nine-game World Series against the Cincinnati Reds, with bookmakers laying five-to-one odds. If the White Sox lost in an upset, a gambler could make a lot more money betting on the World Series than the players were being paid themselves. In fact, members of the team were disgruntled with their meager salaries and the stinginess of White Sox owner Charles Comiskey, who made the players wash their own uniforms instead of sending them to the laundry. On September 21, a few days before the Series was to begin, a group of eight players assembled in the Ansonia hotel room of the first baseman, Arnold "Chick" Gandil, and agreed to throw the series for $10,000 a man, financed by Arnold "the Big Bankroll" Rothstein, the king of New York's gambling houses. According to Eliot Asinof's book *Eight Men Out*, Rothstein was supposed to be signaled that the "fix was in" during the first game when the White Sox pitcher, Eddie Cicotte, would "accidentally" hit the first batter with the ball. Rothstein was in a room at the Ansonia crowded with gamblers who had bet on the game, and when he heard that Cicotte had hit the Reds' second baseman, Morrie Rath, in the back with a fastball, Rothstein walked out of the hotel and out into the afternoon rain a happy man. He made an untold fortune on the Series, but he was never caught for bankrolling the fix, although the players were. The White Sox played so clumsily that by the time they were only three games into the Series, rumors were rife that the game was crooked. The Sox lost five games to three, and as a wail of "Say it ain't so, Joe," went up across the country from baseball fans, the court invalidated the 1919 World Series, and Jackson and the other seven players were charged with criminal conspiracy to defraud the public. All eight were found innocent of charges in a 1921 jury trial, but they were banned from baseball for life.

To add to the constant air of melodrama and excitement at the hotel, Florenz Ziegfeld moved into a ninth-floor suite of thirteen rooms in one of the towers. He lived with his first wife, the singing siren Anna Held, who was the greatest of all his *Follies* stars. When Held became pregnant, Ziegfeld demanded she undergo an abortion in the apartment so as not to inconvenience her performance schedule. Held also reportedly took baths in tubs filled with milk, her complexion was so fair, and as a publicity stunt Ziegfeld arranged for the milkman to sue him for unpaid bills. The showman also kept a gold-painted, life-size statue of his voluptuous wife in the entrance foyer of their apartment, and in an apartment on the thirteenth floor, Ziegfeld kept an equally voluptuous mistress, Lillian Lorraine.

Years later Lorraine ended up destitute, living in a walk-up on Ninety-sixth and Broadway. The story goes that a reporter searched her out and asked, "What happened, Miss Lorraine? Ziegfeld said you were the greatest beauty he ever had in the *Follies*."

"He was right," Lorraine explained. "He had me in a tower suite at the Hotel Ansonia and he and his wife lived in another tower suite. And I cheated on him . . . I had a whirl! I blew a lot of money, I got loaded, I was on the stuff, I tore around, I had abortions, I gave fellers the clap. So that's what happened."

The appalled reporter stammered, "If you had your life to live over again, what would you have done differently?"

"I never should have cut my hair," Lorraine said.

## I I I

IF REAL LIFE at the Ansonia had operatic overtones, it was appropriate to the dramatic music that seemed to fill its every room. It has been written, apocryphally, that Stokes intentionally built the Ansonia for musicians, which is why the doors to each apartment were double width, so grand pianos could easily be moved in and out, or that he built the hotel to be soundproofed to attract musicians, which was in truth an ancillary benefit of the fireproofed walls. It's also been claimed that the building's purported constant seventy-degree temperature, a great benefit for sinuses, lured singers to the hotel, but there's really no solid explanation as to why it, of all the hotels in New York, turned into a "Palace for the Muses," as West Side historian Peter Selwen named it, except for destiny.

One thing is for certain — the Ansonia's popularity with the opera crowd wasn't for its proximity to the Metropolitan Opera House, which was then located thirty-one blocks to the south, on Thirty-ninth Street and Broadway. Opera was enjoying a renaissance in society at the time, not because of the music or the singing but because between January and the end of Lent, every Monday night, the opera was Mrs. Astor's regular outing to be seen in her "social throne" — box number seven in the Golden Horseshoe ring of the Metropolitan. Monday-night attendance at the opera became a de rigueur event for society, except that no one watched the opera, they watched one another, and the same dozen or so familiar productions with the same familiar singers and sets were mounted each year — nothing too sad or too gory.

This was all about to change in 1903, the Ansonia's inaugural year, when Otto Kahn was asked to join the board of directors of the new

Metropolitan Opera. Kahn was a respected banker and patron of the arts who was himself an amateur musician and the first Jew on the board. At the time the Met was a private concern that held the lease on the opera house, and it hired various impresarios to produce and stage the operas. Over the next few years Kahn became more involved in the day-to-day operations and slowly began to buy up most of the stock until he became the principal financial patron and guiding spirit. One of Kahn's first decisions was to appoint as the new director of the Met the highly regarded but staid German opera impresario Heinrich Conried, who made a splash his first season by presenting Enrico Caruso at his American premiere in *Rigoletto* in 1903. This is when Caruso allegedly stayed at the newly finished Ansonia Hotel. Historians dispute whether the great tenor actually stayed in the building. It is generally agreed that more significant to the building's association with opera was Otto Kahn's enticing the legendary manager of La Scala, Giulio Gatti-Casazza, to assume the role of general manager of the Metropolitan (upon Heinrich Conried's retirement in 1908) and moving him into the Ansonia. Gatti-Casazza was the Ziegfeld of opera, a new-age showman who produced and booked all aspects of his productions. In turn, he insisted that Kahn also hire La Scala's world-famous conductor, Arturo Toscanini, to work with him, and Kahn brought Toscanini and his family to America to live at the Ansonia Hotel.

The presence of Gatti-Casazza and Toscanini at the Metropolitan Opera caused a sensation in the opera world. Along with the novelty of "popular" stars such as Caruso emerging, the arrival of the La Scala singers helped revive interest in opera as more than just a Monday-night social outing. Dozens of great opera stars moved to New York to be part of the new Metropolitan, almost all renting at the Ansonia.

Gatti-Casazza and Toscanini were followed into the building by the glamorous Geraldine Farrar, the principal soprano for the Metropolitan Opera for next fifteen years; Antonio Scotti, the Met's principal baritone; the celebrated Russian bass Feodor Chaliapin; bass Ezio Pinza, who arrived in 1926; maestro Ettore Panizza, who in 1934 became the new chief conductor of the Metropolitan; coloratura soprano Lily Pons and her husband, conductor André Kostelanetz; the tenor Tito Schipa; soprano Roberta Peters, and her world-famous voice coach, Eleanor McLennan; and Lauritz Melchior, the foremost Wagnerian tenor in the world, who lived in the building from 1926 to the early 1950s and used his stuffed trophies for bow-and-arrow practice in the hallway, causing the other tenants to call the police.

At night the lobby came alive when the stars would return from the opera house, hungry for dinner. Each great artist had his or her own claque of fans who congregated in the lobby, loudly debating the merits of their favorite stars. When Caruso or Toscanini or Geraldine Farrar swept into the Ansonia, the fans would erupt into applause and cheers. During the day the hotel was sleepy, but an hour before the curtain a long line of cars and carriages appeared to take the great singers and maestros to the opera house. Because so much business of the Metropolitan Opera depended on tenants of the Ansonia, its switchboard began to function as a message board, secretary, and factotum.

The world of professional opera was like opera itself: bigger than life, filled with drama and tragedy. Opera singers were basically theater people, hot-blooded and temperamental. Their apartment doors were kept open, the wine flowed freely, love affairs were played out in public, hearts were broken, and lovers came and went with the season's repertoire.

## I V

THE ANSONIA EVEN brought love to W. E. D. Stokes again; a twenty-four-year-old titian-haired beauty from Colorado named Helen Elwood, who was a hotel guest visiting her sister. Stokes and Elwood eloped in February of 1911 to Jersey City, where he lied on the marriage license about his age by twelve years. When the bride's mother, back in Denver, found out that her daughter had eloped with the notorious W. E. D. Stokes, she fainted, reported the *New York Times* in the wedding notice.

Helen Elwood had some other surprises in store for her besides her husband's real age. In June, only four months after their wedding, the police found Stokes clinging to a banister on the fourth-floor landing of the Verona apartment house on West Eightieth Street, bleeding profusely from three gunshot wounds in his legs. He was the victim of the wrath of two showgirls, Miss Lillian Graham, twenty-two, a vaudeville backup act booked as "the Great Emotional Psychic Actress," and her girlfriend, Ethel Conrad, a "dressmaker's model." The duo had a fat packet of billets-doux that Stokes had written, and when he went to retrieve them — or buy them back — the shooting broke out.

The subsequent trial was the biggest tabloid news story of its time, filling the lobby with reporters and the curious for weeks. Stokes never once left his rooms at the Ansonia to testify during the entire trial. Instead, the Ansonia house physician, Dr. Josiah Thornley, told the court that Stokes was gravely ill with "acute indigestion" and could not appear in person; as the trial proceeded, the *New York Times* ran daily accounts of his health. WED STOKES ILL, read a headline on December 1; STOKES NEAR DEATH, BUT RALLIES AGAIN on December 4;

then STOKES MUCH WORSE. The tenth of the month brought STOKES WORSE, THEN BETTER, and finally, on December 12, a specialist, Dr. Bolton Bangs, operated on him in his rooms at the Ansonia for an "abscess of the left kidney." Miraculously, the operation took only forty-five minutes, not much less time than it took the jury to reach a verdict of not guilty for the two girls. The last public record of the accused was a review of their second appearance at the Hammerstein Victoria Theater shortly after the trial, where they sang three songs and danced. "They gave no indication of improvement vocally or histrioni-cally, since their previous appearance," the *New York Times* said.

Stokes's brush with mortality evidently had a serious effect on him, because in December 1911, he further amused New York City by gift-ing his fourteen-year-old son ownership of the Ansonia, then the largest hotel in the world, with an estimated value of $6.5 million. As Stokes had desired, Weddie seemed to have his father's smarts. Unfor-tunately, his mother's beauty had escaped him, and like his dad, he was tall and oafish and given to some unusual passions. At the age of twelve he had built a wireless station on the roof of his father's hotel that broadcast over three states, and two years later he became presi-dent of his own company, the Junior Wireless Club, Limited, and even testified before a Senate committee on interstate wireless communica-tions when he was still a teenager. Weddie attended Andover, Yale, and the U.S. Naval Academy and served abroad during World War I as a lieutenant. He had a degree in law from the University of Chicago. He met his wife in Palm Beach, after he wrecked his sailboat in front of her property, and proposed to her after knowing her for only three days. She later had a nervous breakdown when Weddie was named one of his stepmother's lovers in her divorce lawsuit from his father.

Indeed, Helen Elwood managed to stick it out with Stokes for ten years after the shooting and even gave him two more children: a son,

James, born in 1914, and a daughter, Helen Muriel, in 1915. But after years of abuse she finally cracked when Stokes moved forty-seven chickens into their apartment.* She hoped to end the marriage as quietly as possible and move back to Colorado, but instead what followed, thanks to Stokes, became the greatest divorce scandal of the early part of the century, a four-year saga that was followed by the press with such fervor that even the *New York Times* published seventy-two stories about it, albeit sometimes on the amusement pages.

According to New York State matrimonial laws of the time, if Stokes could prove that his wife had committed adultery, he could end their marriage at little cost, and in March 1921 he sued her for infidelity and named twelve men in affidavits with whom he claimed she had had sex, including his own son Weddie. He even presented the court with a letter from Weddie backing up the assertion. Helen Elwood Stokes promptly sued Weddie for $1 million for libel. There were two full-scale trials, with an ancillary trial for perjury in Illinois, where Stokes had paid witnesses to testify that his wife had worked in an infamous whorehouse. At the first trial in 1922 the judge denied Stokes a divorce on grounds of infidelity, but Stokes's attorney had the verdict set aside on a technicality, and in October 1923 the entire cast of characters reconvened in the appellate division, this time for a jury trial. Simultaneously a grand jury indicted Stokes on nine counts of conspiracy for buying perjured testimony. On November 10, 1923, after one hour and five minutes of deliberation, the appelate jury returned a unanimous verdict that Stokes was not entitled to the divorce because his claims of infidelity had not been substantiated. He

---

*Clearly, by this point Stokes was beginning to lose his mind. He also nailed his wife's bedroom door shut one night in a jealous rage, and when he was ill in bed with a cold, he tied around his toe a string, which trailed out the door, down the stairs, to a room where a nurse sat, waiting for him to pull on it.

settled an $800,000 trust fund on Helen and the two children, and in return she withdrew her libel suit against Weddie. In March 1925 in Illinois, after being found innocent of conspiring to fix a jury, Stokes told the court, "I haven't very long to live, you know, but I'm going to try to do some good in the time that is left me."

He was correct in that he would be dead in a little over a year. He said good-bye to his beloved Ansonia and moved just across the street into 238 West Seventy-third Street, a dreary four-story brownstone, where he died from lobar pneumonia on May 19, 1926, just three days before his seventy-fourth birthday. He left an estate of nearly $10 million. However, at the time of his death there were various claims and judgments against him totaling over $9 million, a great part of it for legal fees.

His son Weddie aged into a stern, difficult man who was afraid of germs and refused to enter the home of a person who was sick with a cold. Weddie invested his inheritance and wrote a book called *Planetary Configurations and Stock Market Sentiment* about the connection between the position of the stars and investing in stocks and real estate. He never cared much about the Ansonia and allowed it to sink into disrepair. In 1911, when his father signed it over to him as a gift, under his father's direction Weddie signed a "net lease" and management contract with the first of many individuals and companies who assumed operation of the building, including John McEntee Bowman, who also owned the Biltmore Hotels in New York and Los Angeles, and in 1928 a character named Mrs. Sue McClary, a Wall Street bond saleswoman, operated the place on a month-to-month basis. In 1929 an entity called the Ansco Hotel System Inc. named Paul Henkel, a celebrity restaurateur who owned Keen's Chop House, the managing director of the hotel, and he tried to spiff up the place by putting handball courts on the roof and had the second-floor ballroom transformed into an indoor miniature golf course, a great novelty that quickly failed as an attraction.

The restaurants and kitchens closed with the Depression, and although the Ansonia kept its "hotel" designation, it stopped being a hotel and turned into a residence with no services. A hundred and fourteen of the suites were converted to "non-tenement[s] by removing various partitions, sinks, and kitchens," according to the filed plans. The brown-and-white-striped bonnets that shielded the windows were stripped and sold, and in 1930 the street level was destroyed. The central entrance on Broadway, the portals through which so many had passed, was sealed, and storefronts were installed instead. In the 1930s more than 100 people died in a fire that raged through a Chicago hotel, fueled by the fluelike updraft of the elevator shafts, and New York City passed new fire-safety laws, forcing the open faces of the Ansonia's elevators to be replaced with solid fireproof doors, and thick firewalls were built between the elevators and the hallways.

In September 1942 the most grievous affront to the building occurred when it was literally stripped of all the glorious metal ornamentation in a patriotic gesture to supply material for bullets and tanks for World War II. There had been some discussion about taking down the metal railings around Central Park, but the Ansonia's manager du jour, Louis Zuch, told the press, "Before we start taking off the metal railings around parks, we should collect all our useless junk." A goal was set to cull 100,000 pounds of "junk" from the Ansonia, and they stripped the copper cartouches that crowned the corner domes, each seven feet tall, weighing one thousand pounds; pried out of the walls several tons of copper pipes, once used for cooling and the pneumatic tubes; and cannibalized the old elevator rails and ancient machinery in the basement. What couldn't be carried away became detritus. Also during the war, the gorgeous skylight window at the top of the dizzying seventeen-floor staircase was tarred over to comply with blackout regulations and has remained that way ever since.

Finally, in 1945 Weddie Stokes sold the Ansonia out of family hands, and it wound up being owned by a crooked landlord named Samuel Broxmeyer, who literally milked the building by offering tenants rental discounts to get them to pay two and three years' rent in advance, then used the money to buy more apartment buildings before eventually absconding. Broxmeyer got five years in prison, and the building wound up as an asset in bankruptcy court. It was sold at auction for a pitiful $40,000 to one of the mortgage holders, Jake Starr, who determined that in the long run the Ansonia was more trouble than it was worth, and decided to demolish it.

## V

JAKE STARR, THE "great lamplighter of Broadway," was a pugnacious little man who wore a long black coat and a homburg that came down to his ears. Every day he strode up Broadway to the Ansonia Hotel from Forty-second Street, where he ran the family business, Artkraft Strauss, the famous sign company that made 90 percent of all the theater marquees, block-long billboards, and pulsating neon signs that earned Broadway the sobriquet the Great White Way.

Starr would spend part of his day in Times Square literally counting the number of people who walked by his signs, separating them in his mind into native New Yorkers and what he called "furriners." He charged tens of thousands of dollars a month in rent for his billboards based on a rate of "human circulation." In the trade his specialty was known as a "spectacular," such as the forty-foot model of a

Trans World Airways Super Constellation with four whirling propellers, which he built in 1955 and put on the roof of Toffenetti's restaurant on Broadway, or the legendary Camel cigarette billboard above the hurly-burly at Forty-fourth Street that blew giant smoke rings onto the Great White Way. Starr originally was a steelworker and tinsmith in Ukraine. He emigrated to America in 1902 and took a job with a small sign-making company on the Lower East Side. By 1909 he had opened his own sign-making business and had invented an electric starter for automobiles, which he sold to Pierce-Arrow.

It was his combined interest in electricity and signage that prompted him to obtain the North American license to a new French technology called neon. After Starr got the license, every time a neon sign glowed in the United States, it was said, a penny went into Jake Starr's pocket. Starr was best known by the public for the New Year's Eve ball he first made in 1907 out of iron and electric lights, which became the first lit ball to ever drop from the top of the Times Building on New Year's Eve. Despite his success, he was notoriously nasty in business, "a vulgar and uncouth little man," Harry Garland, the president of the Ansonia Residents Association, called him, and he was so hard on his employees and family that *Inc.* magazine called its 1991 article on Starr and the Artkraft Strauss company "Daddy Dearest."

"Make your trademark a landmark," Starr always told his customers. If Starr thought that by buying the Ansonia he was buying an icon, he showed no recognition of it. He put up a measly $200,000 cash and held a $1.5 million mortgage, and although the *New York Times* announced, when he bought the place, THE HOTEL ANSONIA TO BE MODERNIZED, no modernization was forthcoming. Starr discovered to his great dismay that the Ansonia had never obtained a certificate of occupancy from the city, because it was built before there was such a thing. It was, in effect, operating illegally as a hotel, which it really wasn't anymore anyway — a situation that the law demanded be remedied immediately. However, the problem with getting a certificate of occupancy was that the building needed to be brought up to code, which would cost Starr millions of dollars. The infrastructure was disintegrating: the original piping was rusted through, the roof leaked in dozens of places, and the balconies were attached with wire. It didn't need modernizing, it needed gutting and rebuilding beyond the old man's means. So instead of doing anything, Starr did nothing. He let the building deteriorate while hundreds of complaints against him began to pile up at the Department of Buildings.

In 1967, as a way to generate income from the building, Starr rented the abandoned basement swimming pool and Turkish baths to a former opera singer named Steve Ostrow, who fit in perfectly with the great tradition of oddball entrepreneurs at the Ansonia. Ostrow believed that in the new era of gay liberation and openness in New York, the time was ripe for a luxurious gay bathhouse, "reminiscent of the glory of ancient Rome," said the ads, except with an orgy room. In retrospect, the Continental Baths, as he named the place, was more Disneyland than hard-core sex. It had palm fronds, flattering lighting, a waterfall that emptied into a crystal-clear blue swimming pool, its own discotheque, a barbershop, and in one cubicle, Puerto Rican drug dealers. It also had a candy machine with K-Y jelly and a warning system of colored lights that tipped off patrons when the vice squad made its periodic visits — somehow never managing to catch anyone having sex. But perhaps the most remarkable thing about the Continental Baths was its famous cabaret, to which the public was invited fully dressed.

By the early 1970s, going to the cabaret at the Continental Baths to watch an emerging act and sitting alongside the naked young men covered by skimpy white towels lounging by the swimming pool became the au courant destination for the fast-lane crowd looking for the next sensation. It was as if Dionysus had hired a press agent. The line to get into the cabaret on a Saturday night went down the block, as long as the line of limousines discharging passengers. The crowd was a mix of women in mink coats with husbands in suits and ties, and gay men in leather jackets with their boyfriends. The author Edmund White remembered that "it struck me for the first time at the Continental Baths that gays were being seen as chic and exemplary." In some ways it was the precursor to that other exotic mix of entertainment and public sex, Studio 54.

Part of the success of the Continental was that Steve Ostrow managed to book an impressive group of budding stars, including most famously Bette Midler, then known as Bathhouse Bette, who was just at the start of her career, as was her accompanist, Barry Manilow, who played piano for her dressed in only a towel. Singers Melba Moore, Peter Allen, John Davidson, ventriloquist Wayland Flowers, and the jazz vocal group Manhattan Transfer also appeared at the Continental early in their careers, and one night in 1973 the Metropolitan Opera House produced and recorded a live performance there of acclaimed soprano Eleanor Steber — who lived upstairs — called *Live at the Bath House.* The men in the audience wore "black towels" in lieu of formal wear.

As the years passed, the old building and its problems began to drive the irascible landlord "insane," according to Harry Garland, one of the many voice coaches who lived and worked there. Garland was a former Fulbright Scholar from Knoxville, Tennesee, who moved into the Ansonia in 1959, when the Wagnarian opera singers still sang carols in the hallways at Christmas. In 1968, when the New York City housing codes and laws were changed and residential "hotels" fell under the protection of the Rent Stabilization Board, Garland helped form the building's first tenants association, the Ansonia Residents Association (ARA). The tenants pooled their money and hired a lawyer who successfully petitioned the court to freeze the rents until vital repairs were made to the building. Starr was so angry at Garland that "people were concerned for my safety," Garland said.

The frozen rents brought Jake Starr — then nearly eighty years old — to a spiteful decision: the Ansonia would be better off demolished. In its stead would be built a new, forty-story residential tower that would "better serve the neighborhood," as one of his lawyers put it when inaugurating the long legal process to evict all the tenants and bring in the wrecking ball. At first, Garland and the ARA tried to find a rich benefactor to buy the building from Starr to prevent him from demolishing it, and approached the Ford and John D. Rockefeller Foundations, among others, to take over the building. Failing that, they decided to fight Starr by outwitting him. They hired their own attorney to appeal to the New York City Landmarks Preservation Commission to have the Ansonia declared one of New York's only 1,023 landmarks, rendering it impervious to alteration or demolition. This made Starr hopping mad. "You'll never get it landmarked," he sputtered to Garland when he ran into him in the lobby. "I have the most powerful men in Washington representing me." His representatives were also ruthless. At a preliminary hearing at the Landmarks Preservation Commission on April 28, 1970, Starr's attorney called the building an "economic liability" and told the commission, "The hotel's architectural appearance is not worthy of designation of a landmark. I am not, nor is the owner, aware of any particular historic significance to the building."

Of course, when word spread throughout the great building of the attorney's contention that it wasn't "of any particular historic signifi-cance," it served to galvanize the tenants. A weeklong protest and demonstration was organized for October 1971, and more than 25,000 signatures were collected on petitions urging New York's mayor, John V. Lindsay, to have the building declared a landmark. The finale of the week was a five-hour live performance held in the middle of Seventy-third Street, which was closed to traffic, featuring many of the building's illustrious tenants, including actress Geraldine Fitzgerald. Finally, on March 15, 1972, after the intervention of Congresswoman Bella Abzug, the New York City Landmarks Preservation Commis-sion designated the exterior of the Ansonia Hotel a landmark, which Starr could not demolish. However, the *interior* of the building was not under the purview of the commission, and it washed its hands over what Jake Starr did with it.

Thus, the building became a decaying shell. In 1973 the Continental Baths closed. Gay men, it turned out, wanted to get down to business without straights in suits and dresses ogling them, and they abandoned the Continental for dozens of hard-core bathhouses that were open-ing all over the city. Once the men in the towels were gone, so was the Continental charm. Steve Ostrow moved to Australia where he founded an organization named MAG (Mature Age Gays) and is writing his autobiography, *Saturday Night at the Baths.*

Jacob Starr died at age eighty-seven. He left his money in a trust that was forbidden to make a contribution to the upkeep of the build-ing, which was left to his grandchildren. His heirs were eager to sell the building, but with all its frozen rent and legal problems, it seemed like a hopeless task.

In October of 1977 the former Continental bathhouse was rented to Larry Levenson, a fat, fortyish man who once made his living

selling cans of soda from a shopping bag on the beach at Coney Island
and later as a manager of a McDonald's. In recent years he had become known as a promoter of "swinging," the practice of couples'
trading partners for sexual encounters. Levenson signed a long-term
contract to reopen the abandoned Continental Baths as a swingers' club
called Plato's Retreat. Levenson added a fifty-person Jacuzzi and lined
the floor with mattresses in the orgy room, and suddenly the Ansonia
became famous yet again, but this time for much less benign reasons.
Plato's Retreat attracted an assortment of kinky types from the suburbs: dry cleaners and their wives or fat men in toupees with their
heavily made-up girlfriends. There was a "membership" fee at the
door of $30 per couple — no single men allowed — and free booze
and a "hot buffet." To add to the seedy atmosphere, on the street level,
between the entrance to Plato's Retreat and the north entrance to the
Ansonia, an X-rated sex shop that sold pornographic movies and latex
toys rented a storefront. Single men who were denied admission to
Plato's began to hang around the entrance to the building and solicit
women, and eventually the north doors had to be sealed up for security reasons as well as to psychologically block off the unpleasantness
of what was happening on West Seventy-third Street. Vincent Joyce
remembered that one of the building maintenance workers made
a hole in the wall of the basement so the employees could check up
on the activities, and they charged the delivery guys $2 for a few min-
utes' peek.

As a crowning touch, about that time the ramshackle Ansonia
began to attract as tenants, for unfathomable reasons, all sorts of
mediums, psychics, spiritualists, and fortune-tellers, many of whom
talked to ghosts. One of them, Clifford Bias, held a quasi-religious
service in a chapel off the lobby on Sunday afternoons. One Sunday

Dr. Bias was blindfolded and summoning up the dead when the great singer Geraldine Farrar appeared from the great veil to deliver a message: "The Ansonia isn't what it used to be when I was there."

## V I

"I'VE GOT THESE plans *somewhere*," Jesse Krasnow said quietly, searching through a jumbled pile of papers and computer printouts stacked on a hanging shelf on the wall of his office. Finally, on an upper shelf, he spotted the roll of building plans and tried to slide them out from under a pile, only to bring everything on the shelf tumbling onto the lower shelves and eventually onto the floor in a heap.

Krasnow mumbled apologies and knelt to scoop up the raft of papers in his arms and replaced them on the shelf, now even more precariously balanced than before. He is a bespectacled man with calm blue eyes and a round, open face. He has a balding pate that is fringed with a brush of white hair, and his manner is mild and distracted, like an absentminded professor. His small office in a midtown building was stacked with piles of papers — on top of filing cabinets, along the windowsill, on his crowded desk — piles of statements and bills and inventories from the many buildings that Krasnow owned. There was not much evidence of the Ansonia in sight, except for one small framed photograph on the wall of the waiting room, taken at the turn of the previous century, and another, larger photograph of the building in the conference room, where there was also a framed photograph of a huge library in Ramla, Israel, which Krasnow and his family helped raise the $92 million to build. The library has since been destroyed in the Palestinian intifada.

Krasnow unrolled a copy of the original plans of the Ansonia across his desk and peered at them as if for the first time. He began pointing out obscure details of the original main floor, unrecognizable from the lobby of today. "Here is the original entrance," he said. "This is Broadway and you came through here. The reception desk was here" — he pointed — "and behind it were offices. And over here was the writing room. When we took down a wall over here, we found steps that led down to the arcade level. This area that was once the dining room is now a theater school — the American Musical and Dramatic Academy — it's one of the best in the country, and we gave them a great leasing deal so we could keep them there. It seemed appropriate to the musical legacy of the building. And over in this area, last week we took down one of the walls in a store on the Broadway side to renovate it for new tenants and we found an original archway that was part of the lobby. So we're going to save it and try to take it out whole, so it can be reconstructed."

Krasnow, it turned out, had been saving bits and pieces of the Ansonia for years, including door hinges and windowpanes and pieces of terra-cotta. There were filing cabinets full of arcana in the sales office at the hotel, including ancient leases of long-dead tenants and photos of the ballroom in the 1920s with its columns gussied up with thousands of intertwined lilies. Krasnow might have had only a summary appreciation of the provenance of the Ansonia when he bought it, but over the next twenty-five years he became enraptured with the building. It became the great love of his real estate holdings as well as the bane of his professional career.

"I love buildings," he said. "When I'm driving in the car my wife yells at me because instead of watching where I'm driving, I'm looking at the buildings. I find Harlem fascinating," he said. "If not for rent control, Harlem would be like the Oklahoma land rush." He was born in the Bronx and he was attending the Wharton School at the University of Pennsylvania when his family started to invest in real estate. Now he was the head of an investment company called Lefferts Fore, whose most profitable activity over the years has been to act as a "converter" of distressed buildings. "Around nineteen sixty-eight we started acquiring properties that had either financial or physical problems," Krasnow said. "You might call them 'workout' properties that had more debts than they could carry, or they had physical problems. For instance, we had a joint venture at the Alden at Two twenty-five Central Park West." The Alden is a large, brick B building with an A location, directly north of the Beresford on Central Park West. Krasnow converted the Alden from a dumpy residential hotel into a desirable modern co-op with 338 apartments. "We also took over the Nevada," he said, referring to a thirty-story dark-brick apartment tower stuck on the traffic-riddled triple intersection of Sixty-ninth Street, Broadway, and Amsterdam Avenue. "The Nevada was about ninety percent complete in construction, but it was in bankruptcy. They ran out of money around nineteen seventy-six, and then we stepped in and took over control of it and opened the building in nineteen seventy-seven. There was a tremendous number of creditors, and we had to work out settlements with all the creditor groups to get the property to an operating level that was sustainable, and we didn't finally settle with the creditors until after we had been open for two years already."

To buy the Ansonia, an investment partnership was formed of eight different family groups representing twenty-one individual investors — including Max M. Kampelman, chief U.S. negotiator with the Soviet Union on nuclear arms — who each invested approximately $100,000. The first thing that Jesse Krasnow did was to get Plato's Retreat out of the basement. Krasnow not only wanted it gone, he *had* to get rid of it; mortgage lenders didn't want to be seen financing a building that sheltered a swingers' club, and banks were leery of giving Krasnow a mortgage. He paid Larry Levenson $1 million to break his lease and close down Plato's. Levenson begged him to let him stay the summer of 1980 until the Democratic National Convention was over, and Krasnow gave him three more months. In September Plato's moved to the ground floor of a factory building on West Thirty-fourth Street and Tenth Avenue, where it operated for five more years before the authorities shut it down for violating the city's new AIDS-related sexual practices in public places law. Levenson was later convicted of federal tax evasion and died of heart failure in 1999 at the age of sixty-two.

In the past when Krasnow bought a building, he was able to use income from the rents to help sustain the costs, but he knew he wouldn't be able to do that with the Ansonia, because the rents were frozen. His first task, then, was to fix the building violations that Starr had let pile up and ask the Rent Stabilization Board to unfreeze the rents. Thus began a civil war between Krasnow and the tenants. "This wasn't simple cosmetics," Krasnow said. "The plumbing was wrought-iron, and the building was in need of tens of millions of dollars of repairs." As each individual apartment was repaired and each violation satisfied, Krasnow would send the tenants a notice — to which they legally had only seventy-two hours to respond — that he was going to ask the city to unfreeze the rent in that apartment to "compatible levels." In some cases, tenants who lived on Social Security payments and had been paying only a few hundred dollars a month to live in squalor under Jake Starr would now have plumbing that worked but would face rent increases of 300 percent — an impossible amount for them. Outraged, the tenants accused Krasnow of doing only patchwork repairs instead of rectifying the serious structural problems, and the leaky roof was refurbished so many times that it became a joke in the building. "Every year the sap flows," complained one tenant, "and every year Krasnow tars the roof of the Ansonia and it still leaks." Krasnow put $3.5 million alone into the repair of the roof, and it still sometimes leaks.

Of all the accusations leveled against Krasnow the one that galled him the most was the charge of "aesthetic abuse" against the building. In particular, he was still vexed by an article that ran in the *Village Voice* in early June 1980 with the headline BARBARIANS RAPE ANSONIA. Krasnow had redone just one floor, the twelfth, as a model for his interior-design plans, and the tenants hated it so much that they started a new petition to have the interior of the Ansonia declared a landmark as well, to protect it from Krasnow's changes. "After *umpteen* years," he said, "that nobody did *anything*, we put in new carpeting and new lights and the tenant groups didn't like it. As a matter of fact," he said, searching for another file folder, "at the time I was kind of angry, so I hired a photographer. This is what the place looked like when we bought it in nineteen seventy-eight." He presented a set of photographs of what looked like the hallways of a medieval mental ward. "The halls were yellow. Dreary. Discolored linoleum, fluorescent lights, bare bulbs, and old tiles." He held up a close-up, like a crime-scene photo, of portions of the linoleum in the hallways, with sections ripped and missing. "This is what the floors looked like," he said passionately. "This is what the marble looked like before we refinished it. These were the light fixtures. When you came out of the elevator, this is what you saw."

Unfortunately, no matter how good his intentions, there was something middle-class about the taste level of the renovations, and the coup de grâce was delivered by architecture writer Paul Goldberger later that June. In a *New York Times* column titled "Rescuing the Ansonia from Its Rescuers," Goldberg wrote, "Its lobby at times looks like something out of a George Price cartoon: its elevators could be in a factory, and its corridors look like bowling alleys from the wrong side of the tracks.... The corridor has dropped ceilings ... with grotesque, modern chandeliers of the sort that would cheapen even a Ramada Inn. There are two kinds of rust-colored carpeting and two kinds of wallpaper, which manage neither to be attractive in themselves nor to go at all well together."

Krasnow persisted, undaunted, with some modifications, and redid every floor, elevator, and staircase in the building. Within two years Lefferts Fore had gone from a $2.5 million cash investment to holding over $21 million in mortgages on the building, all of it used to make repairs and improvements, Krasnow said, in addition to putting $4 million into a reserve fund to show the tenants good faith. Yet Krasnow continued to enrage some tenants, no matter what he did, including finding financial relief and income by opening a 100-car garage in the basement. In March 1980 the Ansonia Residents Association declared a rent strike. ARA members paid their rents into an escrow account (where over $2 million in cash accumulated) and used the interest from the account to hire a lawyer to sue Krasnow. When that group seemed close to negotiating a compromise with Krasnow, another, more radical splinter tenant group formed, the Ansonia Tenants Association, and its members began to pay their rents into an escrow account, too, and use the interest to sue Krasnow. For the next decade the Ansonia Hotel became the single most litigated residence in the history of New York City. A Manhattan housing court judge was assigned full-time to the case, and over the next ten years Krasnow repeatedly found himself cast in the role of one of the city's most villainous landlords.

Krasnow realized that in the long run, the best solution to making the building functional again and settling all the lawsuits was to pay off the tenants who were the unhappiest, and Krasnow shelled out hundreds of thousands of dollars for disgruntled residents to leave. In 1990 the tenants accepted a condominium plan allowing them to either continue to rent their apartments or buy them at a 60 percent reduction in price. That meant a one-bedroom apartment would cost $125,000 — way beyond the means of most Ansonia tenants. (Today, a one-bedroom apartment at the Ansonia is valued at around $600,000.) At present 29 percent of the building is still rent-protected, and the modest rents of those tenants do not cover the cost of their maintenance. Krasnow has continued to subsidize that share, and he has claimed that over the years he's put almost $100 million into the building.

In 2003 he moved his offices into the Ansonia. He enjoyed mingling in the building every day with the residents, most of whom didn't recognize him. "The newer tenants don't care about me," he said, "and the older ones still have a good deal." Of all the diverse history of the building, the resident that most fascinated him was Babe Ruth. Krasnow kept a curio cabinet made by his grandfather in his office with several shelves' worth of Babe Ruth memorabilia. He's spent the past twenty-five years trying to track down which apartment Ruth lived in. But nobody knows for sure — not Babe Ruth biographers, not the Baseball Hall of Fame. If the apartment is ever identified, it will instantly triple in value and become the most famous apartment in the building, Krasnow predicted. One apartment that has been identified with some certainty is the apartment in which W. E. D. Stokes once lived. A TV producer named Daniel Arndt paid $1.3 million for two adjoining apartments in the northeast turreted corner, and in the process of renovating them, his workmen opened up a wall and found a ledger page addressed to W. E. D. Stokes, a good claim to provenance. The three-bedroom apartment recently changed hands for just under $4 million, and there is another currently for sale for $5 million.

Still, for all the big numbers the apartments are fetching, the Ansonia Hotel remains a bit funky. There is occasionally a resident having a doze in the odd lobby seating area (although the dusty dried floral display has been removed), and no matter how hard they try, the building somehow never looks as chicly decorated as most other high-priced condominium buildings. But a little dowdy is probably the way the Ansonia should look. The building's senior concierge and historian, Vincent Joyce, is still behind the front desk during the day shift. "Lots of new people here," he lamented in his beautiful brogue. "People with children and nannies. There's a lot of that now." He wondered if he should think about retiring, because his left hip hurt him but he was afraid of the long recovery period if he had it replaced, living alone the way he did. But one of the older tenants brought him some sort of pill from Israel and since he started taking it, the pain went away. Anyway, the lobby desk isn't far to go to work every day, just downstairs from his apartment, and although he pretended not to know, he realized that he was just as much an irreplaceable piece of Ansonia history as anyone else in the past 100 years.

# EIGHT

# BILLION-DOLLAR
# BROKER

I was here just last week," Dolly Lenz shouted over the grinding noise of construction, "but this building is going up so fast, it looks different every time I come."

It was a hot, overcast day in August 2003, and the din at the Time Warner Center was like listening to the hollow roar of a seashell, only amplified by 2.8 million square feet. Lenz, forty-five, was leading the way along the perimeter of the Fifty-eighth Street side of the construction site, searching for the new entrance of the south residential tower, a half-finished steel-and-concrete skeleton that towered eighty stories above her. Lenz cut a determined figure as she wended her way past piles of debris and concrete barricades, a big pocketbook and plastic tote bag in one hand and a roll of floor plans in the other. She was dressed in a black Chanel suit, white silk blouse, and sensible low heels. Her large oval glasses and the way her dark hair was tightly pulled back in an austere ponytail contributed to her prim, businesslike look. Except for the spotlessly clean white hard hat she wore on her head, she could have been a high-school principal marching a student off to detention instead of the city's top real estate broker about to show a writer the raw innards of a $30 million apartment.

"Last week when I brought a customer from California to see one of the thirty-million-dollar penthouses," Lenz shouted in her fast-paced, clipped New York accent, "there wasn't even an indoor elevator, let alone a lobby." On the previous visit to the building she took her client up in an outside freight elevator, little more than a wire-mesh cage on a hoist attached to scaffolding on the side of the building. "It was like riding a roller coaster. Very exposed," she said. "It was scary. But a good kind of scary. Especially if the guy doesn't have good control of the brakes. The customer I was with thought he was going to die. He was flipping out, but I loved it." But now that one of the indoor elevators in the residential tower was in operation, the building's developer, the Related Companies, had nixed the outside joy rides, much to the disappointment of Lenz, who considered it one of the perks of visiting the rapidly changing building.

Lenz wasn't the only one surprised at the speed with which the Time Warner Center was being built. For those who lived in midtown and saw it changing every day — in particular, the co-op owners on Fifth Avenue whose skyline was forever being transformed by the Twin Towers of Condo Doom — it was like watching stop-action photography. The 750-foot-tall buildings were sprouting up at the rate of one floor every two days, and almost as quickly, a few floors below, the steel skeleton was veneered in a glittering blue-white glass, manufactured one-third thicker than normal to prevent distortion. Everything about the building was supercharged, like a skyscraper on steroids. At $1.7 billion in construction costs, it is the largest, most expensive mixed-purpose building ever built, the biggest construction project undertaken in the city since the World Trade Center. Because of its many components, the building is a three-dimensional jigsaw puzzle, so complicated that it has had seven different kinds of architects and has six different addresses. David Childs from the design firm of Skidmore, Owings & Merrill gets credit for the building's eighty-story twin towers and its massive, seventeen-story curving-arc base. The towers contain 200 luxury condominiums, as well as a nineteen-story Mandarin Oriental hotel embedded in the north tower and designed by the noted German firm of Brennan Beer Gorman. The international headquarters of the media conglomerate Time Warner was being carved out of the base, 900,000 square feet of it, which includes studios for its CNN television unit with a dramatic glass backdrop that overlooks Columbus Circle and Central Park South. The Boston-based architectural design firm of Elkus/Manfredi Ltd. contributed the Shops at Columbus Circle — a glass-enclosed 150-foot atrium and vertical shopping mall, five stories tall, with 350,000 square feet of commercial space. In the basement, by way of an attenuated escalator ride, the Whole Foods chain was building a massive 59,000-square-foot supermarket that will make Harrods Food Halls look like a deli. Below that, three stories underground, there is a 504-car garage with twenty-four-hour valet car service and a lounge for napping chauffeurs waiting on call for their employers upstairs.

The building is also committed to the Upper West Side's cultural heritage, and the north side of the base contains 100,000 square feet of performance space for the new home of Jazz at Lincoln Center, a satellite of Lincoln Center seven blocks uptown. The firm of Rafael Viñoly Architects designed four different performance halls, including a 1,200-seat auditorium with movable seats and a 600-seat amphitheater with a "suspended glass wall" that will turn opaque during performances to shield the performers and audience from the distraction of traffic swirling around Columbus Circle below.

And those are just the headlines.

To piece all this together by its opening date of late 2003, more than 3,000 construction workers — the largest construction crew ever assembled for a single building in New York — including 250 Mohawk Indian ironworkers who were brought in to weld the 28,000 tons of steel beams, toiled over the building like worker bees, while hundreds of heavy trucks trundled in and out of the labyrinthine underground garages with materials and supplies. The building was moving so fast that even part of its name blew off in the wash: it was originally called the AOL Time Warner Center, but when the Internet service provider turned out to be an unpopular merger with Time Warner, its initials were lopped off.

The people who had undertaken the construction loan on all this — yes, the largest single mortgage ever granted in the United States, for $1.4 billion — were known collectively as the Related Companies, a group of investors headed by a prominent Manhattan developer named Stephen M. Ross. The Related Companies would have preferred that Lenz not take her clients up in the building while it was under construction, because it was dangerous and an insurance liability, but since Lenz had already sold over $100 million worth of apartments in the complex, and would probably sell another $100 million more, whatever Dolly wanted, Dolly got. In New York if you're a condominium developer such as Stephen Ross or Donald Trump, and Dolly Lenz decides she wants to take clients up in your unfinished building to seal a deal, you just say yes. In Manhattan residential real estate, Dolly Lenz is a combination Babe Ruth and Jack the Ripper. She's been the number one broker at every brokerage she's been with for the past fifteen years, with a career batting average of nearly $3 billion in apartments, along with a trail of bloodied cobrokers. "I'm playing chess while every other broker is playing checkers" is Lenz's explanation for her no-holds-barred reputation. "I will get that deal. If my eye is on a prize, I will make that deal."

One familiar plaint from brokers is that she steals clients. "Name me one client I stole, I exhort you!" Lenz excitedly demanded when confronted by Deborah Schoeneman from *New York* magazine. "I would never do anything to endanger my real estate license," she later added. "There is nothing that anybody can point out that is not in the interest of my seller or buyer." That being said, she readily confessed that she has sued more than twenty sellers — not brokers — for commissions she felt she deserved. Lenz herself was once sued for interfering with a sale, by broker Michele Conte, when Conte's customer, Dennis Kozlowski, the CEO of Tyco Corporation, backed out of buying a condominium at 1049 Fifth Avenue and instead wound up buying an apartment through Dolly Lenz at 950 Fifth, for $18.6 million. Kozlowski spent several hours in deposition before the lawsuit was dismissed by summary judgment. Three years later Lenz testified at Kozlowski's federal trial when it turned out that the $18.6 million he paid for the apartment, as well as other sundries, such as a $6,000 shower curtain, was taken from company funds that belonged to Tyco shareholders. Kozlowski was charged with grand larceny and securities fraud. The case ended in a mistrial.

It was Kozlowski who nicknamed Lenz "Jaws," a sobriquet she proudly acknowledges by keeping a stuffed plush shark with a bow tied around its head on a shelf in her office. Yet the bespectacled lady in the white hard hat with small beads of perspiration on her forehead searching for the south tower lobby entrance in the muggy heat didn't seem the least bit shark-like. She seemed, in fact, more like a middle-class Jewish mother in a good suit, except that she isn't Jewish, despite all the good Yiddish words she knows. Her maiden name is Idaliz Dolly Canino, and her mother and father are Spanish. Lenz was born in the Bronx and raised a Catholic, but she feels and acts Jewish, she said, because she married a *yeshiva bucher*, her CPA husband, Aaron; and their two children, thirteen and fourteen, are being raised Jewish. "He went to Yeshiva University and came from a kosher home and then he brought me home to his mother. Oy, poor guy," she said. "We got married in City Hall on a Thursday and I never converted. As far as I'm concerned, I am Jewish, because my mother's mother was Jewish, so that makes me Jewish."

Lenz didn't take all her clients to see the unfinished space in the Time Warner Center. "The developers don't want me to take just anybody up in the building," Lenz explained. "It has to be somebody who is really committed to buying; otherwise, it's too challenging for someone who doesn't understand raw construction to see all this," she said, gesturing to the frenetic activity around her. "And they have to want to buy a penthouse, or a half a floor — and they start at eleven million."

Customers who couldn't afford to pay $11 million were relegated to choosing their apartment from a model in a marketing office at the Metropolitan Tower, a building about half a mile away from the Time Warner Center, on West Fifty-seventh Street. This suite of rooms was rented by the Related Companies at a cost of $1 million a year, and it was well worth it: although buying an apartment sight unseen from a marketing office may seem like a nonchalant way to spend $5 million or so, 99 percent of all the preconstruction apartments in the Time Warner towers were sold from this office — over $300 million worth. The sales personnel joked that they were selling "air"; square footage that at the time existed only in the sky, without walls or floors around it. But what they were really selling was amenities, the bells and whistles, brand names and status chips that give the building cachet and set it apart in the competitive marketplace.

Its "airplane views" are the Time Warner Center's greatest appeal, and the location of the marketing office was chosen, in part, because as soon as a visitor walked into the office there was an unimpeded view through a huge picture window of the center's twin towers soaring over the midtown Manhattan skyline. Just in front of this impressive vista stood a computerized scale model of the real building in the background. The model could be animated by pressing a combination of buttons to show off different features of the building; individual apartments could be made to light up, the theaters darken, the shopping mall twinkle. Prospective buyers could determine exactly where their condo would be in the finished tower by choosing individual units to light up. There was also, built into a wall of the offices, one of the actual floor-to-ceiling windows from the towers, and behind it a startlingly realistic, true-to-perspective, full-color reproduction of Central Park as it would look from one of the towers.

Instead of a full-scale model, only fragments of the finished apartments were built into the marketing office, including the actual kitchens and bathrooms by designer Thad Hayes. The models were dressed like a stage set, as if a very fussy, elegant person actually lived there, with fresh flowers in the vases, lit scented votive candles, real vintage bottles in the built-in humidity-controlled wine cabinets, caviar on the shelf inside the refrigerator, and scented soap in the marble soap dishes. So carefully was all this chosen that Lenz claimed that Related Companies president Stephen Ross, who was admittedly obsessed with every detail of the construction of the Time Warner Center for fifteen years, actually sat on the toilet seat of the model (with the top down) and contemplated the view that potential buyers would have from the commode.

In one part of the suite there were samples of the moldings and flooring (not the standard ⅛ inch, but ¾-inch oak in a herringbone pattern "stained on premises" to the buyers' specifications), and customers were offered a soft drink or coffee while they relaxed on a sofa and watched a slick video on a huge plasma screen about the wondrous perks of living in the towers, which are wondrous indeed. Each apartment comes prewired with sixteen different kinds of telecommunications lines, including T1, PBX, DSL, and phone and cable lines, making it "broadcast-ready," capable of live TV transmission for teleconferencing business meetings, or if your life becomes a reality show. All this technology, including the ultra-high-tech security systems, will be monitored twenty-four hours a day in a command center hidden deep within the building with so many closed-circuit cameras, computer screens, and alarms that it looks like the War Room of the Pentagon.

The north tower, which is really on Sixtieth Street, also has a made-up address, 80 Columbus Circle. Owners of the sixty-five condominiums for sale in this tower are included in a plan offered by the Mandarin Oriental Hotel and are considered "permanent residents of the hotel," which means that all the concierge services of the Mandarin are available to them — typically, room service, maids, dog walkers, massages, and limousines. A la carte living in this hybrid condominium/hotel is designed to appeal to the huge influx of wealthy foreigners who want a pied-à-terre in New York and maintain a chief residence with a full staff elsewhere. The south tower has amenities that were attracting families, mostly from New York, such as the woman with six children to whom Lenz sold a penthouse for $32 million. When both towers are sold out, they will each have generated half a billion dollars' worth of sales.

The south tower holds the record for the second-most-expensive apartment sold in New York, a 10,000-square-foot duplex on the seventy-fifth and seventy-sixth floor that was purchased for $42.5 million. Conventional wisdom in the industry is that this huge sale price was so stunningly reassuring to the condo market that it ignited a spate of luxury-condo sales over $10 million throughout the city. The buyer was David Martinez, a forty-six-year-old financier who has offices in London and New York. A bachelor, Martinez first became interested in the building when it was only a huge excavation hole. He and his broker, Robby Browne, were scheduled to take a helicopter ride above the site on the afternoon of September 11, 2001. They intended to hover at the approximate height of the apartment he was interested in buying for a dramatic presentation of the kind of views it would have. For obvious reasons the helicopter trip that day was canceled. Yet even after the destruction of the World Trade Center, Martinez remained undaunted in his desire to live in the city's newest twin towers, and he bought the apartment anyway. In fact, the association of having twin towers and being a terrorist target has had no effect on the building's popularity; in the four-week period following September 11, $46 million worth of apartments were sold at the Time Warner Center. When Dolly Lenz asked one of her buyers if he wanted out of his contract to buy a 3,500-square-foot duplex, he said, "Absolutely not, I'm not going to let those terrorists mess up my life."

When the sales presentation in the marketing office was over, customers were sent home with a "goody bag" of floor plans that measured a jumbo six by three feet; stacks of promotional booklets printed on the finest stock, slipped into embossed sleeves tied in grosgrain; and a Baccarat crystal, five-pointed star paperweight with the logo FIVE STAR LIVING engraved on it, a phrase that the Related Companies has trademarked.

## 11

THAT HOT AUGUST day at the bustling Time Warner Center construction site, not much Five Star Living was apparent yet, nor was the residential lobby. Although the address Lenz was searching for is called 1 Central Park (also sometimes written as One, depending on how pretentious the marketing team is trying to be), it was actually located on West Fifty-eighth Street. The fancy address was invented by the Related Companies and approved by the city in an effort to help make the building sound more portentous. When Lenz finally discovered it behind a temporary plywood barricade, it wasn't a lobby at all: no marble floors, wood paneling, wall tapestry, or glass-and-polished-steel marquee extending protectively from the front door to the curb. There was only an exposed infrastructure of the building's innards with bare lightbulbs hanging from the ceiling grids, an elevator bank, and a few test slabs of white onyx that would soon cover the walls. A loud portable radio blasting rock music could hardly be heard over the whirring and grinding noise of construction, and when the only working elevator eventually arrived on the lobby floor — the call button hadn't been installed yet, so all Lenz could do was wait for it to show up — it turned out to be a tiny lift swathed in heavy padding, big enough for only three or four people. At the controls, subbing for the not-yet-installed digital-fingerprint scanners that apartment owners will use in lieu of a door key, was a construction worker in work pants, T-shirt, and hard hat who was manning a panel of push buttons.

"To the top," Lenz requested.

"To the top?" he repeated.

"To the very top," she said.

The very top in this case is actually the fifty-third floor, although it is marked 80 in the building plans and 80 will be the number on the elevator button. That's because, like addresses, floor numbers get fudged in the world of luxury condominiums. "Construction counting," as they call it in the trade, is different from "marketing counting" because many of the newer condominium buildings are multiple-use and have office space or hotels on the lower floors, so the ceiling heights can differ wildly throughout the building. At the Time Warner Center the fifty-third floor would be the eightieth floor if the building were residential from the ground up and all the floors had nine-foot ceilings; when the residential floors start, the floor number jumps from 23 to 51. This tricky counting method was first used in 1985 by developer Harry Macklowe, who described his Metropolitan Tower building on West Fifty-seventh Street as having seventy-eight floors when it actually has only sixty-eight. It is the justification that Donald Trump uses to advertise the Trump World Tower building across from the United Nations as the "tallest residential building in the world" at ninety stories, when in reality it is only seventy-two stories tall. There is not much more justification to call all five top floors of the Time Warner Center "penthouses," either, which should refer only to the uppermost floor of a building and technically describes a structure that sits on the roof. The Time Warner Center penthouses begin at a setback on the seventy-fourth floor and are each being sold as a single, undivided apartment with a massive 8,300-square-foot footprint.

No matter how the Time Warner Center towers are numbered, when the elevator came to a stop and the door opened, the concrete ledge in the sky onto which Lenz stepped was very high up. "It's high, but it's not surreal," Lenz said. Yet it *was* surreal. Because on the top five floors there were few support beams, except for the central core that held up the building, the panorama was literally river to river, New York Harbor to Harlem. This is what they mean by "airplane views": it was like being in an airplane that was standing still. No model or slick video in a marketing office could approximate the sheer rush of being so high above the city. Manhattan had turned into scale-model-size, yet seemingly more urgently alive than on the ground, with the bustle of people and vehicles so easily visible on the grid of streets stretching out below. It was the perfect divide. A view of refined old money from the pinnacle of new money.

Central Park was lush in August and deeply green, and peering up behind it were the stolid co-operative buildings of Fifth Avenue, like one-dimensional dioramas in a pop-up book. There was big sky, too, a blue-gray miasma through which glided tiny slivers of airplanes to and from the three major airports surrounding the city, and below them what must have been a score of helicopters buzzing above Manhattan like gnats. No wonder Lenz wanted to bring high rollers to see the view. The idea of living with that view every day made all the luxurious trappings of Fifth Avenue seem meaningless, all the stately beauty of Rosario Candela and the grand rambling apartments on Central Park West seem unimportant.

Only one building, the rectangular monolith of Trump International Hotel & Tower at the apex of Central Park West and Broadway, marred the view. Trump bought the forty-five-story office building previously owned by Gulf + Western in 1995 and had it gussied up by architects Philip Johnson and Costas Kondylis in golden-black glass with a brassy gold trim. The *New York Times* said that it looked like "a 1980's gold lamé party dress." Trump turned the bottom twenty-nine floors into a luxury hotel and the top floors into very expensive condominiums with views of Central Park and the Fifth Avenue skyline, but lower than those of the Time Warner Center. Trump was delighted that his building marred the view from the Time Warner complex, and he liked to rub it in. To goad his competitors, Trump put a series of large signs across the windows of the uppermost floors of his building facing the Time Warner Center with the message SEE, YOUR VIEWS AREN'T SO GOOD, ARE THEY? He justified the taunt by saying, "What these guys did was piss me off. The apartments [at the Time Warner Center] have shit views, they look at the back of my building. Worse, when you go higher you can see the pile of shit on the roof [of his building]. It's the only building where I store the garbage on the roof." Trump took the sign down after he had his fun.

A far more commanding aspect of the view than the Trump International was the north tower of the Time Warner Center, in whose mirror-perfect glass surface the south tower was reflected. The parallelogram shape of the two towers, which follows the curvature of Broadway around Columbus Circle, was designed so that from a certain angle the two buildings disappear behind each other. The distance between them is surprisingly close; it is the exact six-car width of Fifty-ninth Street — had it continued through the fountain at Columbus Circle and down the middle of the building. This is called a "view corridor," which the developers were obliged to include in their design so the building wouldn't cast a black swath across Central Park. The shadow that would have been thrown by a denser building became a rallying issue for New York City activists in 1985 when Jacqueline Kennedy Onassis joined hundreds of other New York City protesters demonstrating in Central Park by opening a sea of black umbrellas to illustrate the size of the umbra a solid building would cast.

Lenz pointed out that on all the other floors the apartments were preconfigured, while the five top floors were an empty canvas. "People bring their own architects," she said, "and they build a home in the sky. It's not like a co-op, where there are structural walls that are holding up the building. You can build whatever you want. The services are almost anywhere under the floors, so you can put a kitchen or bathroom anywhere you please and nobody is going to stop you. One couple I showed this to wanted to make it into a one- or two-bedroom apartment, with Zen-like rooms in between that weren't really rooms but 'floating' rooms. The people looking at the floor below us have three children, so they need three bedrooms just for them, then a master suite, a guest room, a maid's room, and they wanted a large library.

"So?" Lenz smiled, standing in the middle of the large unfinished space, her shoes covered in concrete dust. "It's thirty million dollars, as is, no walls. Should I wrap it up?"

## I I I

REAL ESTATE ISN'T just a vocation for Dolly Lenz; it is an obsession. And while many good salespeople are obsessed with the marketplace, Lenz's preoccupation with real estate has caused her to move her family in and out of at least fifteen different apartments in the past twelve years, including seven apartments at the Parc Vendome on West Fifty-seventh Street. Her colleagues joke that the reason she sometimes has a limousine pick up her children after school is so that they'll know where to go home. She made a profit on every move, she admitted, "but not enough to be in it for the money." Not *just* the money, at least. She's also in it for the gamble, the pitch, being on the come, the excitement of change — the excitement, period. Like riding in the outside elevator at the Time Warner Center. And she doesn't become attached or sentimental about her surroundings. "I don't pack everything myself each time I move," she said. "I have a packing company come and do it for me — if I take my furniture, which I don't often do. I like to buy everything new when I move. Every place I buy is so different that you can't take furniture, it doesn't look right."

Her interest in Manhattan real estate started twenty-five years ago, when Lenz and her husband made a pact that they would forgo the luxury of living in a one-bedroom apartment and live in a studio and buy a second studio as an investment. It was the most basic real estate get-rich plan, the kind that silver-tongued salesmen hawk on late-night TV. Dolly and Aaron Lenz put 20 percent down on a studio apartment, took out an 80 percent mortgage, and rented the studio for a small profit. After a few years Lenz and her husband owned thirty-one studios and held nearly $4 million worth of mortgages. It was at one of those mortgage closings, Lenz recounted, when the commission check to the broker was $24,000, "My husband took me outside and said, 'That broker did nothing, *nothing*, and she made twenty-four thousand dollars. You should do that.'"

It was a month after Lenz's tour of the top floor of the Time Warner Center, and she was eating lunch at the Ritz-Carlton Club Lounge, a private club on the second floor of a hotel-and-condominium conversion at which Lenz had sold $143 million worth of apartments. She finished off a plate of food with gusto and headed back to the buffet table for a second helping. She is self-conscious about being zaftig, and she said that she overeats for energy, but it's not hard to discern that she also eats for comfort and that beneath her easy charm there can be roiling discontent. Like many brilliant salespeople who have bravura on the job and learn to deal with frequent disappointment, Lenz is surprisingly insecure and easily wounded.

"Every time I meet a new client, I feel like I'm onstage and I get stage fright," she confessed. "I worry, 'Do I look okay? Did I say the right thing? Did I say the wrong thing?' No, I tell myself — 'I'm me — forget it.'" At company functions she finds it hard to make small talk and she is distant and aloof from other brokers, fiddling with her handheld BlackBerry, answering her e-mail messages.

In Lenz's family women were not supposed to work. Her father was a dredging mechanic and her mother worked as a manager at a Bronx supermarket — "When my father let her work," Lenz said, "because my father was very old-fashioned." Lenz herself was a teenage cashier in a Waldbaum's Supermarket on 234th Street before she went off to City College to study accounting and then get her master's degree in auditing at the New School. She traveled for a while, doing "black book" auditing for United Artists pictures in Los Angeles in disputes about movie grosses, and she adjudicated claims for major shipping companies with interests in the Middle East — she lived in Egypt for six months and learned to read numbers in Arabic. Back in New York, married and in her early thirties, "I was not a happy accountant," she said. That was when she took her husband's advice and got her real estate license and started selling apartments, first at a small mom-and-pop shop and later at the mid-level firm of L. B. Kaye.

When Lenz started in residential real estate, condominium apartments were looked down upon as housing for buyers who couldn't get past co-op boards. Although condominiums have boards and bylaws, unlike co-ops, no one can be turned away. Basically, anyone with the cash to buy an apartment can get in. In the condominium plan an owner buys outright the floors and walls and even the apartment's "air space." It can be sold, rented, mortgaged, traded — all without the consent of neighbors. In a condominium a resident can never be sure what kind of an undesirable neighbor might wind up living next door, or on the floor above.

The word *condominium* is from the sixth-century B.C. Roman "law of condominium." This was the first time in recorded history that a legal definition was instituted over joint ownership of property. Modern-day condominiums were popular in South America and Puerto Rico long before they became an accepted form of ownership in the United States in 1961, when the Federal Housing Administration was authorized by Congress to provide mortgage insurance for them. Over the next thirty-six months, forty states in the United States passed legislation adopting condominiums as a legal form of ownership, including New York in May 1964. A scant eight months later the first condominium in Manhattan was opened: a thirty-three-story building called the Saint-Tropez at 340 East Sixty-fourth Street, considered swank at the time because it had an outdoor swimming pool on its fifteenth-floor setback, despite its outré location on First Avenue.

By the mid-1980s condominiums had become the predominant form of new development in New York, and between 1985 and 1988 more than 15,000 condominiums were built. What was at first presaged as a "condo glut" in the industry completely sold out. This unleashed a secondary wave of condominium development, this time increasingly high-end luxury buildings, such as Dag Hammarskjold Plaza near the United Nations on Second Avenue, and the fierce competition between new buildings trying to outdo one another with bells and whistles began in earnest.

Lenz remembered telling her manager at L. B. Kaye, "'You know, I really think condos are the wave of the future. We should start a condo division.' My manager said to me, '*Condos?* What are you talking about? You're going to sell *condos?* They have ads in the papers with their own sales offices and big marketing budgets. Customers don't need you to buy a condo — they can buy a condo themselves. But they need you to buy a co-op because they can't walk in the door of a co-operative by themselves.'"

"I thought to myself," Lenz said, "'My job is to make money and to make transactions happen. Why should I do what everybody else was doing and follow the pack?' I decided I was going to preclude the buyer from going to a sales office and I was going to develop a condominium business."

At that particular moment one of the largest sectors of buyers in the condominium market were wealthy South Americans, many of whom were looking for a simple way to move cash out of the turbulent economies of their homelands. While most brokers weren't interested in selling condominiums to South Americans, Lenz was delighted to cultivate a Latin clientele; Spanish was her mother tongue and she understood the culture. She began to actively quarry the Spanish-speaking market by buying her own advertisements in upscale South American and Mexican magazines and newspapers, and she soon created a word-of-mouth reputation as the broker to call for rich foreigners who wanted to buy in New York. Within two years Lenz became the top-earning broker at L. B. Kaye, with as much as 95 percent of her sales in condominiums.

When Lenz was poached away from L. B. Kaye to be the "condominium specialist" at upper-crust Sotheby's International Realty, she quickly learned that there was nothing lower than a "condominium specialist." The power at Sotheby's real estate division (which Edward Lee Cave had started so many years before) then resided in a clique of old-time biddy brokers, the "Dragon Ladies," as Lenz called them. A bunch of similar Dragon Ladies exists at almost every upscale agency in Manhattan. They are upper-class brokers who sell only upper-class co-ops to upper-class people. "Everybody at Sotheby's thought I was weird because I sold condos," Lenz said.

Lenz pointed out that her clientele was hardly society's dregs. As condominiums became more sumptuous and even more expensive than co-ops, the stigma of buying a condo because there's no board scrutiny became an anachronism. "There are many different reasons that clients don't want to face a co-op board. Maybe they're extremely private and they don't want to give their tax returns up. Or maybe the customers can't buy the apartment in their own name, like co-op boards demand, because that could subject all their income worldwide to U.S. taxes, and they need to purchase it in a corporate name. So it's not that my clients *can't* pass muster, because they *can* pass muster; it's that they didn't want to pass muster. And as condominiums get more and more luxurious, there's no need to put up with the problems presented by a co-op."

But it was the "bulks" that really put her on the map. "What I do is different than Edward Lee Cave or Alice Mason," Lenz said. "They sell apartment by apartment. I try to sell 'bulks' of apartments. Although I do sell 'homes' to live in, I think of apartments a little bit differently than most brokers; I see them as a commodity." Lenz got the idea to sell "bulks" when she discovered that Sotheby's had collectibles auctions touring throughout the Far East. These auctions were a trunk show of treasures, crisscrossing Asia, from Taiwan to Japan and Malaysia. Sotheby's set up pre-auction viewings in hotel ballrooms and courted wealthy Asians, who were pouring billions of dollars into investment-grade collectibles. Lenz figured that condos were as good an investment as collectibles, and she asked Sotheby's to let her go out on the road with the auctions, set up a booth, and try to sell condominiums.

But Sotheby's would not underwrite such a gambit, so Lenz wrote a business proposal for Donald Trump, asking him to bankroll her, and he agreed to shell out $110,000 to send her on the road. In 1992 Lenz, accompanied by her husband, spent six weeks in Asia, armed with display stands, photographs, CD-ROMs, and videotapes of luxury buildings and their interiors. Some customers were referrals; others were people she met who came up to her small booth. "I said to these potential investors, 'I can sell you a block of ten apartments in a condominium building and here's the internal rate of return. Here's the cash-on-cash return. Here are the projections. Let's go to your bank and let's see what they'll finance. If you buy ten apartments, I'll rent them for you. My husband is an accountant in New York and he'll manage them for you. We'll collect the rents and pay all the bills, with no headaches to you.'"

Over the years Lenz cultivated a network of high-rolling real estate investors, mortgage bankers, and private wealth throughout the Far East. "I'm not sure that I invented bulk sales," she said, "but in my world of residential real estate, I did. In my world, nobody was doing that. My first year at Sotheby's, I was the top broker. And every year after that, I was the top broker, so they could not-like me all they wanted."

Lenz said that technically she was the top broker at Sotheby's for two years even *after* she left in 1999, until all of the international deals she set up had closed — although Sotheby's contested this, and the parting was acrimonious. Lenz didn't make a soft landing at Douglas Elliman, either, where she went next and two of the top players in the company quit or were let go within six months of her arrival. "From the second Dolly walked in the door there were fights," said Paul Purcell, then president of Douglas Elliman, who hired her.

"I didn't know I was walking into a snake pit," Lenz said. Whatever environment she found herself in, Lenz flourished. She sold both co-ops and condos and she became chummy with key members of the real estate press. Her reputation was burnished on the pages of the *New York Post* and the *New York Observer*. Other brokers learned to stay out of her way. As her fame spread she began to receive hundreds of requests each month from sellers and buyers, soliciting her services. The two-hour testimony she gave at the trial of Dennis Kozlowski piqued the public's interest in her and she was profiled on ABC's 20/20 show. Condominium developers courted her to sell in their buildings, and periodically she would make trips to the Far East to market her "bulks" to bankers or potentates. There was no way of telling for sure, because the earnings of many of the top brokers at other agencies are never revealed, but as far as anyone could tell, Lenz was the top-earning broker in the business, a powerhouse that no one could touch.

It was in July 2001, when real estate prices in New York were soaring and Lenz had too many customers to handle by herself, that she met a handsome and ambitious young broker at Douglas Elliman named Michael Shvo. Lenz soon took the young broker under her wing, and for the next year and a half they became inseparable friends and business associates.

And she has regretted it ever since.

# NINE

# NUMBER 1

W e stole it!" Michael Shvo sang out. "From two-eight to two million! We fucking stole it!"

Shvo was in all his glory. He had just closed a deal for his client at a much lower price than was asked. "It's better to make a deal for less money than no deal at all" is one of the credos Shvo tells his trainees; others are "There is no deal too small" and "The client doesn't know what the fuck he wants."

Shvo began to manically punch numbers on the telephone console atop his desk's sideboard and then pounded on the wall behind him so hard that a framed "brucha" — a prayer for good business in Hebrew — nearly fell off.

"Wha-at?" a man's voice called from the other side of the wall.

"We stole it!" Shvo shouted at the wall. "For two million dollars!"

The muffled response from the other room was drowned out by the penetrating booooping tone of his desk intercom, followed by the voice of his assistant, Samara, announcing a phone call for which he had been waiting. Shvo said, "Put her on double-oh-seven" — the number of his private line — and flipped the receiver into his palm.

"Elaine? Michael!" he crooned. "Hi, honey! Did Donald get you? We're doing apartment fifty-eight for two million. No!" He laughed. "The Donald — don't even go there. If he wants to, let him call me, or let him talk to my boss, Howard Lorber, who owns me. Let him talk to Howard." Shvo speaks in a mellifluous voice tinged with some charming accent whose origin sounds more fashionably Continental than Israeli, which it actually is. "Honey, you have, in the next twenty seconds, in your fax, all this information — buyer's name and address, the lawyer — how fast do you want me to work? You know? What do we need to do this?"

Michael Shvo was putting on a show, and he wasn't shy about it. He is tall, slim, and handsome. Everything about him is suave — his navy blue suit; his beautiful blue dress shirt with azure cuff links; his patterned, dark blue Hermès tie; and his habit of distractedly pushing his thick, chestnut-colored hair back from his forehead with the same kind of coy self-awareness that very handsome men have on television soap operas. His worldly, self-confident manner belies his tender age; he is just a few days shy of his thirty-first birthday.

Samara, a petite young woman with a ponytail, appeared at the door with a letter for him to approve, and Shvo began to read it aloud: "'Please find enclosed information . . . for Mr. Wolfson for the purchase of blah blah blah. . . .'" He crossed out some words with a great flourish of his pen. "That was struck today, what the fuck is wrong with them? Why the fuck do you write it? And put my numbers somewhere so she can find them — and a little quicker — yeah?" Samara gave him the resigned look of a long-suffering gal Friday and moped out of the room.

It was 6:30 P.M. on a frigid weekday night in December 2003, and most of the fluorescent-lit, utilitarian cubicles of Douglas Elliman's Madison Avenue offices were deserted except for Shvo and his staff of factotums, known as the Shvo Group in the company, his own little agency within the agency. Even after hours, when there was no pressing business, employees of the Shvo Group were expected to be in the office, ready to spring into action if a customer looking for an apartment called after 8:00 P.M., or even midnight. The Shvo Group had turned Michael Shvo into one of the highest-earning brokers in the business. Shvo had 150 "exclusives" at the moment, the most of any broker in the company, from $300,000 studios on the Lower East Side to $30 million condos. He was such an expert at getting people to give him exclusives on their apartments that he lectured on the subject to new Douglas Elliman brokers. But 150 apartments are way too many for one person to handle, so he created a team of "mini-me's," as he called them, "that I try to make into duplicate Michaels." His mini-me's did most of the showing and selling on the lower-end deals; Shvo supplied the clients and took a 40 percent share of commissions. He claimed that the competition for jobs with the Shvo Group was so fierce that brokers sent him candy and gifts, hoping to get his attention, but he only hired people with no previous real estate experience. "Common sense," he said. "If you're doing this for two years and you're not successful, then you're obviously doing something wrong. There are two things that you need to succeed in real estate. You need at least an average IQ and a strong will to work. That is all you need to succeed." His acolytes pulled their own weight; members of the Shvo Group had to bill a minimum of $300,000 a year in commissions. "If not, they're out the door," he said.

Shvo's attention flickered under a barrage of stimuli: a musical note signaling an e-mail chimed from one of the three flat-screen monitors on his desk; simultaneously one of his three cell phones and two handheld BlackBerrys, lined up like toy soldiers on the windowsill, began to vibrate and buzz; and there was a member of the Shvo

Group at his office door asking for her commission check. "Money? I have no money," Shvo said playfully as he produced a check from his desk drawer that pleased the young woman, who thanked him profusely before she shut the door behind her.

Then, for just a brief moment, there was quiet in the room and Shvo tried to focus on a question that had been posed to him earlier: "What makes Michael run?"

He laughed a charming but studied laugh, showing beautiful white teeth. "I don't do drugs, I don't drink, I don't smoke," he said. "I work eighteen hours a day and I don't sleep. I think sleeping is a waste of time. All of the energy that you see is from real estate. That's why I sell better than anybody else — because there is nobody that can be so excited." He scoffed at the prolific gossip about his being the office lothario. ("Think Warren Beatty in the movie *Shampoo*" is the way one of his coworkers described him.) "I have no private life," he said. The beautiful girl in the framed picture sitting on the windowsill in his office was his sister. "I'm in the office sometimes until midnight. If you find a girl that would marry me and let me work eighteen hours a day, let me know." He said he lived alone and relaxed at night by playing classical piano, which he studied in Israel. "Sometimes I play a Beethoven sonata before going to bed," he said, "or Mozart's Fantasy in C minor." He also fills his lonely hours with the opera, he said, where he has a regular seat, and he subscribes to "seven different series at Carnegie Hall" as well. On Friday nights he attends Sabbath services at a synagogue, and he observes the Sabbath on Saturday — the one day of the week he does not go to the office. Every Tuesday night he would invite a rabbi from a Chabad House, the messianic sect of Orthodox Judaism, to teach the Torah in his office, and would invite everyone in the company to join them and participate.

Shvo's account of his life and accomplishments is colorful and dramatic. He grew up in Arsuf, a beach community in Israel, where in his youth there was no running water, he said. He visited the United States many times as a child, mainly on vacation with his parents, who were college professors. He said that after an obligatory stint in the Israeli army, he became a successful stockbroker. "I finished the army at the age of twenty and a half, when I started my financial business," he said. "I made lots and lots of money and I learned what it was to be very rich. I could have retired when I was twenty-two if I wanted to."

Curiously, instead of retiring, he headed for New York City and wound up driving a cab. He said that after the plane landed at Kennedy Airport, "on the way into the city in the cab I asked the cab driver how driving a cab worked. Two and a half months later, I owned fifteen yellow cabs and had forty drivers working for me, dispatching them from, like, a street corner." One night, said Shvo, he was standing on Broadway in the West Sixties, distributing flyers to hack drivers passing by, when "I was looking up at this building. I said 'What a beautiful building, this is where I want to live.' Bottom line is, I live there now. And I own more than one apartment there."

Somehow Shvo transitioned from driving a cab into a brief marriage during which he dabbled in the nightclub business, he said, and eventually took a job as an apartment rental agent. As it turned out, Israeli-born men predominantly staff the rental field of Manhattan real estate, probably because of the dogged persistence and long hours it takes to make any money doing it. "My first year at J. Sopher I did over three hundred rentals," Shvo said. "All I did was show apartments. I used to show forty apartments a day and I did at least one deal a day. I think the most expensive apartment I netted my first year was three thousand dollars a month. That period showing rentals was what made me what I am today, because now, after a year, I know every building. I've dealt with a million different kinds of clients. I know the inventory better than any other broker in the city."

Is it possible to learn all the subtleties of New York City real estate from a year in rentals? Doesn't it take a seasoned broker to understand the nuances between Beekman Place and Sutton Place? Brokers like Alice Mason and Edward Lee Cave have spent decades studying the pedigree and provenance of Manhattan co-ops.

"Co-ops are a thing of the past and people don't give a shit about Sutton Place anymore," Shvo sneered. "Why do you think the Time Warner building is such a success? Because people want to be where the action is. The prices in TriBeCa now are *sick*. I was showing *fifteen-million-dollar* apartments in TriBeCa last week. Today they're selling one-bedrooms in Chinatown for one million. Do you think a thirty-eight-year-old partner in Goldman Sachs who makes eighty million a year knows who Alice Mason or Edward Lee Cave is?

"You know what?" Shvo asked. "They're all going to drop dead soon, or they're going to be too old to be able to walk. I mean, think about it, who's going to sell apartments ten years from now? I'm the new generation of real estate broker. I don't do social real estate. I don't care who I sell to. I have, in my opinion, created how real estate is done in New York."

Two weeks later, in early January 2004, Michael Shvo, newly turned thirty-one years old, was enjoying a leisurely dinner at his favorite table at Daniel, the pricey, four-star restaurant on East Sixty-fifth Street. Daniel is one of only two restaurants at which Shvo will regularly dine, he said, the other being Nobu, the hip celebrity sushi joint in TriBeCa. Shvo was again elegantly turned out in a dark suit, white shirt, and Hermès tie. He was drinking dessert wine from a fluted crystal glass, and after just a few sips he got a softer, sleepy look in his eyes and sank back into the pillows of the banquette. His dinner had been a cholesterol-be-damned feast of pâté de foie gras, filet de boeuf, and his favorite creamy dessert à la maison.

Shvo was evidently a valued customer at Daniel. The maître d', also in a Hermès tie, twice came to his table to fawn over him and trade tips on trendy ski resorts. Later, Daniel Boulud, the restaurant's namesake chef, made a trip out of the kitchen to trade stories with Shvo about the relative leg room of a BMW and an S500 Mercedes sedan, like the chauffeur-driven Mercedes Shvo had waiting for him outside. Boulud confided in Shvo that he was thinking of opening another restaurant, smaller and more intimate, like a bistro, and asked Shvo if he had a suggestion for a location available to lease.

Shvo said he knew just the place, a commercial building with a storefront in the East Seventies that was on the market for about $7 million. "But I don't want to spend seven million on a building," Boulud protested. "I just want to lease some restaurant space."

Shvo said, "Daniel, if I have you as the tenant in the street level, getting the seven million from somebody to buy the building upstairs will be no problem at all." Shvo promised he would do some research on a location; Boulud thanked him and left.

Shvo was in a celebratory mood that night because the comptroller at Douglas Elliman had compiled a ranking of the top-grossing brokers within the company for 2003, and the Shvo Group was the number one producer in the company and Shvo was going to be named the number one broker. The ranking of all the top brokers in the company was going to be announced at an awards ceremony held on February 11 in the Grand Ballroom of the Pierre Hotel, attended by 1,000 employees. The personal earnings of the company's top brokers were going to be revealed in an elaborate ceremony. News of Shvo's ranking had become the talk of Douglas Elliman. For the first time in recent memory, Dolly Lenz was demoted to number two broker, and Shvo was making no secret of his pleasure in it.

When Shvo and Lenz met in the summer of 2001, Dolly was famous in the business and had exclusives on some of the best apartments in the city. Shvo was ambitious and wanted to work with her. "Dolly had an exclusive that I wanted to share," he said, "so I went to meet her in the lobby of a building. The first time I saw her she was dressed like a slob, chewing gum, talking on the cell phone. I said to myself, 'No way this is Dolly Lenz. I wouldn't let her clean my apartment.'" Shvo claimed he asked, "*You're Dolly Lenz?*" His incredulity quickly dissipated after spending a few minutes listening to her talk about the real estate market and realizing how smart she was. Shvo gave her his guarantee that if she would share the exclusive on the apartment with him, he would sell it for her. "She said to herself, 'Okay, who's this little *pisher* that's coming in?'" Shvo said. "I showed the apartment only five times before I sold it, and Dolly ended up screwing me on the deal." Shvo said he was on his way to the airport to catch a plane for Israel when he found out that Lenz had claimed the apartment was already in contract for a higher price with her own client and there would be no commission for Shvo. He canceled his flight to Israel and took a taxi to Lenz's office, where he sat down uninvited in a chair next to her desk and refused to budge. No matter how many times she asked him to leave, he stayed where he was and kept talking. According to Shvo, by the end of the day Lenz so admired his gumption that she finally agreed to close the deal with his buyers. After that, they were new best friends.

Paul Purcell, who was then president of Douglas Elliman, remembered when Lenz and Shvo paired up. "They were joined at the hip," he said. "They never went anywhere without each other. It was perverse, to be honest with you."

"We became very good friends," Shvo admitted, a tinge of wistfulness creeping into his voice. "We were partners for quite a while. We were very close — very close. We used to talk seventeen times a day. We were as close as two people that were not married could be. Or probably closer than two people that are married. She made a great contribution to my knowledge in real estate. Obviously, I learned a lot of good stuff from her and I learned a lot of bad things. But I loved her to death at the time. I was closer to her than her husband. Her children came to me for advice. Many weekends I flew out by helicopter to her house in the Hamptons."

Shvo savored another sip of his dessert wine. "Recently, though, our relationship was terminated. We don't speak." What caused so much animosity between them? "If you ask about the end of the relationship, you could write your next book about it," he said. He contemplated the loss of his friendship for a moment, searching for the right words. "The truth is," he said finally, "I broke her heart."

## I I

IF MICHAEL SHVO broke Dolly Lenz's heart, it was by claiming that he made more money than she did.

"Broke my heart?" she repeated, nearly apoplectic, her eyes wide behind oval eyeglasses. "*Close* to my children? *Helicopter?* He never took a helicopter to the Hamptons to my knowledge." She was talking faster than ever; there was color in her cheeks and blood in her eye. It was late January and Lenz was sitting on an upholstered stool at the bar of Jean Georges on the ground floor of the Trump International Hotel & Tower. She looked surprisingly streamlined. After years of feeling dumpy and uncomfortable with her body, she put herself on a strict diet and exercise regimen a few months before, and her figure had changed dramatically. She looked almost as sleek as the new Time Warner Center behind her, visible through the giant lobby-level windows of the restaurant. The building's official black-tie opening was still a week away, and already it had been declared a sensation. The building looked particularly glamorous at night, with the glass skin of the towers reflecting the sparkle of the city, like glitter on silk, and the five levels of retail shops inside the seventeen-story base lit up like boxes within boxes. Up in the towers almost 80 percent of the condominiums were sold, and the five new restaurants in the atrium with views overlooking Columbus Circle and down Central Park South, with its romantic hansom cabs, were already booked months in advance. In an example of perfect New Yorkese, the *New York Post* ran a boldface headline proclaiming that A BEAUT IS BORN. Urban planners and architecture critics joined in lauding the rejuvenating effect of the building on the Upper West Side and credited it with having a positive psychological effect on the entire city; its towers were being hailed as a symbol of the city's phoenixlike resilience after the destruction of September 11, 2001.

Lenz had sold $130 million worth of condos in the towers behind her — roughly $7 million in commissions — but was oblivious to their existence at the moment because she was so consumed with Michael Shvo. Her diatribe against him was interrupted only when Jean-Georges Vongerichten, the restaurant's eponymous owner, heard that Lenz was "in the house" and came out of the kitchen to chat with her about his chances of selling his apartment; Lenz was the exclusive agent for an investment apartment Vongerichten owned upstairs in the Trump International and she gave him some reassuring words that it would sell for his price. He kissed her good night on each cheek and left. The maître d' soon summoned her, and after a pit stop to say hello to movie producer and real estate investor Keith Barish in the lounge, Lenz was shown to a table in the main dining room. She ordered a nine-course tasting dinner for herself and her companion and nursed another glass of wine along with a grudge.

"Listen, don't get fooled by Shvo because he's so cute," she admonished. "He's about not knowing when to stop. He is about not having rules, and if there are rules, he thinks they don't apply to him and he will do what he wants. It's simply not true that he's number one in the company," she said. "I knew there was trouble when the company comptroller went over my earnings last month. Nobody has ever done that before. Shvo wants them to change the way they count income. It's already unfair. Let's say Shvo earned a million dollars last year. Four hundred thousand of that might come from his own efforts — and six hundred thousand comes from the efforts of the people in the Shvo Group, because he gets forty percent of what they make. That was already unfair to say he earned one million. But now he wants to go even further than that and include the other sixty percent of all the Shvo Group's income as well — money he didn't even personally earn! You can't calculate me, an individual broker, against a group. If you looked at the results individually, he was number ten, and I was number one."

When Shvo was asked to comment on the equity of pitting the earnings of the entire Shvo Group against Dolly Lenz as an individual, he shrugged. "Dolly Lenz could have formed her own group," he said. "But she has no group because Dolly cannot give out power. She cannot just let go. That's Dolly."

Lenz accounts for the intensity of their friendship as "business close," she said. "He and I both work the same way. We work twenty-four hours a day, seven days a week, and when you work twenty-four/seven you wind up spending an awful lot of time together." If she sounds hurt, it's because "I trusted him," Lenz said. "I figured, look, I put a million dollars in this child's pocket, the last thing I have to do is worry. . . ." What about his contention that he broke her heart? Lenz laughed. "I thought I broke *his* heart."

Lenz said that things began to unravel when, she alleged, he began poaching her clients — ironically, the same complaint that many brokers have had about her. "One day an Israeli client of mine called me up," she said. "This guy is worth like six billion dollars. He was given to me as a client by the vice chairman of Goldman Sachs. He called me up and said, 'Who is Michael Shvo? Did you have him call me?'"

Furious, Lenz said she went to Shvo and demanded, "'Why did you call this Israeli guy?' and he said, 'Oh, is he your client?'" The two stopped working together soon after, and Lenz claimed that she found crowbar marks on her locked office door and that her client list had been downloaded from her computer, all of which she reported to the owners of the company. Over the next year Lenz and Shvo lodged accusations of every kind against each other, business and personal, and their open feuding became one of the juiciest topics of interoffice gossip.

But no matter how nasty the sniping became, things didn't turn really ugly until Shvo insisted that he be named the number one earner at the company and there was blood of honor spilled in the hallways of Douglas Elliman.

## I I I

INTO THE MIDDLE of this internecine warfare stepped the redoubtable Dorothy Herman, fifty, of Syosset, Long Island.

"Dottie" Herman was the undisputed queen of suburban residential real estate. She was a local Long Island gal who worked her way up from a certified financial planner at a small mom-and-pop real estate agency to the principal partner and CEO of Prudential Long Island Realty, a sprawling suburban outfit with forty offices and $2.4 billion in annual sales. For over a decade Herman had longed to cross the East River into Manhattan, where there was no Prudential brand and the streets were paved with real estate gold. She even had a company slogan picked out: "From Montauk to Manhattan." But she could never figure out how to do it — buy an existing company, or build from the ground up? Her financial partner, Howard Lorber, fifty-three, the president of New Valley Corp., a Miami-based, publicly traded real estate company, who also owned Nathan's Famous hot dogs, was prepared to write a $50 million check to finance a foray, but the logistics of starting a company from scratch in the crowded New York market and finding brokers to staff it were daunting. Even harder was finding an existing company to swallow whole. The New York real estate community was already reeling from a frenzied consolidation of small and medium-size companies being snatched up by huge financial holding corporations to create behemoth firms with near-unlimited financial resources, Internet technology, and marketing clout, such as the 800-broker firm Corcoran, owned by the New Jersey–based Cendant Corporation. Midsize firms such as Warburg Realty, Stribling & Associates, and William B. May were besieged with offers from national companies for buyouts, and tiny boutique firms like Alice Mason, with only eighteen employees and a minuscule marketing budget, had become grains of sand on a vast beach. Even the fiercely independent Edward Lee Cave with a thirty-member staff was in negotiations with the bigger Brown Harris Stevens about becoming a subsidiary.

Most daunting of all, perhaps, for Dottie Herman in entering the Manhattan market was the community's opinion of her as a carpet-bagger and Prudential Long Island Realty as a meat-and-potatoes outfit that made its sales volume in the resale of low-end suburban houses. The Prudential FOR SALE sign was a familiar totem on the front lawn of postwar tract houses in developments all over Long Island. Even Herman herself was denigrated as too "up-Island," too blond and brassy for the clubby environs of New York residential real estate. In 1999, when she opened up her first Prudential office in the posh Hamptons, local brokers predicted she wouldn't last a year in that snooty market, and *New York* magazine ran an article about her arrival titled "Broker from Another Planet." But her Hamptons offices lasted far more than a year; within a year Herman had *five* offices in the Hamptons, and she managed to infuriate the other agencies by hiring away their best brokers and capturing a major share of the market.

That's why in March of 2003 the xenophobic New York real estate community was dismayed to discover that Dottie Herman and Howard Lorber had shelled out $71.75 million to purchase the revered Douglas Elliman Company, established in 1911 by one of the great salesmen of real estate history, from Andrew Farkas and his Insignia Financial Group. What Herman and her partner paid all that money for was thirteen offices in key locations throughout the city (some with high rents), 800 nervous brokers wondering if they were going to become part of the next "Costco of real estate chains," and the goodwill of the Douglas Elliman name — which they kept in New York, eventually renaming the company Prudential Douglas Elliman. The resources of the Long Island and New York companies were integrated to create a regional behemoth with more than 2,000 brokers, 51 offices, and $6.5 billion dollars a year in sales. An additional $150 million was earmarked for expansion, and one of Herman's first moves was to double the size of the company's Madison Avenue headquarters to 60,000 square feet and to buy more desks, chairs, and telephones and start hiring brokers to use them, allegedly by offering heavy hiring bonuses and generous commission splits.

Suddenly, the Belle of the 'Burbs was the Bane of Manhattan.

"Douglas Elliman would roll over in his grave," a broker told *New York* magazine on the occasion of Herman's arrival.

Welcome Dottie Herman.

"One broker from another agency actually called to ask me if I was going to put lawn FOR SALE signs in front of co-op buildings," Herman said, repeating one of her favorite stories about her catty reception in New York ten months before. It was nearly 8:00 P.M. and Herman was in her fourth-floor office at the company's Madison Avenue headquarters, waiting to take some of her brokers and marketing staff out for dinner. "I have no idea to this day if that person who asked about the lawn signs was serious or if they were being mean, but you know what? The bottom line is, in this world you have to have faith in yourself."

Herman is hardly the brassy broad from the suburbs that her rivals have painted her to be. She is engaging and attractive, and one smart cookie; the only thing Long Island about her is her accent. She was wearing a low-cut black Chanel-like suit, a gold bracelet, and high heels that showed off her long, tanned legs. She has a warm, loopy smile that shows an impressive array of white teeth and, occasionally, the gum she chews. Many of her brokers regard her with near-fanatic devotion, and indeed, she is genuine and nourishing, more the hard-nosed, loving mother than the hard-nosed CEO — the broker with the heart of gold.

This nondescript office is one of her four offices, if you count the backseat of the chauffeured car where Herman spends a great part of her day working while in transit, answering phone calls and e-mail. She divides her week among a rented pied-à-terre at the Essex House; her family home in Syosset, Long Island, which she shares with her husband, attorney Jay Herman; and her beach house in Southampton, where she looks in on her highly profitable Hamptons offices on weekends.

When in residence in her office she leaves the door open to encourage brokers to drop in and chat. She believes closed doors create "barriers" in an office and promote an unhealthy business atmosphere. "When I first bought the company I had lines of brokers out my door," she said. "I tried my best to get to know as many people as I could, but sometimes people would say to me, 'You know, I don't feel good — you don't know me.' And I would explain to them, I'd say, 'Look, I have eight hundred and ninety people to get to know and I can't know them all inside of a month or two.' But I did try, and I did listen. But I also understood myself that you just don't walk into a company and get trust and respect because you bought a company or because you have a title. You have to earn it."

Herman was disturbed by the amount of viciousness she discovered in Manhattan real estate, outside of Elliman and within. "I believe that it's a tough business to be in for brokers. You try to build a team one day and the next day the members of the team are competing with each other on the same deal. I want people to respect each other's differences, but I learned in life that you can't win every battle." Still, she ruminated over dinner that night with her marketing staff on how to develop a more nurturing environment, and she continues to travel from office to office, meeting with brokers, listening to their problems, cheering them on. She spends at least part of her day drying tears with a promise of "we're not going to let you starve."

She also keeps a copy of former GE chairman Jack Welch's Six Rules for Success in her purse, which include "Be candid with everyone" and "Don't manage, lead." She's also partial to the last one, "Control your own destiny, or someone else will." Herman understands destiny. When she was ten years old, her family was returning from a ski vacation in Vermont. "We had a very bad car accident," Herman remembered. Herman and her mother were thrown from the car. Her mother was killed and her father was maimed. "Was that a life-changing event?" she asked. "Ten years old, you don't really realize that." She spent the rest of her adolescence caring for her father and her siblings. "What I understood at an early age is, life isn't forever," she told *New York* magazine upon her purchase of Douglas Elliman in 2003. "In having no one to nurture me, I pretty much did it for myself. I was always an achiever. I was willing to do whatever it takes to be successful."

Willing to do whatever it took to engender a kinder, gentler Prudential Douglas Elliman and yet aggressively find the brokers with whom to expand was a fine line to toe. Word on the street was that Herman was offering brokers at other agencies hefty marketing budgets and perks (for instance, assistants paid for by the company) to jump ship. Her tactics were so ruthless that she allegedly called top brokers at every rival company to make offers, including signing bonuses as high as $250,000, and inflated commissions. Most brokers get 50 percent of the commission, with the rest going to the company;

Herman was allegedly offering as much as 75 percent commission on the first $150,000 in sales for the first year, a deal too lucrative for the company to make any money if marketing dollars were factored in. One rival brokerage was so incensed by her tactics that it reported her to the Real Estate Board of New York, which determined she was doing nothing unethical.

Herman wasn't immune to poaching from other agencies, either, and by one account in the first year she lost fifty brokers who packed up and took their real estate licenses elsewhere. One idea that Herman developed to stop brokers from leaving Prudential Douglas Elliman was to offer them the opportunity to start their own "groups." The idea was that brokers could build a "business within a business," as Herman put it, like owning their own company but protected by the corporate stepparent. "Ten years ago a big agent would have left to open his own offices and it would cost millions to do," Herman said. "This way you can have your own office within our office and the expense is on the owners."

It was Herman's "group" idea that made Michael Shvo into a star in the real estate business and a handful for Herman to contend with. On February 9, 2004, two days before the awards ceremony, in an emotional conversation, Shvo told Herman that if he wasn't named number one broker in the company, he would quit and move the entire Shvo Group to Sotheby's International Realty. Thanks to the speed of e-mail, Shvo's ultimatum was the chief bit of company gossip by lunchtime that day. Dolly Lenz claimed she got eighty e-mails congratulating her on Shvo's imminent departure, but Lenz was dubious he would really leave.

That night Lenz and Dottie Herman had dinner at the Four Seasons Hotel restaurant on East Fifty-seventh Street, just around the corner from Prudential Douglas Elliman headquarters. In the ten months since Herman had bought the company, she and Lenz had become fast friends. "I was immediately in love with Dottie," Lenz said. "She spoke my language and she spoke from the heart. She knew what I was thinking." That night at dinner Herman was thinking she was about to lose the second-biggest producer in her company less than a year after she bought it. Lenz assured her, "Don't worry, Shvo's not leaving."

"He's gonna quit," Herman fretted.

"So let him fucking quit," Lenz answered flatly.

Herman spent most of the next day trying to fashion a compromise with Shvo. She pointed out to him that he would be the most honored broker in the company. He was going to be honored for "most sales transactions" of 2003, a remarkable 119 of them. He was going to be given an award for the "most sales exclusives." He was going to receive fourth place in "most rentals." As an individual he would be honored for earning over $750,000 in gross commissions. And the Shvo Group was going to be named the "number one group," and it would be the last award — *after* Dolly Lenz's award — the position of highest honor.

But she also made it clear that Dolly Lenz was going to be named the company's number one individual broker, not him.

Herman cajoled and massaged Shvo through the day of February 10, 2004, and spoke to him on the telephone as late as one o'clock the following morning, trying to persuade him to show up at the awards ceremony, but Shvo was torn, according to Herman. "He even had to call his spiritual adviser in Israel," she said.

By 9:00 A.M. the morning of the awards breakfast, no one had any idea if he was going to show up.

## I V

THE DRIVING TECHNO beat of Moby's "We Are All Made of Stars" was percolating over the sound system of the Pierre's Grand Ballroom on the morning of February 11, 2004, as 1,000 of Prudential Douglas Elliman's highest-earning brokers arrived for the awards breakfast. They were a handsome bunch, dressed mostly in dark clothes, each as impeccably groomed and fastidiously coiffed as any of the clients to whom they were showing apartments later that day. Many of them were even richer than most of their clients. They were an ambitious group; most had already stopped at their offices that morning to answer their e-mails or pick up daily listing sheets so they could leave directly from the ballroom to show apartments. No doubt many were aware that twenty-one stories above the ballroom's trompe l'oeil blue sky ceiling and celadon chandeliers, in the half-hotel, half-cooperative building owned by the Four Seasons Hotel chain, one of the most expensive apartments in the city was for sale: the co-op of Mohamed al-Fayed, the father of Dodi al-Fayed, who died with Princess Diana in a car crash in Paris, was on the market for $25 million.

Waiters in black tie circulated with pitchers of orange juice, silver pots of coffee, and piping-hot plates of scrambled eggs while company-hired videographers and photographers captured the arriving crowd. Brokers from different offices greeted one another with hugs and kisses and found their assigned seats at the packed, gaily set tables. At every place setting there was a small stuffed teddy bear and red heart with the words *I Love You* written on it, a personal touch chosen by Dottie Herman.

There was no dais, but there was an unofficial VIP table stageside, just next to the podium and below a huge screen upon which a live video of the proceedings was being projected. Dolly Lenz was at this table with her bosses, Herman and Lorber. It was more than apparent from the new, more revealing clothes she was wearing that she had stuck to her diet and exercise routine with the same dedication with which she sold real estate; she had shed over forty pounds from her torso and ten years from her looks.

The Shvo Group was assembled at a table toward the center of the room, looking like a hapless troop without a leader. "He's not gonna show," Herman said, nervously scanning the room for Michael Shvo.

"He'll show. I'm telling you. He'll show," Lenz assured her.

It was a scant few minutes before the awards ceremony began that Shvo appeared in the doorway of the ballroom, looking cool and collected. He sauntered to his table, dressed in a dark suit, smiling charmingly at whoever caught his eye as he made his way through the crowded tables. Up front, next to the stage, Lenz said "I *told* you he would show up. I told you he would never quit."

The program began with introductory comments by Jeff Rothstein, the manager of the West Side office, who looked out at the size of the crowd and sighed, "We're not small anymore." He asked that those several hundred new brokers who had joined the ranks of the company within the past year stand up at their seats, and he also acknowledged the sixteen new "superstar brokers" who had been in the top 5 percent of producers in their old companies before jumping ship to Douglas Elliman. Finally, after some sophomoric potshots at the competition's slogans and hairdos, a surprise speaker was announced who brought the crowd to its feet: Donald Trump, then riding the crest of the success of his TV show, *The Apprentice.* The crowd cheered and applauded as a spotlight picked out the developer at the front entrance of the ballroom, dressed in a bespoke dark suit and bright pink tie, and followed him as he preeningly made his way across the room. In acknowledgment of his warm reception, when he reached the podium he hailed the audience as "a group of killers," a compliment that was greeted with a roar of knowing laughter.

"Brutal, brutal people, brokers," Trump said to more laughter. "What can I tell you? We're all brokers when we get down to it." Trump admiringly described Dottie Herman as "the greatest killer in the world," and as for dealing with Hollywood executives, "we have worse killers," he said. "This may be the only business where the people we deal with are worse than in Hollywood," he said proudly.

A face he recognized in the crowd distracted Trump's attention. "Oh, hello!" he crooned. "Look who we have here!" He was pointing to Dolly Lenz. "One of the great killers of all time!" he proclaimed. There was a loud burst of laughter, and Lenz laughed good-naturedly along with the rest. "I never knew your breasts were so large," Trump unexpectedly said to Lenz, who had removed the jacket to her suit to reveal her new, curvy figure. The audience howled. "I never noticed how attractive you were until this morning." (Lenz later said, "It was the weirdest experience I ever had; people my age don't think about their boobs.") Trump shook his head in fake amazement. "This is the first time I've seen Dolly Lenz blush," he told the audience. "She's a real ballbreaker, but she's *good* at what she does — she's *real* good.

"But enough about real estate," he said. "Who the fuck wants to talk about real estate?" Laughter. Just then the familiar chirping sound of a cell phone penetrated the ballroom. All attention focused on the source: it was Lenz's phone. *"Turn off that goddamn phone, Dolly!"* Trump bellowed, and the audience had another good laugh.

The awards part of the affair began with a short introduction by Howard Lorber, who explained to a riveted crowd that of the $6.4 billion that Prudential Douglas Elliman grossed in 2003, $168 million of it was paid in commissions to its brokers. Sitting before him that day in the ballroom were some of the best-paid brokers in the business. In proof, the presentation of the awards began, the highlight of which was a succession of awards to brokers who earned net commissions in three categories: from $250,000 to $499,000; $500,000 to $749,000; and $750,000 and above. As each broker's name was announced it was projected onto a large screen to the right of the stage and the broker was given an ovation as he or she stood and went to the stage to collect the award and gift and pose briefly for a corporate photograph with Dottie Herman and Howard Lorber. Eventually, they got to the last, most important category, the Top Ten Brokers in the company. Dottie Herman noted that inclusion in this category put these brokers in the top .5 percent of all residential real estate brokers in the United States.

Howard Lorber began the countdown and called each broker to the stage to receive an award and a kiss and be photographed. When he reached the number one spot, unaware that his lapel microphone was still on, he turned away from the podium and asked Dottie Herman, "Do I have to tell them the difference between 'best group' and 'individual'?"

Herman exasperatedly shook her head no.

Lorber went back to the podium and announced, "The number one broker of the year is . . . Dolly Lenz."

Lenz stood up with a fixed smile on her face and made her way to the stage to warm applause from her colleagues. She took her award, posed for a few photographs, and quickly went back to her seat.

"I now present the award not only for number one as a group," Lorber said, "but for the all-time sales earning record *in history* as far as anybody can tell — *the all-time leading commissions,* Michael Shvo!"

Shvo's name was met with another convivial round of applause as he stood and made his way up to the stage for a fourth time that morning. He posed for a photograph with Herman and Lorber, the three of them happily grinning at the camera. Then Shvo whispered something in Herman's ear, and she responded by enthusiastically gesturing to Lenz at her table that she should join the group onstage. At first Lenz resisted, but then Howard Lorber started gesturing to her, too, and after a brief pause she stood up and the applause gently increased as she walked back up to the podium. The four of them posed for a picture together, Lenz and Shvo smiling brightly at the camera. Then they leaned toward each other and air-kissed as the strobe lights went off one last time.

## V

TWO MONTHS LATER Dolly Lenz broke all cost-per-square-foot records in Manhattan by selling a duplex on the top floors of the north Time Warner Center tower for $4,100 a square foot, totaling $25.5 million. The buyer of this apartment was a Wall Street investor named Jack Silver who was president of SIAR Capital, a private firm that invested in emerging-growth companies. Silver and his wife were yet another couple deserting the graciously sized rooms of a Rosario Candela apartment, this one at 920 Fifth Avenue, for the Big Sky vistas of the Time Warner Center. "At first they only wanted to look at prewar on Fifth Avenue," Lenz said, but the couple soon discovered that there were few co-ops for sale in the Good Buildings of New York. Despite stock market volatility and rising interest rates, apartment prices were ballooning yet again, this time because of the lack of inventory. It was almost as if so many A list Manhattan apartments had been traded in the gluttonous market the year before that there was nothing left to sell. Lenz, who was impatient with the narrowness of the Upper East Side luxury market, tried to persuade the Silvers to look at a floor in the Time Warner Center, but "they refused. They didn't even want to see it. Then one day we were out looking at apartments and I took them to lunch in one of the restaurants at the Time Warner building and I said to them, 'As long as we're here, why don't we go upstairs to see the apartment?'" The view did it. But after weeks of negotiation between the developer and the buyer, they were still $1 million apart on the price and Lenz couldn't seem to close the deal. "At twenty-five million you wouldn't think that a million dollars would kill a deal that big, but there was also another buyer hovering and I was flipping out," she said. In an unusual move, she asked Howard Lorber to close the deal for her by having a private lunch with Jack Silver. "It was alpha male to alpha male," Lenz said. "It was the only way to get it done."

While $25.5 million sales are nothing to scoff at, Lenz was not happy with the numbers at which Manhattan real estate was trading and she was concerned about what it portended for the near future. "In my mind, the numbers aren't beginning to make sense," she said. "The gap between earnings and the cost of real estate is huge, and that's the beginning of not a good thing. The prices are so high that foreigners are priced out of the market; they think these prices are out of their reach, and they're right. If you're an outsider, you can't come into the New York market. I don't think that prices are going to take a dive, but I think that soon the residential market will totally plateau." As a hedge, she was turning her attention downtown, where the prices weren't quite as inflated. "Development is clearly in lower Manhattan," she said. "The uptown market is all resale business — the same twenty brokers fighting for the same exclusive." In 2004 Lenz was named executive vice president and managing director of Prudential Douglas Elliman, and as of this writing her accumulative gross sales have exceeded $3 billion. In 2005 she sold the most expensive residence ever in the Northeast, Burnt Point, in Wainscott, New York, for $45 million.

With a combined 2,580 brokers, Prudential Douglas Elliman is the largest real estate sales company in the region. With gross sales nearing $6 billion, 2004 was a banner year for the company, and in 2005 Herman and Lorber expect Prudential Douglas Elliman to surpass that figure with the addition of a commercial real estate division. Additional residential offices have been opened or acquired in Brooklyn and in Queens, where about 200 Chinese-speaking brokers have been hired in that borough popular with Chinese immigrants. The next major expansion is planned for Florida, where Herman has already opened offices in Palm Beach, Boca Raton, and Miami, and immediately hired away one of the top brokers in that city to manage her new office.

"Is it a bubble?" Herman asked. "Will the bubble burst? No, I don't think the bubble is going to burst in Manhattan. There were many years when I said, 'It can't go up any more,' but everything is based on supply and demand, and there's a limited supply of land in New York. What will save it is that Americans now have a completely different relationship with real estate than they did just ten years ago. Real estate used to be about the place you lived and spent the rest of your life; it wasn't an investment. Owning a home wasn't considered liquid. Now, with refinancing and home equity loans, you have access to some portion of your equity, and homes have become a major part of every American's portfolio. The only difference is here in New York when people sell their homes, it makes the newspapers. In New York, real estate has become like Hollywood, and the brokers become the stars."

As for the animus between Michael Shvo and Dolly Lenz, Herman learned that there are some battles she will never win, although she stubbornly holds out hope for goodwill among her competitive tribe. Lenz and Shvo never talked to each other again for as long as they worked together at Prudential Douglas Elliman, even when they passed side by side in the hall.

The Shvo juggernaut continued. His group's transactions topped $300 million in sales, his mini-me's grew to twenty-seven, and his commissions put him in the top 3 percent of all residential brokers in the country. Dottie Herman actually cried when he left the company; she was fond of him and felt somehow responsible for not being able to keep him on board. In the spring of 2004 the Corcoran Group filed multiple complaints against Shvo with the ethics committee of the Real Estate Board of New York. Although it has no legal power to fine or punish individual brokers, save for suspension or public censure, in early autumn of 2004 the committee's recommendation was for Michael Shvo to take a course in ethics with a real estate professional, which Shvo indignantly refused to do. Reluctantly, Herman realized that they had come to the end of their professional association, and on October 18, 2004, the Shvo Group's telephones were disconnected, the office locks were changed, and Michael Shvo's name and fantastic list of exclusive co-operatives was taken off the Prudential Douglas Elliman website.

Shvo immediately announced the formation of his own real estate sales and consulting company, also to be called the Shvo Group, and public assurances were made to the press on both sides that his departure from Prudential Douglas Elliman was amicable and had nothing to do with complaints lodged against him with the Real Estate Board. He told the *New York Observer*, "I wanted to branch out on my own. . . . There are lots of great things to be done in real estate." To which Dottie Herman responded, "I think in light of everything, people need to do what they need to do."

# A NOTE ON SOURCES

OF THE MANY texts about New York that were consulted in writing this book, the most invaluable to me include *New York, New York; How the Apartment House Transformed the Life of the City (1869–1930)* by Elizabeth Hawes (Henry Holt, 1993); *Alone Together: A History of New York's Early Apartments* by Elizabeth Collins Cromley (Cornell University Press, 1990); *Manhattan Manners: Architecture and Style* by M. Christine Boyer (Rizzoli, 1985); *Fifth Avenue: The Best Address* by Jerry E. Patterson (Rizzoli, 1998); *Fifth Avenue* by Theodore James Jr. (Walker & Company, 1971); *On Fifth Avenue: Then and Now* by Ronda Wist (Birch Lane Press, 1992); *Mansions in the Clouds: The Skyscraper Palazzi of Emery Roth* by Steven Ruttenbaum (Balsam Press, 1986); and *New York 1930: Architecture and Urbanism Between the Two World Wars* by Robert A. M. Stern, Gregory Gilmartin, and Thomas Mellins (Rizzoli, 1987). The city's luxury buildings and apartments have been extensively and expertly cataloged by Andrew Alpern, whose books about Manhattan include *The New York Apartment Houses of Rosario Candela and James Carpenter* (Acanthus Press, 2002); *Historic Manhattan Apartment Houses* (Dover, 1996); *Luxury Apartment Houses of Manhattan* (Dover, 1993); and *Apartments for the Affluent* (McGraw-Hill, 1975). The writings of the prolific *New York Times* architecture historian and author Christopher Gray were also indispensable to my research. The New-York Historical Society, the Seymour B. Durst Old York Library at the Graduate Center of the City University of New York, and the Avery Library at Columbia University were also sources of immeasurable help.

# ACKNOWLEDGMENTS

I AM DEEPLY indebted to Linda Stein for her personal support during the writing of this book and her generosity in sharing her encyclopedic knowledge of the real estate business with me.

My gratitude as well for the time and trust of the many people who contributed in some way to this text, including Betty Sherrill, Alice Mason, Dominique Richard, Edgar Lansbury, Fredrick Peters, Susan Bird, Allison Utsch, Stephanie Stokes, John Berger, Michelle Kleier, Marci Lippman, Dan Douglas, Tom McGrath, Heather Cohane, Sharon Baum, Hall F. Willkie, Les Lieberman, Kent Karlson, Robby Browne, Edward Lee Cave, Kathy Steinberg, Dottie Herman, Dolly Lenz, Howard Lorber, Leonard Steinberg, Charles Curkin, Steven Gottlieb, Steve Sweetland, Diane Ramirez, Gil Neary, Helene Luchnick, Esther Mueller, Clive Davis, Peter Marra, Paul Purcell, David Patrick Columbia, Paul Goldberger, Dominick Dunne, Kirk Henckles, Earnest Gilmont, Peter Mickel, A. Laurance Kaiser IV, David Paler, Marshall Brickman, Arthur Carter, David Fink, Charles

Stevenson, Conal O'Brien, Alexandra Kuczynski, Dorrie Swope, Richard Johnson, Michael Shvo, John Doyle from the Real Estate Board of New York, Roger Erickson, Vincent Joyce, Harry Garland, Jesse Krasnow, Howard Margolis, Nadine Woloshin, Miller Samuel Inc., the Real Estate Board of New York, Tom Allon of Manhattan Media, Carl Swanson, Deborah Schoeneman, and Joel Weinstein.

My personal thanks to Frank and Sophia and Antony DiGiacomo; Bob Balaban and Lynn Grossman, and their daughters, Mariah and Hazel Balaban; Robert Wiesenthal, Linnea Conrad, and Richard Wiesenthal; Ellen Wiesenthal; Sydney Butchkes; Joseph Olshan; Maer Roshan; Jonathan Canno; Roberta and Frank Wolf; Gali and Alon Lefkowitz; Andrea Ackerman and Harry and Alex Fischman; Tara Newman; Carolyn Beegan; Wally Smith and Bonnie Grice; Frank Miller; and Wayne Myers.

This task would have been impossible for me without Martha Trachtenberg, my longtime and talented editorial assistant, and Gali Ettner Lefkovitz, who helped in the final preparation of the manuscript. My sincere thanks to Steve Lamont, Heather Rizzo, Heather Fain, and Aysa Muchnick at Little, Brown, who all graciously godmothered this project to fruition.

Some books come easier than others. My wise and savvy editor, Bill Phillips, knows this well. He and my publisher, Michael Pietsch, deserve awards for their faith, forbearance, and professionalism while I wrote this book. No author could have better advice, guidance, and encouragement from anyone, or know a nicer guy, than my agent, Richard Pine.

*Steven Gaines*
*Wainscott, New York,*
*2004*

# INDEX

Abzug, Bella, 196
Acosta de Alba, Rita Hernandez de,
    158–59, 166–69, 171–72
Acosta, Mercedes de, 167, 168, 172
Acquavella, William, 25
Adams, Al, 178
Adams, Franklin, 97n
Aga Kahn, 69
Aga Kahn, Princess Yasmin, 143n
Agnelli, Giovanni, 44
Airman, Noel (fictional character), 129
Alden, the (225 Central Park West), 200
al-Fayed, Dodi, 246
al-Fayed, Mohamed, 246
Alfred, the (Sixty-first Street), 124
Alice F. Mason, Ltd., 15, 240; see also
    Mason, Alice F.
Allen, Armin, 35
Allen, Charles, 55
Allen, Paul Gardner, 35
Allen, Peter, 142n, 194
Allen, Soon-Yi, 13
Allen, Woody, 13, 14, 69, 124
Ammon, Ted, 7
Amory, Cleveland, 167
Anderson, Mary, 81

Annenberg, Moses L., 107
Ansonia Hotel (2109 Broadway)
    described, 150–58, 173–77
    development of, 165, 169–71
    history of, 155, 186–96
    landlord-tenant battles at, 158, 195,
        201–3
    musicians and, 183–85
    rehabilitation of, 198–205
    reputation of, 177–82
Ansonia Residents Association, 192, 195,
    203
Ansonia Tenants Association, 203
Anti-Defamation League of B'nai B'rith,
    18
AOL Time Warner Center. See Time
    Warner Center
apartments
    history of, 75–77
    renovations of, 28, 30, 31, 47, 58, 71, 107,
        108, 141–48
    studio, 83–84
Apprentice, The (television program), 247
Arafat, Yasser, 13
Arbus, Diane, 143n
Architectural Digest, 120

# Index

Arc, The (Sutton Place), 101–2
Arc Tenants Association, 102
Ardsley, the (320 Central Park West), 63
Arndt, David, 204
Artkraft Strauss company, 191, 192
*Arts and Decoration* magazine, 97
Ashforth, Adams, 94
Asinof, Eliot, 181
Astor, John Jacob, IV, 8, 73
Astor, John Jacob, Sr., 95
Astor, Mrs. Vincent, 105
Astor, Mrs. William Backhouse, Jr., 3, 16,
    183
*Avenue* magazine, 25

Backer, Baroness Renée de, 26
Balsan, Jacques, 109
Bangs, Bolton, 186
Barish, Keith, 237
Barrymore, Ethel, 102
Baruch, Bernard, 17
Bass, Anne, 54
Baum, Sharon, 122
Beatty, Warren, 116–17, 230
Beaux, Ernesta, 68
Beekman, James, 95–96
Beekman, Mrs. James, 95–96
Beekman Place
    No. 1, 37n, 47
    No. 2, 16, 63, 93
Beekman Terrace (Fifty-first Street),
    97
Beresford, the (211 Central Park West), 56,
    145
Bergen, Candice, 54
Bergerac, Michel, 54
Bernstein, Carl, 13
Bernstein, Leonard, 62
Bernstein, Richard, 80
Bias, Clifford, 197–98
Billings, C. K. G., 24
Birmingham, Stephen, 164
Birnbaum, Arthur, 158
Blass, Bill, 92, 111

"Block Beautiful," 97
Bobst, Elmer, 107
Bogart, Humphrey, 98
Boldini, Giovanni, 171
Bonner, Hugh, 171
Bono, 129, 144
Booth, Lavinia, 77
Boulud, Daniel, 12, 233
Bowman, John McEntee, 189
Boy-Ed, Karl, 178–79
*Boy Leading a Horse* (Picasso), 24
Brennan Beer Gorman company, 208
Brevoort, Henry, 4
Brickman, Marshall, 143
Brinkley, Christie, 58, 116
Broadway, 131, 162–63
    *See also* Ansonia Hotel
Brokaw, Isaac V., 7
brokers, real estate, 119–21, 210, 232,
    243–44
Brolin, James, 63
Browne, Robby, 93–94, 214
Brown Harris Stevens Residential Sales,
    57, 240
Brown, Helen Gurley, 13
Broxmeyer, Samuel, 191
Bryan, J. Shelby, 107–10
Buatta, Mario, 65
Burroughs, William S., 80
Burry, Mrs. Edward C., 17

Campanile, the, 97–98
Candela, Rosario, 88, 93, 104, 217, 250
Cannon Point North (Sutton Place), 102
Cantor, Arthur, 47
Cantor, Eddie, 143
Carey, Mariah, 63–65
Carnegie, Andrew, 74, 100
Carnegie Hall, 74
Carnegie Hill, 36, 38
Carter, Arthur, 54–55
Carter, Jimmy, 13, 14
Caruso, Enrico, 184, 185
Cave, Anna Blanche Compton, 40

Cave, Edward Lee, 2, 66, 91, 224, 240
   on co-ops, 33–36, 44–45, 52
   experience of, 39–40, 223, 232
   Stein and, 137, 141
   Stein and Stein, 114
Census Bureau, U.S., 41
Central Park
   820 Fifth Avenue and, 23
   crime in, 40
   homeless in, 98
   real estate prices and, 81, 99
   status and, 2, 5, 39
   views and, 217, 218
Central Park Apartments (Central Park
   South), 81–82
Central Park West
   described, 125–32
   development of, 163
   Good Buildings and, 36
   real estate prices on, 44, 127
   status and, 36, 39, 125, 128–29
   Time Warner Center and, 217
   vs. Fifth Avenue, 1, 126, 131
   No. 41 (Harperley Hall), 62
   No. 50, 127 (*see also* Central Park West,
     No. 55)
   No. 88, 57, 116
   No. 91, 64
   No. 101, 129
   No. 115 (the Majestic), 127, 129
   No. 151 (Kenilworth Building), 143
   No. 211 (the Beresford), 56
   No. 225 (the Alden), 200
   No. 271, 127
   No. 279, 124
   No. 320 (the Ardsley), 63
   *See also* the Dakota; the San Remo
Central Park West, No. 55, 132–33
   Karan and, 123–25
   renovations and, 141–42
*Central Park West* (television series), 125
Chaliapin, Feodor, 185
Champion, George, 69
Chanin, Irwin, 129

Cheatham, Owen, 69
*Chelsea Girls, The* (film), 80
Chelsea, Hotel (West Twenty-third
   Street), 79–80
Chelsea (West Side neighborhood), 37, 38
Cher, 62
Chicago White Sox, 153, 180–82
*Chic Savages* (Fairchild), 90–91
Childs, David, 208
Chinatown, 232
Churchill, Winston, 106
Church, Norris, 12
Cicotte, Eddie, 181
*Citizen Kane* (film), 134
*City Observed, The* (Goldberger), 126
civil rights violations, 49–50
Clarke, Arthur C., 80
Clark, Edward Severin, 164
Clinton, Bill, 13, 14, 66, 108, 109
Cochrane, Lucy (C. Z. Guest), 106–7, 108
Cogan, Marshall, 142n
Cogan, Maureen, 142n
Cohn, Roy, 71
Comiskey, Charles, 181
Commissioners Plan of 1811, 3
Commission on Human Rights, 49–50,
   71
condominiums
   about, 46, 221–22
   at Ansonia Hotel, 155, 204–5
   Lenz and, 222–26
   market for, 44, 213–14, 216
   status and, 221–23
Conrad, Ethel, 186
Conried, Heinrich, 184
conspicuous consumption, 42–43
Conte, Michele, 210
Continental Baths, 193–94, 196, 197
co-op boards
   application packages for, 24–25, 29,
     51–56, 136
   Cave on, 44–45
   condominiums and, 224
   diplomats and, 20

co-op boards (*cont.*)
  discrimination and, 8–9, 18, 19,
    49–50
  Hilfiger and, 29
  interviews with, 19, 56–58, 62, 64,
    108–10, 136–37
  lawsuits against, 7, 47, 49–50, 67–72,
    158
  letters of recommendation and, 9, 29,
    55–56, 62, 136
  Mason and, 20–22
  power of, 2, 46–47, 68–69
  prequalification and, 27n
  renovations and, 141, 142n, 144–45
  turndowns by, 49–50, 61–67, 69, 72,
    91–92
co-op buildings
  broker experience and, 232
  flip tax at, 59–60
  history of, 50–51, 72–74, 77–84
  market for, 43–44
  as neighborhood, 45–46
  proprietary lease in, 46–48
  status and, 221–24
  tax advantages of, 48
Copperfield, David, 135
Corcoran Agency, 31, 239
Corcoran, Barbara, 122
Corcoran Group, 253
Cosby, Bill, 9
Costello, Frank, 129
Coward, Noël, 97
Crane, Louise, 2, 27
Crane, Mrs. W. Murray, 27
Crane, Winthrop, 27
Crawford, Joan, 69
Cronkite, Betsy, 12
Cronkite, Walter, 12
Crosby, Harry, 53
Cross & Cross, 88, 104
Curran, Charles C., 83
Curry, Agnetta, 91
Curry, Brownlee, 91
Custer, Elizabeth, 77

Dag Hammarskjöld Plaza (Second
    Avenue), 222
Dakota, the (1 West Seventy-second
    Street), 36, 47, 62, 164–65
Dash, Dame, 116, 140
Davidson, John, 194
David-Weill, Michael, 54
*Dead End* (Kingsley), 98
DeLorean, John, 8
Dempsey, Jack, 143n, 179
Diamond, Howard, 6
Diana, Princess of Wales, 246
Dichter, Cipa, 142n
Dichter, Misha, 142n
Dietrich, Marlene, 167
Diller, Barry, 12
diplomats, 20–21
discrimination, 8–9, 18, 19, 49–50
Dodge, Mary Maples, 81
Dodge, Mrs. Marcellus Hartley, 59
Dodge, Phyllis B., 167
dogs, 57–59
Douglas Elliman Company
    awards banquet of, 246–50
    Browne at, 93
    Herman and, 239–43
    Lenz at, 9, 225, 226, 252
    Shvo at, 228, 229, 233–34, 238, 253–54
Douglas, Michael, 42
Draper, Dorothy (Mrs. George
    Tuckerman), 101
Duboy, Paul Emile, 170
Dumond, Frank, 83
Dunne, Dominick, 6, 13, 87, 122
Dutchtown, 163
Dyson, Anne, 6

Earhart, Amelia, 105
East End Avenue
  No. 1, 37n
  No. 120, 37n
  No. 180, 50
East River, 96–97, 99, 100, 103
East River Drive, 89

East Side, Upper, 36, 37, 129, 251
  vs. Upper West Side, 126, 127–28
  *See also particular streets*
East Village, 38
Edelman, Asher, 2
Edward Lee Cave Inc., 35
  *See also* Cave, Edward Lee
Eighteenth Street, East, No. 142, 76
*Eight Men Out* (Asinof), 181
Eisner, Michael, 9
El Dorado, the (Upper West Side), 129
Elkus/Manfredi Ltd., 208
Ellison, Larry, 127
Elwood, Helen, 186–89
Erickson, Roger, 122
Ertegun, Mica, 92
*Esquire* magazine, 36
estate condition, 142
ethics, 62, 244, 253
Everett, Rupert, 112–15, 141
evictions, 20, 47–48, 59, 195
exclusive listings, 121, 252
  Lenz and, 234, 236–37
  open houses and, 138–39
  Shvo and, 229, 234, 245, 253

Faber, Eberhard, 23
Fairchild, John, 90–91
al-Faisal, Prince Saud, 20
Farkas, Andrew, 240
Farrar, Geraldine, 185, 198
Farrow, Mia, 164
Fawcett, Farrah, 171
Federal Housing Administration, 222
Feigen, Richard, 54
Field, Mrs. Marshall, III, 67
Fifth Avenue
  described, 3–5
  development and, 100
  Good Buildings and, 36
  Jews and, 7–9, 128
  real estate prices on, 43, 44, 99, 127
  scandal on, 6–7
  status and, 1–2, 5, 8, 9, 35, 38, 250

Time Warner Center and, 217
  vs. Central Park West, 1, 126, 131
  No. 1, 47
  No. 640, 20
  No. 800, 59
  No. 810, 37n, 142n
  No. 814, 7
  No. 817, 6, 66 (*see also* Fifth Avenue, No. 820)
  No. 825, 27, 37n (*see also* Fifth Avenue, No. 834)
  No. 909, 6
  No. 912, 132
  No. 920, 132, 250
  No. 927, 62–63
  No. 930, 124
  No. 950, 25, 54
  No. 953, 37n
  No. 960, 7, 37n, 54, 210
  No. 969, 25, 126, 140
  No. 990, 25
  No. 998, 37n, 54
  No. 1009, 6
  No. 1020, 37n
  No. 1030, 37n, 54
  No. 1040, 25, 27n, 37n, 54
  No. 1049, 24n, 210
  No. 1107, 9
  No. 1125, 7
  No. 1133, 6, 21–22
  No. 1158, 9, 24n
Fifth Avenue, No. 820, 8, 22–23, 37n
  board package for, 54
  dogs and, 59
  Hilfiger and, 1–3, 10, 22, 28–30
  residents of, 23–25
  Vanderbilt and, 16
  Wrightsman and, 24–28
Fifth Avenue, No. 834
  application package for, 53–54
  co-op board of, 19
  real estate market and, 43, 44
  residents of, 8–9
  status of, 37n

Fifty-first Street, East, 97
    No. 425, 50
*54* (film), 119
Fifty-ninth Street, East, 78
Fifty-second Street, East, No. 435
    (River House), 36–37, 67–72,
    98–99
Fifty-seventh Street, East, 36
Fifty-seventh Street, West
    No. 140 (Metropolitan Tower), 211,
    216
    No. 152 (the Rembrandt), 74, 78
    No. 340 (Parc Vendôme), 219
Fitzgerald, F. Scott, 181
Fitzgerald, Geraldine, 196
Five Points (Foley Square), 73
Flack, Roberta, 62
floor numbering systems, 216
Flowers, Wayland, 194
Forbes 40 richest people, 42
Forbes Inc., 17
Ford, Charlotte, 47, 110
Ford, Gerald, 41
Ford, Harrison, 129, 135
*Fortune* magazine, 129
Four Hundred list, 16
Francis, Clarence, 101–2
Franlin Street, No. 90, 65

Gabellini, Michael, 135, 148
Gandil, Arnold "Chick," 181
Garbo, Greta, 97, 167
Garland, Harry, 192, 194–95
Gatti-Casazza, Giulio, 184–85
Geffen, David, 119
Gekko, Gordon (fictional character), 42
Getty, Ann, 24
Getty, Gordon, 24
*Ghostbusters* (film), 133
Gilbert, Eddie, 21–22
Gilmartin, Joseph, 174
Gladys Mills company, 15
Goelet, Robert, 23
Goldberger, Paul, 126, 202–3

Good Buildings, 59, 63, 67, 122, 250–51
    application package for, 53–54
    described, 36–37, 39, 51, 88
    discrimination and, 8–9, 50
Gorcey, Leo, 98
Gottlieb, Steve, 137
Gould, Jason, 63
Gould, Jay, 23
Grace Church, 4
Gracie, Archibald, 95
Gracie Square, No. 10, 37n, 141
Graham, Lillian, 186
Gray, Christopher, 164n
Great Depression, 98
Greenspan, Alan, 13
Greenwich Village, 37, 38, 202
Gross, Arthur, 132
Grubman, Allen, 28
Grubman, Deborah, 28, 31
Grunwald, Henry, 12, 54
Guest, C.Z., 106–7, 108
Guest, Fredrick E., 106
Guest, Winston, 106
Guinzburg, Tom, 45
Gutfreund, John, 8
Gutfreund, Susan, 108
Gwathmey, Charles, 142n, 143, 145

Hale, Nathan, 96
Hall, Huntz, 98
Hamilton, Philip. *See* Hubert, Philip
Hanson, Steve, 155
Harman, Jay, 242
Harman, Jerry, 133
Harperley Hall (41 Central Park West),
    62
*Harper's Weekly*, 163
Harsenville, 163
Hartford, Huntington, 47–48
Hassam, Childe, 83
Hauptmann, Bruno, 129
Hawthorne, the (East Fifty-ninth Street),
    78
Hayes, Thad, 212

Hayworth, Rita, 143n
Hearst, Veronica, 54
Heatherton, Joey, 62
Heinz, Mrs. Drue, 104
Held, Anna, 182
Helleu, Paul, 160
Hemingway, Mariel, 125
Henkel, Paul, 189
Henry, O., 80
*Here Lies the Heart* (Mercedes de Acosta),
    167
Herman, Dorothy
    awards banquet and, 246–50
    Douglas Elliman Company and,
        239–43
    Lenz and, 244–45
    real estate market and, 252–54
Hewitt, Don, 125
Hilfiger, Susie, 29
Hilfiger, Tommy, 1–3, 9–10, 22,
    28–30
Hines, Gregory, 9
Hirschfield, Abe, 65–66
Hirschfield, Zipora, 65–66
Hoffman, Dustin, 127
Hooker, Janet Armstrong, 107
Hotel des Artistes (1 West Sixty-seventh
    Street), 83
*House of Mirth* (Wharton), 3
*How the Other Half Lives* (Riis), 73
Hubert, the (East Fifty-ninth Street), 78
Hubert Home Clubs, 78, 79–80
Hubert, Philip, 72–75, 77–82, 84
Hudson River, 96
Huerta, General Vincent, 178–79
Huffington, Arianna, 13
Hunt, Richard Morris, 76, 103
Hyde, Henry B., 168

Imber, Gerald, 6
immigrants, 130
*Inc.* magazine, 192
Ingrao, Tony, 111
Insignia Financial Group, 240

*In the Form of a Person* (Pyne), 85
Irish Gold Coast, 39
Irish residents, 17, 18
Irving Place, 102
Ivor, Richard, 12

Jackson, Janet, 44
Jackson, Shoeless Joe, 181, 182
James, Charles, 80
Jay-Z, 38, 116
Jazz at Lincoln Center, 208
Jennings, Peter, 13, 129
Jewish buildings, 55, 129
Jewish residents, 7–9, 18–19, 55, 128–30,
    165
Jobs, Steven, 144
Joel, Billy, 58, 62, 116
John, Elton, 117
Johnson, Elizabeth "Libbet," 27–28, 44
Johnson, Lady Bird, 88
Johnson, Lyndon Baines, 88
Johnson, Philip, 217
Johnson, Richard, 118
Jones, Paula, 66
Joop, Wolfgang, 92
Joyce, Vincent, 150–52, 156, 197, 205
J. Sopher, 231
Judelson, David (Jim), 91
Junta, Jan, 68

Kahn, Otto, 7, 183–84
Kaiser, A. Laurence, IV, 48, 122
Kampelman, Max M., 200
Kaplan, Jack, 21
Karan, Donna
    55 Central Park West and, 123–25,
        146–48
    Stein and, 113, 132–33, 135–37, 141
Keaton, Diane, 62, 69, 142n
Keller, Louise, 17
Kenilworth Building (151 Central Park
    West), 143
Kennedy, John F., Jr., 38
Kennedy, Rose, 109

Key Ventures, 122
Kidd, Captain, 95
Kingsley, Sidney, 98
Kissinger, Henry, 69, 71, 72
Klein, Calvin, 133, 137
Klemperer, Werner, 61, 62
Kline, Kevin, 7
Knickerbocker, Suzy, 17
Knopf, Alfred A., 17
Koch, David, 54
Koch, Frederick, 2
Kondylis, Costas, 217
Kostelanetz, André, 185
Kozlowski, Dennis, 210, 226
Krasnow, Jesse, 158, 198–205
Kravis, Henry, 52, 91
Kroft, Steve, 13

Ladd, Parker, 93
Landmarks Preservation Commission,
    62n, 170, 173, 177, 195–96
lang, k.d., 133
Lansbury, Edgar, 146
*Last Resorts* (Amory), 167
Lauder, Leonard, 29, 54–55
Lauder, Ronald, 54
Laurance, William L., 101
Lauren, Ralph, 9
Lawford, Patricia, 25, 109
Lawford, Peter, 25
lawsuits
    brokers and, 210
    co-op boards and, 7, 47, 49–50, 55, 65,
        67–72, 158
    co-op *residents* and, 7, 66
L. B. Kaye company, 221, 222, 223
lease, proprietary, 46–48
Lefferts Fore company, 200, 203
Lefkowitz, Louis, 62
Lennon, John, 62, 164
Lenz, Aaron, 210, 220, 224
Lenz, Dorothy (Dolly)
    about, 206–7, 210–11,
        219–21

awards banquet and, 247, 248, 249,
    250
condominiums and, 222–26
co-op boards and, 9, 49, 64
at Douglas Elliman, 9, 225, 226, 252
Shvo and, 226, 234–38, 244–45, 253
Time Warner Center and, 209, 212–19,
    250–51
Leo, Jackie, 143
Levandusky, Ronald, 47
Levenson, Larry, 196–97, 201
Levin, Ira, 164
Levy, Jack, 24
Levy, Leon, 91
Lewis, Loida, 9
Lewis, Reginald, 9
Limbaugh, Rush, 24n
Lincoln, Abraham, 77
Lincoln Center, 131, 208
Lindbergh, Charles, 129
Lindsay, John V., 63, 196
Livingston, Mrs. Goodhue, 102
Logan, Josh, 72
Lorber, Howard, 228, 239, 240, 251, 252
    awards banquet and, 247, 249, 250
Lorillard, Pierre, 23, 42n
Lorraine, Lillian, 182
*Los Angeles Times,* 120
Lower East Side Tenement Museum, 73
Luce, Clare Booth, 97
Luchnick, Helene, 122–23
Lyceum, the (Fourth Avenue and
    Fourteenth Street), 79
Lydig, Major Phillip M., 171
Lydig, Rita. *see* Acosta de Alba, Rita
    Hernandez de
Lyon, Mrs. J. Denniston, 59

Macklowe, Harry, 216
Madero, Francisco, 178
Madie, Michel, 156
Madison Avenue, 5, 34, 78
Madonna, 27n, 28, 61–62, 118, 133
Madrazo, 171

Mailer, Norman, 11, 12, 15
maisonettes, 5–6
Majestic, the (115 Central Park West), 127, 129
Mandell, Cora (fictional character), 87
*Manhattan, Inc.,* 14
Manhattan Transfer, 194
Manilow, Barry, 142n, 194
*Manners: A Handbook of Social Customs* (Marbury), 102
Marbury, Elisabeth "Bessy," 102
market, real estate, 40, 236
    brokers and, 119–20
    consolidations and, 239–40
    growth of, 43–44, 250–53
    *See also* prices, real estate
Martin, Bradley, 101
Martinez, David, 214
Martin, Steve, 143n
Marx, Groucho, 67
Mason, Alice F., 224, 232
    co-op boards and, 20–22, 55
    dinner parties of, 10–16
    Hilfiger and, 28–31
    *Social Register* and, 16–19
Mason, Christopher, 125
Mason, Dominique
    Alice Mason and, 12, 15, 19, 321
    co-op boards and, 57
    Hilfiger and, 28, 30
Matchabelli, Prince, 23
Mathison, Melissa, 135
Maxwell-Pearl, Elsa, 14
Mayer, Louis B., 106
Maynard, Jane, 65
McAllister, Ward, 3, 16
McCarthy, Patrick, 119
McClary, Sue, 189
McLennan, Eleanor, 185
McMillen, Inc., 87, 88, 94
Melchior, Lauritz, 185
Melhado, Louise, 12
Mendl, Sir Charles, 102

Menil, Adelaide de, 124
*Men in White* (Kingsley), 98
Metropolitan Museum of Art, 26, 27n, 30
Metropolitan Opera House, 107, 183–85, 194
Metropolitan Tower (140 West Fifty-seventh Street), 211, 216
Meusel, Bob, 179
Michael, Prince of Kent, 107
Midler, Bette, 194
Miles, Sylvia, 118
Miller, Arthur, 80
*Millionaires* magazine, 42
Mockel, Fred B., 175, 180
Monroe, Marilyn, 16
Moody's Investors Service, 41
Moore, Demi, 142–43
Moore, Mary Tyler, 142n
Moore, Melba, 194
Moranis, Rick, 129
Morgan, Anne, 103
Morgan, J. Pierpont, 103
Morningstar, Marjorie (fictional character), 129
mortgages, 50
Moses, Robert, 131
Mostel, Zero, 142n
Mottola, Tommy, 28, 64, 135
Mueller, Carl, 69
Murdoch, Rupert, 9n, 44
Murray, Arthur, 23
Murray, Kathyrn, 23
Museum of Modern Art, 27

Nash, Paul, 101
National Press Club, 41
Naumburg, Aaron, 83
Navarro, the (Central Park Apartments), 81–82
Navarro, Juan de, 81
Neeson, Liam, 64
Nevada, the (Sixty-ninth Street), 200
New Valley Corp., 239

New York City Department of Buildings, 71, 193

*New York Daily News*, 41, 62

*New York Journal American*, 17

*New York* magazine, 14, 93, 118, 122, 125, 210, 241
 on Herman, 240, 243

*New York Observer*, 2, 110, 120, 225, 254

*New York Post*, 72, 118, 120, 225, 236

*New York Times*, 65, 71, 77, 81, 120, 125, 147
 on Ansonia Hotel, 192, 202–3
 on co-ops, 50, 61
 on the Dakota, 47
 on nannies, 128
 on renovations, 142
 on Stokes, 161, 186
 on Sutton Place, 90, 103, 104
 on Trump International Hotel & Tower, 217
 on wealth, 42, 43

New York Yankees, 179–80

NFO World Group, 42n

Niarchos, Stavros, 24

Nichols, Mike, 12, 54, 137

Nico, 80

Ninety-sixth Street, 1–2, 9, 36, 38, 182

Nixon, Patricia, 65, 67

Nixon, Richard, 65–67, 107

Norris, Bruce A., 20

Norwich, Billy, 118

Notorious B.I.G. (Biggie Smalls), 64

O'Brien, Conal, 155

O'Doul, Lefty, 179

offices, professional, 5–6

Olatunji, Baba, 156

"Old Guard" aristocracy, 3n

Olmsted, Frederick Law, 76

Onassis, Jacqueline Kennedy, 25–26, 27n, 218

One Central Park. *See* Time Warner Center

One Sutton Place South. *See under* Sutton Place South

open houses, 138–39

open listings, 121

*Opulence* magazine, 42

Orentreich, Norman, 6

Ostrow, Steve, 193–94, 196

Otis, Elisha Graves, 176

"Our Crowd" Jews, 18, 19

Paley, Babe, 23–24

Paley, William, 23–24

Paltrow, Gwyneth, 116

Panizza, Ettore, 185

Parc Vendôme (340 West Fifty-seventh Street), 219

Parish-Hadley company, 40

Park Avenue
 Good Buildings and, 36
 Jews and, 128
 status and, 38, 39
 vs. Central Park West, 126, 131
 No. 550, 37n
 No. 555, 37n
 No. 635, 37n
 No. 640, 37n
 No. 650, 18
 No. 655, 19
 No. 720, 18, 37n, 54
 No. 730, 18, 37n
 No. 740, 36, 37n, 53–54
 No. 755, 51
 No. 760, 21
 No. 765–75, 37n
 No. 770, 37n, 44, 62
 No. 778, 37n
 No. 784, 139–40
 No. 791, 49
 No. 812, 37n
 No. 895, 18
 No. 1124, 56–57

Parker, Dorothy, 97n

P. Diddy, 28

Peabody, Polly, 35

Pearsall, Thomas, 99

Pei, I. M., 144

Penn, Sean, 61
*Penthouse* magazine, 61
*People Like Us* (Dunne), 87, 122
Perella, Joseph, 54
Perelman, Ronald, 2, 119
Perry, Richard, 110–11
Peters, Roberta, 185
Petrek, Jeanne, 114
Petrie, Carroll, 53
Phelps, Caroline, 162
Phelps, Stokes & Company, 162
Phipps, Amy, 105–6, 108
Phipps Company, 100–101, 104
Phipps, Henry, 100–101, 105
Picasso, Pablo, 24
Pinza, Ezio, 185
Piscuskas, David, 110
*Planetary Configurations and Stock Market Sentiment* (Stokes), 189
Plato's Retreat, 153, 197, 200–201
*Playboy* magazine, 61
Poitier, Sidney, 9, 24
Pons, Lily, 185
Portnoy (fictional character), 129
Post, Marjorie Merriweather, 9
Potter, Codman, 81
prices, real estate, 36, 81
    at Ansonia Hotel, 155, 204
    on Central Park West, 44, 127
    changes in, 43–44, 75, 98–99, 120, 226, 232, 250–51
    co-ops and, 48, 51, 53–54, 60
    on Fifth Avenue, 43, 44, 99, 127
    on Park Avenue, 44
    rent protection and, 11, 130, 155, 201, 204
    on Sutton Place, 107, 110–11
    at Time Warner Center, 44, 211, 213–14, 250
Prudential Douglas Elliman. *see* Douglas Elliman Company
Prudential Long Island Realty, 239, 240
Puff Daddy, 64n
Pulitzer, Joseph, 168

Purcell, Paul, 225, 234–25
Putnam, George, 77
*Putnam's Magazine*, 76
Pyne, Ann, 85

race, 8–9, 50, 70–71, 131, 155
Rader, Dotson, 14
Radziwill, Lee, 25
Rafael Viñoly Architects, 208
Ramones, the, 133
Randall, Tony, 143n, 146
Ranger, Henry Ward, 83
Rath, Morrie, 181
Rattner, Steven, 54
Real Estate Board of New York, 244, 253
Redford, Robert, 117
Reed, Rex, 62
rejections. *See* turndowns
Related Companies, 209, 211, 212, 214, 215
religion, 17, 18, 19, 49, 50
    *See also* Jewish buildings; Jewish residents
Rembrandt, the (152 West Fifty-seventh Street), 74, 78
renovations, of buildings, 101, 102, 103, 158, 199, 202, 204
rent protection, 11, 130, 155, 201, 204
Rent Stabilization Board, 195, 201
Renwick, James, 4
Ribicoff, Abe, 92
Ribicoff, Casey, 92
Richard, Dominique Mason. *see* Mason, Dominique
Richard, Francis, 15
Richards, Marty, 69
Richardson, Frank, 23
Richardson, Nancy, 23, 27, 31
Richardson, Natasha, 64
*Right to Be Well Born, The* (Stokes), 166
Riis, Jacob, 73
Rivera, Diego, 106
River House (435 East Fifty-second Street), 36–37, 67–72, 98–99

Riverside Drive, 130
  No. 5, 61
Rockefeller, Laurence, 9n
Rockefeller, Mary "Tod," 142n
Rockefeller, Mrs. John D., Jr., 27
Rockefeller, Nelson, 62, 142n
Rockefeller, William, 59
Rodin, Auguste, 171
Roehm, Carolyne, 91
Rohatyn, Elizabeth, 142n
Rohatyn, Felix, 142n
Roosevelt, Franklin Delano, 3n
Root, Elihu, 86
*Rosemary's Baby* (film), 164
Ross, Courtney Sale, 53–54
Ross, Marshall, 54
Ross, Stephen M., 209, 212
Ross, Steve, 54
Roth, Philip, 129
Rothschild, Jacob, 144
Rothstein, Arnold "the Big Bankroll," 181
Rothstein, Jeff, 247
Roth, Steven, 44
Rubenstein, Serge, 7
Russell, Walter, 83
Ruth, Babe, 153, 180, 181, 204

Safra, Lily, 31
Saint Patrick's Cathedral, 8
Saint-Tropez, the (340 East Sixty-fourth
    Street), 222
San Remo, the (145 Central Park West),
    60, 126, 127, 129
  Karan and, 124, 141, 147
  Madonna and, 61–62, 118
  renovations and, 141–45
  status of, 36, 125
Sargent, John Singer, 171
*Saturday Night at the Baths* (Ostrow),
    196
Sawyer, Diane, 12, 54, 137
Scaasi, Arnold, 92–93
scandal, 6–7
Schang, Wally, 179

Schiffer, Claudia, 135
Schipa, Tito, 185
Schlossberg, Edwin, 27n
Schmidt, Mott B., 102, 103
Schoeneman, Deborah, 210
Schrager, Ian, 127
Schwartz, Simon I., 132
Schwarzman, Stephen, 36
Scotti, Antonio, 185
Second Avenue, 222
Sedaka, Neil, 55
Seinfeld, Jerry, 145–46
Selwen, Peter, 183
Semel, Jane, 25
Semel, Terry, 24–25
September 11, 2001 terrorist attacks, 43,
    214, 236
Sevilla, the (Madison Avenue), 78
Seventieth Street, East
  No. 2, 37n
  No. 33, 139
Seventy-ninth Street, East
  No. 21, 37n
  No. 31, 18
  No. 39, 37n
  No. 66, 37n
  No. 79, 37n
Seventy-second Street, East
  No. 4, 37n, 139
  No. 19, 37n, 65
  No. 36, 37n
  No. 117, 37n
  No. 160, 37n
Seventy-second Street, West, No. 1 (the
    Dakota), 36, 47, 62, 164–65
Seventy-seventh Street, East , No. 50, 37n,
    58
*Sex and the City* (televison program), 125,
    155
*Shampoo* (film), 230
Shantyhill, 163
Sherrill, Betty, 85–92, 94, 101, 107–11
Sherrill, H. Virgil, 87, 91, 94
Short, Bobby, 17, 70

Shvo Group, 229, 244, 245, 247, 253–54
Shvo, Michael, 227–32
    awards banquet and, 247, 249–50
    at Douglas Elliman, 228, 229, 233–34,
        238, 253–54
    Lenz and, 226, 234–38, 244–45, 253
Sidney, Sylvia, 98
Silk Stocking District, 37
Silver, Jack, 250–51
Simmons, Gene, 62
Simon, Neil, 143n
*Six Degrees of Separation* (film), 24
Sixty-fifth Street, East , No. 142, 66–67
Sixty-first Street (the Alfred), 124
Sixty-fourth Street, East
    No. 32, 45
    No. 32 (the Verona), 62
    No. 34, 20
    No. 340 (the Saint-Tropez), 222
Sixty-seventh Street, East , No. 2, 54
Sixty-seventh Street, West, No. 1 (Hotel
    des Artistes), 83
Sixty-sixth Street, East
    No. 4, 35, 37n, 54
    No. 131, 91
    No. 131–35, 37n
Skidmore, Owings & Merrill (firm), 208
Sloan, Alfred, Jr., 23
Smith, Alfred E., 23
Smith, Jean, 25
Smith, Liz, 93
Smith, Stephen, 25, 109
*Social Register,* 16–19
society, 2–3, 128
*Society-List and Club Register,* 16
SoHo, 124
Sonnenberg, Ben, 34
Sotheby's International Realty, 119, 122,
    244
    Cave at, 34, 35, 40
    Lenz at, 223, 224–25
Spanish Flats (Central Park South),
    81–82
Spielberg, Steven, 115, 143–44

Stallone, Sylvester, 117
Stanfill, Francesca, 12
Starett and Ven Vleck, 22
Starr, Darren, 125
Starr, Jacob, 152, 191–96, 201
status
    of address, 43–44, 111, 221–24
    of Central Park West, 36, 39, 125,
        128–29
    of Fifth Avenue, 1–2, 5, 8, 9, 35, 38, 250
    Good Buildings and, 37
    letters of recommendation and, 29
    of Park Avenue, 38, 39
    signs of, 38–39, 135
Steber, Eleanor, 194
Steinberg, Kathryn, 36
Steinberg, Saul, 35–36
Steinem, Gloria, 13
Stein, Linda, 57, 127, 137–41
    clients of, 112–20, 149
    Karan and, 123, 133–37, 146–48
Stein, Seymour, 133–35
Stern, Isaac, 145
Stern, Robert A. M., 144
Stigwood, Robert, 143
Sting, 57, 116
Stokes, Anson, 162
Stokes, Caroline, 171
Stokes, Helen Elwood, 186–89
Stokes, Helen Muriel, 188
Stokes, James (father of W. E. D.), 100,
    162
Stokes, James (son of W. E. D.), 188
Stokes, Olivia, 171
Stokes, Rita. *see* Acosta de Alba, Rita
    Hernandez de
Stokes, William Earl Dodge
    Ansonia Hotel and, 161–66, 169–71,
        173–74, 178, 183, 186–88, 204
    Helen Elwood and, 186–89
    Rita de Acosta and, 159–60, 166–69,
        171–72
Stokes, William Earl Dodge, Jr.
    (Weddie), 187, 188, 189, 191

Streisand, Barbra, 62–65
Stribling & Associates, 239
Stuyvesant, Augustus Van Horne, 3n
Stuyvesant, Peter, 76
Stuyvesant, Rutherford, 76–77
Sutton, Effingham B., 99–100, 103, 104
Sutton Place, 36, 99, 232
    history of, 99–104
Sutton Place North, No. 25, 37n
Sutton Place South, No. 1
    described, 88–90
    history of, 95, 104–5
    residents of, 91–92
    Sherrill and, 85–87, 107–11
    status of, 37n, 111
Sutton Place South, No. 13, 102
Swanson, Carl, 120

Talese, Gay, 128
*Tales of the Phelps-Dodge Family* (Dodge), 167
Talking Heads, 133
Taubman, Alfred, 8, 53
taxes
    co-ops and, 48
    flip, 59–60
Taylor, Elizabeth, 6
Temple Emanu-El, 8
Tenement House Act, 77
tenements, 96, 98, 100–101, 130–31
    history of, 72–73
Tennant, Victoria, 143n
*Theory of the Leisure Class* (Veblen), 42
Thomas, Clara Fargo, 97
Thomas, Dylan, 80
Thomas, Joseph, 97
Thornley, Josiah, 186
Thurman, Uma, 116
Tilly, Jennifer, 151
Time Warner Center
    described, 206–8, 211–13, 216–18
    Lenz and, 211, 215, 236, 250–51

prices at, 44, 211, 213–14, 250
Shvo on, 232
Tisch, Jonathan, 54
Tisch, Laurence, 13
Tishman Realty & Construction Company, 99
Toscanini, Arturo, 184–85
*Tragic Mansions* (Acosta de Alba), 172
Triangle of Good Buildings, 36, 67
TriBeCa, 31, 38, 64, 232
Trump, Donald, 216, 217, 218, 228, 247–48
    Lenz and, 209, 224
Trump International Hotel & Tower, 44, 127, 217–18
Trump World Tower, 216
Tuckerman, Mrs. George (Dorothy Draper), 101
Tufo, Peter, 12–13
turndowns
    of celebrities, 61–66, 69–72
    co-op boards and, 49–50, 61–67, 69, 72, 91–92
    lawsuits and, 67
    rates of, 61
Twain, Mark, 25
Tweed, William "Boss," 99
Twenty-third Street, West (Hotel Chelsea), 79–80
20/20 (television program), 226

Union of American Hebrew Congregations, 8
United Nations, 20–21, 96, 104
United Nations Plaza, 47
Utsch, Allison, 141, 146

Vallée, Rudy, 133
Vanderbilt, Alfred Gwynne, Jr., 16, 18
Vanderbilt, Alva, 103
Vanderbilt, Anne Harriman, 103, 104
Vanderbilt, Gertrude, 3
Vanderbilt, Gloria, 67, 69–72, 98

Vanderbilt, William Kissam, 103
*Vanity Fair*, 35, 118
Vaux, Calvert, 75–76
Veblen, Thorstein, 42
Verona, the (32 East Sixty-fourth Street), 62
Versace, Gianni, 27n
Viele, Egbert, 128
*Village Voice*, 202
von Bülow, Claus, 7
von Bülow, Sunny, 7
Von Furstenberg, Diane, 12
Vongerichten, Jean-Georges, 127, 236
Vonnoh, Robert, 84
von Papen, Franz, 178–79

Wallace, Mike, 45, 62
*Wall Street* (film), 42, 118
*Wall Street Journal*, 35, 40, 42, 120
Walsh, Christy, 180
Walters, Barbara, 13
Warburg, Felix Schiff, 7
Warburg, Frieda Schiff, 7
Warburg Realty, 239
Ward, Sela, 119
Warhol, Andy, 80
Washington Square Park, 4
wealth
    address and, 1–3, 41–43, 99–100
    co-op boards and, 51–55
Weaver, Sigourney, 91
Webber, Andrew Lloyd, 116
Weed, Clyde, 69
Weicker, Mrs. Lowell, 25
Weisner, Sidney, 49
Weiss, Stephan, 123–25, 135, 136, 148
Welch, Jack, 243
Welch, Raquel, 142n
Wenner, Jane, 140
Wenner, Jann, 140
West Side Association, 163–64
*West Side Story* (film), 130, 131

West Side, Upper, 36, 38, 126–30, 153–54, 177
    development of, 163–65
    immigrants and, 130
    Jews and, 128–29
    Time Warner Center and, 208, 236
    vs. Upper East Side, 126, 127–28
    *See also* Central Park West
West Village, 37, 38
Wharton, Edith, 3
White, Edmund, 194
White, Shelby, 91
Whitney, John Hay, 17
Wilde, Oscar, 102
Willard, Jess, 179
William B. May company, 239
Williams, Robin, 127
Willis, Bruce, 115, 142–43
Willkie, Hall F., 57
Wilson, Woodrow, 178
Winchell, Walter, 129
Winnick, Gary, 142n
Wintour, Anna, 110
*W* magazine, 14
Wolfe, Elsie de, 102, 172
Wolfe, Tom, 36–37, 67
Woodruff, Robert, 69
Woodward, Ann, 6
Woolcott, Alexander, 97
World Trade Center, 214
Wouk, Herman, 129
Wrightsman, Charles, 25, 26
Wrightsman, Jayne, 1, 24–31
Wynn, Steve, 31

Ziegfeld, Florenz, 182
Zion, Sidney, 14
zip codes, 37
Zuch, Louis, 190
Zuckerman, Mortimer, 13, 54
Zuloaga y Zabaleta, Ignacio, 171

# ABOUT THE AUTHOR

Steven Gaines is the bestselling author of twelve books, including *Philistines at the Hedgerow: Passion and Property in the Hamptons, The Love You Make: An Insider's Story of the Beatles, Heroes and Villains: The True Story of the Beach Boys,* and *Simply Halston: The Untold Story.* A contributing editor at *New York* magazine, his investigative journalism has appeared in *Vanity Fair,* the *New York Observer, Los Angeles,* and *Worth.* He divides his time between Manhattan and East Hampton, New York.